CAVE OF TIGERS

Dharma encounters are an integral part of training at Zen Mountain Monastery. They take place six times a year in the main *zendo* of the Monastery, a meditation hall capable of sitting over one hundred students and visitors. All participants sit in the formal zazen posture, with Daido Roshi sitting at the head of the zendo by the altar and his attendant standing behind him. Daido Roshi gives a short talk to present the theme of the encounter, and then makes a formal invitation for participants to come up and ask questions or present their understanding. Students line up in single file and wait for their turn to face the teacher in front of all the other participants. Each exchange begins and ends with a formal bow, and the end of the exchange is marked by the student saying, "Thank you for your teaching," and Daido Roshi's response, "May your life go well."

CAVE OF TIGERS

MODERN ZEN ENCOUNTERS

John Daido Loori

Edited by
Bonnie Myotai Treace
and
Konrad Ryushin Marchaj

WEATHERHILL
New York · Tokyo

Dedicated to those practitioners who willingly entered the tiger's cave

Editor's Note: Most of the references to classical texts used by Daido Roshi come from Master Dogen's *Shobogenzo: Treasury of the True Dharma Eye*. Rather than using a single translation, Daido Roshi has over the years compiled a synthesis culled from the available translations that he feels best represents the dharma that Dogen wanted to communicate to his students. The other two sources are the *Flower Garland Sutra*, quoted on pages 164 and 165, which comes from Thomas Cleary's one-volume translation, *The Flower Ornament Scripture*, published in 1993 by Shambhala; and the chapter from *The Gateless Gate* called "Zen Warnings," quoted on page 238, which is from Zenkei Shibayama's *Zen Comments on the Mumonkan*, published in 1984 by Harper & Row.

First Edition, 2000
Copyright © 2000 by John Daido Loori
Published by Weatherhill, Inc.
41 Monroe Turnpike, Trumbull, CT 06611

Book and cover design: Noble & Israel Design.

Library of Congress Cataloging-in-Publication Data

Loori, John Daido
    Cave of tigers; live Zen dialogues with John Daido Loori
        p. cm.
    ISBN 0-8348-0433-6
        1. Zen Buddhism 2. Spiritual life—Zen Buddhism I. Zen Mountain
    Monastery II. Title

BQ9268.7 .L655 1999
294.3'927—dc21   00-022561

CONTENTS

Foreword

Cave of Tigers is a collection of edited transcriptions of dharma encounters between students at Zen Mountain Monastery and Zen Master John Daido Loori, Roshi. In bringing the words of these live encounters to the page, we run the danger of freezing solid something that is in essence fluid and transitory: the dynamic of intimate spiritual study between Zen teacher and student. However, because the teacher-student relationship has been so often misunderstood, we have attempted to present these dialogues in a way that will illustrate and clarify, not only the form, but also the evolution of this very particular training relationship.

In Zen we place emphasis on making the practice our own, on realizing the truth of our lives, and then taking the confidence and clarity of that realization into every moment of our daily experience. Even though this work can only be done by each individual, the teacher plays an important role in the development of the student's practice, most often acting as a checkpoint or a mirror that reflects clearly what stands in front of it. The teacher constantly tests students to counteract their tendency to mimic or blindly accept what is offered instead of following a process of self-discovery.

Zen study, and especially the teacher-student relationship, is essentially a kind of combat, and when taken on with real honesty, this combat can be one of the most difficult things we will ever do. In the beginning we enter this study with all our pain, our confusion, and—if we are fortunate—with the awareness of our impending death. It is this last realization that creates the pressure to find a true way to resolve the conflict of our painful existence, and as our practice progresses, we bring to it the passionate intensity which in Zen is referred to as "entering the tiger's cave."

At first the student's work consists simply of quieting the mind, silencing the surface chatter in order to make room for the intrinsic questions of our human nature to arise. Then these questions are refined and clarified by the introduction of a koan, a question or statement that echoes the paradox of life and death and asks for a direct and intimate experience of being. Students sit alone with the koan during periods of zazen, Zen meditation, and periodically are asked to present their understanding to the teacher in the private meeting known as *dokusan*. This is the moment when the teacher agrees to enter into our struggle, to fight along with us, to be both our ally and our enemy, and to do whatever it takes over a course of many years to make sure that our freedom is real and unassailable. Walking together along this path requires enormous trust from both parties, and an understanding of the vigor of the work with its potential to hurt, as well as to heal.

The content of dokusan evolves as the student evolves, beginning with a very supportive, almost parent-child relationship that encourages basic trust in oneself and the process of zazen, and which can then grow into a kind of communication that is both spiritually mature and mutually nourishing. The unique characteristic of Zen is the transmission of experience mind to mind, person to person. Descriptive words and ideas become side issues to the very intimate experience of oneself, and this is where the teacher steps in to constantly check that our experience is indeed personal, deep, and sure. This checking is sometimes affirming: the teacher can see that the student sees, but will push to see if the student is capable of flowing into another situation just as freely as the first; other times it is testing: the teacher sees the student holding on to an idea and presses for a more direct expression, tearing away any attachments that seem to fix or hinder them. Eventually the student tests the teacher, working toward the moment when their minds are in perfect accord, communication complete.

Dharma encounter is a public reflection of the private teacher-student interaction that takes place in the dokusan room. The teacher introduces a topic of discussion and then invites students to come face-to-face to present their understanding, or to ask a question. Coming forward is itself half the battle; it means moving to the edge of our practice, being willing to step into darkness and face the fear of self-doubt. It takes courage and the self-granted permission to fail or to be seen as a fool or a fraud, yet this process also allows us to see that the tiger we face is no one but ourselves.

Though the encounters presented here are varied and range over a wide variety of themes, they are similar in that we all deal with certain things by virtue of our common experience as human beings. In fact, the records of Zen teachings throughout the last twenty-five hundred years reveal encounters not very different from those in these pages. At the same time, this is a particular era, with particular problems including everything from environmental issues to ethics, from right livelihood to family life, and each one of us has a particular life history and manner of expression that create a set of unique, personal koans. In the traditional koans presented in the collections we use in Zen practice, the students were usually monastics traveling from temple to temple on religious pilgrimages. Here, the spiritual seekers are primarily laypeople: mothers, professionals, college students, and car mechanics.

Like many Zen teachings, these encounters—especially those involving senior students—need a different kind of listening to hear them well, a listening that involves the heart more than the intellect, the intuitive rather than the analytical aspect of who we are. To really hear what is going on in these encounters requires a leap of trust, especially at that moment when they no longer seem to "make sense" in a way with which we are familiar. Other encounters are much more discursive and seem more akin to ordinary dialogue, but even then they are not simply conversation—at their heart are questions so intimate that they often go unrecognized: Who are you? What are you? Who asks? Regardless of the subject being discussed, the teacher always meets the students where they stand, offering the teaching in a way that is in accord with their understanding.

Over the last twenty years, a number of publications have appeared documenting the teaching of historic masters in India, China, Japan, and Korea. Many of these publications deal with traditional koans, and these dialogues between ancient masters and their students are an invaluable resource. It is important to note, however, that *Cave of Tigers* is not intended to explain or demystify these historical encounters, but instead gives us a chance to see that the mystical teaching of Zen is alive here in America at the turn of the twenty-first century, that it is accessible, and that it is completely relevant to how each one of us live our lives.

An American teacher working with American students, Daido Roshi embraces the problems and capabilities that we present, willingly throwing himself into battle to help us get rid of whatever ideas we put in the way of our realization. These pages provide a rare opportunity to witness this battle, but even rarer still is to take up the battle ourselves, since doing so requires that we come forward and put ourselves on the line. It requires taking a risk and entering the Cave of Tigers with our whole body and mind.

> Tiger,
> Fangs and claws unsheathed,
> Fully present and prepared to die—
> Is thus invulnerable.

Bonnie Myotai Treace, Sensei
Vice-Abbess, Zen Mountain Monastery

Teacher's Invitation to Dharma Encounter

Dharma encounter is a longstanding tradition in Zen. It dates back to the time of Shakyamuni Buddha and to the exchanges that took place between teachers and students as Buddhism migrated out of India. Today we study these exchanges in the form of koans recorded in the collections widely used in Zen practice.

Dharma encounter is a kind of public dokusan—interview with the teacher— and it is one of the five ways in which a teacher and student interact in the context of Zen training. The other kind of interactions are *teisho*, or dharma discourse; dokusan; *mondo*, a question-and-answer session; and finally, informal interaction.

Dharma discourse is a public talk that the teacher presents to the assembly. It is, however, very different from a lecture. In Zen, we say that dharma discourse is dark to the mind but radiant to the heart; it cannot be grasped intellectually, for it speaks to each one of us from the assumption that we are all realized buddhas. In order to hear what is being presented we need to shift our way of hearing; we must let go of our reference system and be intimate with the words being spoken. We must experience the teachings with our whole body and mind.

Dokusan is a face-to-face meeting where teacher and student deal with questions that come up out of the stillness of zazen. It is in this face-to-face encounter that the intimacy of the teacher-student relationship begins to develop and finally matures to the point of the transmission of the Dharma.

Mondo provides an opportunity for students to ask questions in an informal setting. Mondo tends to be explanatory at times, though it does not exclude direct pointing to the Dharma, depending on the students' potential for understanding.

Informal interaction between teacher and student happen at work, sharing a meal, or during any other kind of informal situation in which teacher and student come together. This form of teaching is by far the most subtle, and yet at times it can prove to be extremely powerful.

Finally we have dharma encounter. At one time these encounters used to happen quite accidentally. Monastics wandered around the countryside without a fixed abode, and if they happened to meet another monastic or a teacher along the road, they would engage them in dialogues covering some point of the teachings. After a while, monasteries appeared and monastics congregated there, and little by little dharma encounter became a more formalized kind of interaction. This form continued through China to Japan and later to America, and here at Zen Mountain Monastery we have adopted it as a very important training tool.

Dharma encounter is completely unrehearsed, so the students don't know what subject the teacher will present, and the teacher does not know the questions the students will ask. It is a powerful way of sharpening one's understanding, of taking one's practice to the edge. It provides a way for junior students to receive the teachings, as well as to see how senior students handle the questions presented, and for senior students to test their understanding. It is with senior students that a bit of what we call "head squeezing" tends to happen: a kind of pushing by the teacher to get the student to see beyond what they're already seeing.

Part of the reason that Zen training takes so long—fifteen, twenty years—is that it is very thorough. It is not enough to understand the words and ideas that describe reality; we must realize reality directly, just as Shakyamuni realized it, just as each of the ancestors realized it for themselves. This realization is what we call mind-to-mind transmission, and it has been handed down from person to person through our lineage for the last twenty-five hundred years. The words used in dharma encounter are part of this transmission. They are live words, turning words, words that reveal the truth rather than obscure it, and that always respond to the student in accord with the place in which they stand.

The most important thing in dharma encounter is to participate. It is not necessary to have answers, since ninety percent of the time the questions are resolved by themselves, simply from the tension of coming forward and having to wait on line. Moving to the edge of our practice causes our mind to work in a different way; it creates a space for the teachings to occur; it allows a different kind of communication.

Please take advantage of this opportunity to train. If you have a question, or if you have something to say, come forward. The key is to put yourself on the line; take a risk. It is in that risk-taking that you realize yourself; it is in putting yourself on the edge of your practice that you learn the most. You don't need to think about it. The more you think about it the farther you move away from it. Just put yourself on the line.

CAVE OF TIGERS

1

THE STILL POINT OF ZAZEN

Zazen is the heart of Zen practice. Historically, Zen monastics were known as the meditation monastics, and Buddhism itself originated in the zazen of Shakyamuni Buddha sitting and realizing the nature of reality under the bodhi tree. But the strong emphasis placed on meditation in Zen really dates back to Bodhidharma, who was reputed to have sat nine years facing the wall in single-minded effort. All of the Zen lineages that are traced to Bodhidharma always maintained zazen as their primary focus and the basis of training.

Of course, there are other forms of Buddhism. There are schools that place emphasis on the study and comprehension of the sutras; others dedicate themselves to repeating the name of a buddha. There are forms of Buddhism that focus on liturgy or elaborate esoteric visualizations. In Zen, the emphasis is on zazen. Whether we are talking about Soto school or Rinzai school, whether we are dealing with koan introspection or silent illumination, the cornerstone of Zen is zazen.

It is amazing, however, how sparse is the information published about zazen, and generally how little is known about zazen even among those who supposedly practice it. When you survey the wealth of Zen Buddhist literature, there are volumes published on koans and koan study. There are extensive collections of sayings of great masters, but few historical documents talk specifically about zazen, and usually they are no more than a paragraph or two in length. Master Dogen is an exception to this. All of his teaching was based on zazen; in fact, he wrote one fascicle in his masterwork *Shobogenzo* devoted exclusively to the subject. Yet, we can say that everything that has been published—all ninetyfour chapters of the *Shobogenzo*, all the sutras and discourses of the Buddha, all the ancient teachings

13

and the koans that have been handed down from generation to generation—is nothing but zazen.

The excerpt below comes from an introduction to zazen titled "The Still Point":

From time immemorial, zazen has been the dwelling place of great sages. Wise ones and sages have all made zazen their own chambers, their own mind, their own body. And through these wise ones and sages, zazen has been actualized. However many great sages and wise ones we suppose have entered into zazen, ever since they have entered, no one has ever met a single one of them. There is only the actualization of the life of zazen. Not a single trace of their having entered remains. The countenance of zazen is completely different when we are in the world gazing off at zazen than when we are in zazen meeting zazen. Our consideration and understanding of the activity and the non–activity of zazen should not be the same as the dragon's understanding. Humans and devas reside in their own worlds. Other beings may have doubts about this, or again they may not. Therefore, without giving way to our surprise and doubt, we should study the words and activity of zazen with the buddhas and ancestors. Taking one view, there is the activity of zazen. Taking another, there is the stillness of zazen. At one time there is activity, another time there is stillness. If our study is not like this, it is not the true zazen of the Tathagata.

We should clearly realize that zazen is not meditation, contemplation, visualization, or mindfulness. It is not to be found in the mudra, chakra, mantra, or koan. Neither in its stillness nor its functioning, its seated or its active form can zazen be said to be meditation. Zazen is not single-pointedness of mind, no mind, aware mind, or transcendental mind. It is not revealed in words or letters, and is only transmitted one-to-one, from buddha to buddha.

Master Dogen said, "Cease from the practice of intellectual understanding, pursuing words and following after speech, and learn the backwards step that turns your light inward to illuminate yourself. Body and mind of themselves will drop away and your original face will be manifested. If you want to attain suchness, you should practice suchness without delay. Cease all movements of the conscious mind, the gauging of all thoughts and views. Have no design on becoming a buddha. Zazen has nothing whatsoever to do with sitting or lying down. The zazen that I speak of is not learning meditation. It is simply the Dharma gate of repose and bliss—the practice-realization of total accumulated enlightenment. It is the manifestation of ultimate reality."

Know that the world of zazen is far different from any other realm. At the precise moment of sitting zazen, examine whether time permeates the vertical and horizontal axes, and all of space. And consider the nature of zazen. Is it different from normal activity? Is it a highly vigorous state? Is it thinking or non-thinking? Action or non-action? Is zazen only the full lotus posture or does it exist in the body and the mind? Does it transcend body and mind? We must examine such various standpoints. The goal is to have a full lotus posture of your body and a full lotus posture in your mind. You must have a full lotus posture in a state where body and mind have fallen away.

The zazen of the mind is not the same as the zazen of the body, and vice versa. There is a zazen of shikantaza that differs from the zazen in which body and mind have fallen off. Once the body and mind drop off, we attain the comprehension and experience of the buddhas and ancestors. We must preserve this mind by thoroughly examining all aspects of zazen.

If we do not transmit zazen, we do not transmit the Buddhadharma. Here on this mountain, from the very beginning, zazen has been an essential aspect of our practice. By seven-thirty in the evening on the day we formally arrived to begin our practice here, we began zazen, and it has continued to be our practice. During that first winter there were only six or seven of us sitting in a very cold building, but zazen never stopped for one moment. It is zazen that has created and maintained this sangha. It is zazen that moves out of this monastery to our affiliate groups across the country and across the ocean. It is zazen that unites all of the sanghas of the Buddhist practitioners throughout the world. Zazen is not only the basis of our practice and the process through which we realize ourselves, but realization itself. Zazen is enlightenment.

STUDENT: Master Dogen says that zazen is the actualization of the ultimate reality. I say we should just wash out our ears.
TEACHER: Don't you believe Dogen?
STUDENT: [Gags.]
TEACHER: Does that mean zazen is or is not?
STUDENT: If I had any idea about it, I certainly wouldn't talk about it.
TEACHER: Why not?
STUDENT: I don't know.
TEACHER: How do you practice zazen?
STUDENT: When the bell rings in the morning, I get up. Ching, ching, ching, ching.
TEACHER: May your life go well.
STUDENT: Thank you for your answer.

STUDENT: I'm curious about consciousness. I realize that experiencing different states of consciousness is still separation from zazen.

TEACHER: In a sense, even discussing different states of consciousness separates consciousness from itself. We don't have compartmentalized consciousness; it's all one consciousness.

STUDENT: I know that intellectually, but most of the time it feels very different.

TEACHER: Do you call feeling happy and feeling sad different states of consciousness? These different ways that we feel can be called different states of consciousness, but really it is all the same consciousness.

STUDENT: I know that's true, but I want to be able to arrive at any of those states at will. I know that's completely deluded, but it's something that I desire. So how do I deal with it?

TEACHER: How do you deal with any desire? Holy desires are no less hindering than profane desires.

STUDENT: What do you do with your cigarette addiction?

TEACHER: I smoke.

STUDENT: I use my consciousness in different ways.

TEACHER: Everybody does. When you're happy, you're using your consciousness in a particular way; when you're sad you're using your consciousness in a particular way.

STUDENT: I can make myself happy and I can make myself sad, but I can't grab hold of states that I really desire.

TEACHER: I don't know what those different states that you desire are.

STUDENT: This wonderful, blissful state of ecstasy.

TEACHER: Why are you chasing after that?

STUDENT: Why?

TEACHER: Yes.

STUDENT: Because it is profound.

TEACHER: It is?

STUDENT: [Laughs.]

TEACHER: Picking your nose is most profound. What do you think of that?

STUDENT: It's profane. I can pick my nose any time I want.

TEACHER: Why don't you just throw away all that groping and running and struggling and just take what you have?

STUDENT: Because that seems too simple, too sober, too mundane.

TEACHER: I don't know about mundane. What's mundane? What's holy? You have two nostrils, right? So what's all the searching and chasing about?

STUDENT: I don't know. I can't give it up.

TEACHER: Can't give it up, can't stop thinking, can't do this, can't do that; very difficult. Time to shut up and sit!

STUDENT: Thank you for your answer.

STUDENT: I constantly get hung up with expectations in my zazen, and a lot of people seem to complain about the same thing. In the past you've talked about aspiration versus expectation. What is aspiration in zazen?

TEACHER: Aspiration has to do with just sitting itself. For me, zazen used to be something I had to do—it was good for me, so I did it. Many people approach all sorts of activities in the same way. Eat more bran, more fiber, take multivitamins, exercise regularly—it's good for you. Then, one day, a change happened with me and zazen. I simply realized that zazen was as intimate a part of my life as drinking water. I don't need to practice drinking water. It happens. When I need water, I drink; just like sleeping, or breathing, or any of the other essentials of my life. Zazen became that intimate—important and ordinary. When that happened, I no longer found myself doing zazen. Zazen became a part of my life. It was no longer a chore but a natural part of my functioning, like raising a hand or walking, and that makes all the difference in the world in one's attitude toward zazen.

STUDENT: After that point, were you judging your zazen while you were sitting?

TEACHER: Sometimes zazen was strong, sometimes it was weak; sometimes my *samadhi* was very deep, at other times I was very scattered. It didn't matter; it was zazen. Whether it is good or bad—this morning I sit, tonight I sit, tomorrow morning I'll sit, the next day I'll sit, and I'll sit for the rest of my life. Hopefully my last breath will happen while I'm doing zazen.

STUDENT: So it has something to do with raising one's faith?

TEACHER: I think it's accepting that which is; recognizing that's what my life was, that's what my life is.

STUDENT: Thank you for your answer.

TEACHER: May your life go well.

STUDENT: When I sit, I'm spending most of my time looking for the *hara*, trying to feel it.

TEACHER: Can you feel the solar plexus?

STUDENT: Here? [Points to the center of his abdomen.]

TEACHER: The solar plexus is up a little higher. It's two or three fingers above the navel. Do you know that place? Have you ever felt it?

STUDENT: I think I'm familiar with it.

TEACHER: Fear or excitement usually settles there.

STUDENT: Yes, definitely fear.

TEACHER: Well, the hara is located a few inches below the navel, and it is there that we place our center of consciousness. That's where you put your mind, rather than in your face, where we customarily put our attentiveness. As you develop familiarity with the hara during zazen, you begin to associate the hara with all awareness. Your centeredness and your hara become firmly connected. When something unexpected happens—when somebody yells, "Fire!"—instead of becoming discombobulated, blood rushing to your head, you'll find that it will flow down to the hara, and you will feel warmth there. The circulation of blood increases to that area of your body where you focus your attention. It's an incredibly interesting phenomenon. If you concentrate on your hand, you can actually measure the increase of temperature in your palm. As you develop the ability to concentrate on your hara, when something unexpected happens all of your energy will immediately go to that place, and rather than scattering you, that energy will collect and center you. It's a very powerful connection to observe and practice, worth all the effort that goes into making it your own.

STUDENT: Thank you for your answer.

TEACHER: May your life go well.

STUDENT: I've heard several people say that their zazen energizes them. I usually don't have that experience. I find that I feel tired and drained after sitting. I'm not sure if that's just the way I sit or is there something I have to change?

TEACHER: If zazen is a thing that you feel you should do, and you have no choice, then it becomes an effort to do it; it's a struggle just to keep your mind focused. Some people deal with this struggle by going unconscious—they fall asleep. Other people become very tense, and thus get exhausted. Some people just space out and spend all their time wondering when the bell's going to ring to end the sitting period. All of these situations make sitting hard, but when you finally just acknowledge the fact that zazen is your life, it changes. It's no longer an effort; it's no longer draining, but rather rejuvenating. During zazen, a person in deep *samadhi* breathes three breaths a minute instead of the twenty of a normal person at rest. Metabolism slows down; heart rate, respiration, and blood flow slow down; the body goes into a state of relaxation that you don't experience even in sleep. That's one of the reasons why sleeping time in a monastery is not very long. If your mind and body are free of tensions, you don't have to sleep ten hours a day. Actually, the more you sit, the less sleep you need, so during intensive meditation retreats like *sesshin*, if you are really sitting, you will only need a few hours of sleep. On the other hand, if you're fighting yourself, sitting becomes very draining. It's a phase that people go through, but ultimately your zazen will become revitalizing and nourishing.

STUDENT: I went out early this morning for a walk and realized that this was the first time in a couple of months that I felt emotionally comfortable with my sitting practice. Up till now, I not only felt separate from zazen, but I felt as if I was a living opponent to my practice and I was in some tremendous conflict with it, and I didn't really even know it. It seems to be dissipating now, but it took a couple of months for me to realize that it was happening.

TEACHER: You're lucky! It took me a couple of years. Anything else?

STUDENT: Thank you for your answer.

TEACHER: May your life go well.

STUDENT: I think I agree with Layman Pang: "Difficult, difficult, difficult."

TEACHER: I agree with his daughter: "Neither difficult nor easy."

STUDENT: I agree with his wife: "Easy, easy, easy." But I've never met his daughter.

TEACHER: [In falsetto.] Neither difficult nor easy.

STUDENT: When I finally get my attention in my hara, do you think I'll find it neither difficult nor easy?

TEACHER: No.

STUDENT: But you just said that was one way of finding it.

TEACHER: One way of finding what?

STUDENT: Neither difficult nor easy.

TEACHER: I said that was one way of finding stability and stillness.

STUDENT: Start by putting attention in my hara?

TEACHER: That's a good practice. Is this difficult?

STUDENT: Right here now? No.

TEACHER: Is it easy?

STUDENT: No.

TEACHER: Well, there we have it, and no hara.

STUDENT: That's it? [Laughs.] Okay. I don't have anything else to report.

TEACHER: May your life go well.

STUDENT: Thank you for your answer.

STUDENT: How do I get off the roller coaster of my emotions?

TEACHER: How did you get on it?

STUDENT: I created it. How do I de-create it?

TEACHER: How do you create it?

STUDENT: It's in my mind.

TEACHER: You create it by your thoughts. Those thoughts lead to other thoughts, and the whole stream of thoughts turns into what we call an emotion, a physiological response. Anger, sadness, anxiety, fear, joy—they're all thought-related. If you really probe into these experiences and get to the root of them, below the feelings you will see the thoughts that lead to them. If you go deep enough into the thoughts, you will arrive at the place where the first thought arises, and eventually you get to the place before the first thought. "Before the first thought" is very still and quiet, but as soon as the first thought happens, the chain reaction begins, and the next thing you know, you're responding on an emotional level. What you need to do is to recognize that process. Once you recognize that process and really know, firsthand, that you're the creator and the master of what happens to you—that what you do and what happens to you are the same thing—then your way of dealing with all of life's turmoil transforms automatically. You empower yourself. Going into the anxiety, going into the fear, going into the emotion, then being it, seeing the thoughts that lead to it, frees you.

STUDENT: Sometimes I feel present but not fully there, and those are the best times, but then I still have to go back to face myself more directly.

TEACHER: It sounds like what you're talking about is suppression and denial. That doesn't accomplish anything. It just produces a big boiler inside your gut, and usually whatever you're suppressing will be manifested in some other way. You can't suppress reality, you can't deny it. That's why the only way through a barrier is to *be* the barrier. The only way through a koan is to be the koan. That's what zazen is; that's what practice is. Be intimate with it all—with the whole catastrophe—and in that intimacy you begin to see things in a completely different way. It takes a lot of trust to do it. We are conditioned and respond to situations in terms of years of conditioning, and the only way you're going to break free of that is to do exactly the opposite of what you've been doing all your life. Instead of turning away from a barrier, turn toward it. Be it with the whole body and mind. That's the way you make yourself free.

STUDENT: Thank you for your answer.

TEACHER: May your life go well.

STUDENT: I hear zazen this, zazen that, zazen in the morning and afternoon and evening, zazen over here, zazen over there. If I can't accept the person who I am on my pillow, I'll have nothing to do with it.

TEACHER: Sure. That's what zazen is—intimacy twenty-four hours a day. One moment of zazen immediately actualizes the zazen of thousands of buddhas and ancestors past, present, and future. It's like plugging into the center of the universe. One moment of zazen; one second of zazen. It is with you wherever you go. It is with you before you even leave to go there. May your life go well.

STUDENT: Thank you for your answer.

STUDENT: I love zazen. I hate zazen!

TEACHER: That's how I feel about it.

STUDENT: About what?

TEACHER: Beat's me. Anything else?

STUDENT: No.

TEACHER: May your life go well.

STUDENT: Thank you for your answer.

STUDENT: I'm trying to understand zazen by relating it to ordinary activities. A couple of times when I've gone out hiking, I've gotten to a point where I'm walking along and then I am not. Then I wake up. Isn't that zazen?

TEACHER: In a sense it's zazen. But when you're walking along, before you wake up, is there any understanding?

STUDENT: There is nothing.

TEACHER: So why are you trying to understand zazen? Understanding is not what it's about. When you're really intimate with zazen, there's no knowing it. Just like when you're really intimate with your hiking. There's no knowing it. That's what zazen is about. Otherwise there's self-consciousness; there's the person doing zazen and then there's the watcher, the witness. "Now you're doing zazen, now you're not doing zazen; now it's good, now it's bad." How is it when it transcends good and bad, understanding and knowing?

STUDENT: More than just sitting and counting your breath.

TEACHER: Of course. It's walking or dancing or crying or laughing. Zazen is a way of using your mind and living your life. You can do zazen waiting in the bus station or sitting in a doctor's office. Zazen is also walking to the doctor's office, talking to the doctor. Zazen is our life.

STUDENT: How can I do that?

TEACHER: By doing it and being intimate with it.

STUDENT: How can I sit and really sit?

TEACHER: How can you sit and not sit?

STUDENT: By thinking.

TEACHER: Thinking is not zazen?

STUDENT: Not if I understand what I'm hearing.

TEACHER: Okay. Just think non-thinking then.

STUDENT: I find myself going to sleep.

TEACHER: How do you think non-thinking?

STUDENT: I don't know.

TEACHER: Not thinking. Those are the instructions that Master Dogen left us.
Cross your legs, straighten your posture, lower your eyes, and then think non-thinking. How do you think non-thinking? Not thinking.

STUDENT: No problem. Thank you for your answer.

TEACHER: May your life go well.

STUDENT: As I understand, in Buddhist thinking there's no such thing as a soul,
and when we die we go back to the One. In zazen the same is true, we return
to the One. So why the hell am I going to spend twenty-five years sitting on
the pillow, when in twenty-five years I'll be one with everything anyway?

TEACHER: You don't have to wait twenty-five years. You're the One now, whether
you realize it or not. It's not something that happens to you. You're already
one with the whole universe. When you die, I don't know where you go.

STUDENT: It's a gamble, I guess.

TEACHER: What's a gamble?

STUDENT: Where you go.

TEACHER: What's the difference? When you live, just live. When you die, just die.
When you sit, just sit. Anything else?

STUDENT: No.

TEACHER: May your life go well.

STUDENT: Thank you for your answer.

STUDENT: Zen practice is designed to break habits and free us from conditioning,
but in doing zazen, aren't we creating a new habit? Sitting in the morning, sitting in the evening—I thought we didn't want to develop habitual patterns.

TEACHER: True, true. Definitely don't chase after sounds, definitely don't follow
after form. When the bell rings, why do you put on your *rakusu* and sit zazen?

STUDENT: It's a habit.

TEACHER: You should get rid of that habit.

STUDENT: Then I won't do it anymore.

TEACHER: If you're doing zazen out of habit, you're not doing zazen in the first
place. If you're perpetuating a habit, you're not practicing.

STUDENT: If I haven't experienced that kind of practice, I just have to believe what you're saying. Why should I believe it?

TEACHER: You shouldn't believe it.

STUDENT: So how can I ever get to experience it?

TEACHER: By doing it.

STUDENT: How can I do it without setting up a habit?

TEACHER: It's not a habit.

STUDENT: It is. Sitting in the morning...

TEACHER: If you're practicing it as a habit, then you're not practicing. I'm asking you to practice it without making it a habit. Just do it. Is drinking water a habit? Is sleeping a habit? Is breathing a habit? Arguing is a habit.

STUDENT: I would die if I didn't breathe, but I would not die if I didn't sit zazen.

TEACHER: You wouldn't die if you didn't sit zazen?

STUDENT: No.

TEACHER: Don't sit zazen, and don't die.

STUDENT: But that's not the solution.

TEACHER: The solution is to sit zazen and die.

STUDENT: But that's still something that you're telling me, and I have to believe it to do it.

TEACHER: Please, don't believe it, and I'm not telling you to do anything. You do what you want. I have nothing to tell you. You don't want to sit, don't sit. You want to sit, sit. But whatever you decide to do, don't wobble.

STUDENT: Okay. Thank you for your answer.

TEACHER: May your life go well.

STUDENT: Is it true that zazen itself is enlightenment?

TEACHER: Yes.

STUDENT: So, when I sit and I'm falling asleep, or I'm daydreaming, or I'm not watching my thoughts, is my zazen enlightenment?

TEACHER: The very first thing that the Buddha said upon his enlightenment is that all sentient beings are already enlightened. Obviously that includes our sleeping, our wakefulness, our intelligence, our stupidity. Most people have the idea that enlightenment is somewhere other than where they stand, so they run around looking for it. What Master Dogen is saying is that the process, zazen, and the goal, enlightenment, are not two things, any more than absolute and relative are two things. Form is emptiness, emptiness is form. Delusion is enlightenment, enlightenment is delusion. Good and bad are the same thing. It doesn't compute logically, so what is it?

STUDENT: Yes, I think I'm definitely getting stuck on that.

TEACHER: That's because you're trying to understand it by linear, sequential thought. The fact that you can't understand it doesn't mean that it's not so. Anything else?

STUDENT: No. Thank you for your answer.

TEACHER: May your life go well.

STUDENT: I have been trying to do zazen for years and tonight I feel as confused as ever about what I'm doing. I read a letter by Master Hakuin and he said that if you sit and are not aware of your hara, the zazen is not good at all. Today I feel that I don't know what I'm doing.

TEACHER: Well, I don't know what I'm doing either.

STUDENT: [Laughs.]

TEACHER: Do you have a question?

STUDENT: What am I doing?

TEACHER: You know who you have to ask to get that answer—the doer.

STUDENT: When I sit by myself, my body doesn't ache no matter how long I sit. When I sit in the *zendo* and everyone is here, my body hurts.

TEACHER: Some evening while you are doing zazen here, we'll all sneak out and see if your body stops aching. You know where this is all happening—it's all up in your head.

STUDENT: I know, it's a belief in my head, but I'm not aware of it.

TEACHER: Let it go. Treat it like any other thought.

STUDENT: My practice is to sit with things.

TEACHER: Okay, so sit with it, and hurt. [Laughs.] When you get tired of hurting, you will stop.

STUDENT: But then I'm not letting it go.

TEACHER: Oh, it will go. After it hurts long enough, you'll get tired of it and it will stop.

STUDENT: I'm tenacious.

TEACHER: Good, that's what you need, tenacity. Just keep sitting. Just keep hurting. Just keep laughing. Does it hurt now?

STUDENT: [Shakes her head.]

TEACHER: And we're all here.

STUDENT: [Laughs.]

TEACHER: You are cured already. May your life go well.

STUDENT: Thank you for your answer.

TEACHER: Thank you.

STUDENT: This morning I woke up and I felt like shit, but I've got a crush on zazen, so I came down anyway and the first sitting period was [nods off], second sitting period was [sits alert].

TEACHER: What was that first period?

STUDENT: [Slumps.]

TEACHER: Pile of shit sitting zazen.

STUDENT: [Wipes tears and sniffs.] Little pile.

TEACHER: Little pile of big shit.

STUDENT: Big shit!

TEACHER: Until finally it fills the whole universe, reaches everywhere. Heaven and earth disappear. Is that the only kind of zazen you do?

STUDENT: [Shakes her head.]

TEACHER: What's the other kind?

STUDENT: You really want to know?

TEACHER: Yeah, go ahead.

STUDENT: Well, during sesshin, the morning period right before lunch is spent just trying to stay awake.

TEACHER: Forget about sesshin, forget about dawn zazen, forget about evening zazen—what other kind of zazen do you do?

STUDENT: [Knocks on teacher's wooden platform.]

TEACHER: You blew it. May your life go well.

STUDENT: [Laughs.] Thank you for your answer.

There is no question that zazen is a very disciplined practice and that it is the beginning and the end of Zen training. Unfortunately, true zazen is rarely being practiced these days. Yet unless we realize zazen—sitting Zen—then our walking Zen, laughing Zen, crying Zen are not the Zen of the buddhas and ancestors.

Zazen is the most essential aspect of the mind-to-mind transmission. It is an incredibly powerful tool. It is not just sitting cross-legged. It is not just meditation. There's an incredible unfolding that takes place in zazen. It's endless. It's a precious gift that has come to us, that has been handed down for two thousand five hundred years. Its simplicity can be very deceiving. It is by far the most powerful thing any of us will ever encounter in our lives. Don't take it lightly. Even the zazen of the most rank beginner gives life to countless buddhas and ancestors, past, present and future. Please don't waste this gift.

2 THE PRACTICE OF EVERYDAY LIFE

In the opening lines of "Genjokoan," the seminal chapter of his masterwork *Shobogenzo: The Treasury of the True Dharma Eye*, Master Dogen says,

> When all dharmas are Buddhadharma, there is life and death, enlightenment and delusion, practice, buddhas and creatures.
>
> When the ten thousand things are without self, there are no buddhas and no creatures, no enlightenment and no delusion, no life and no death.
>
> However, the Buddha Way is beyond being and non-being; therefore there are buddhas and creatures, enlightenment and delusion, life and death.

This paragraph is a distillation of the entirety of the *Shobogenzo*. In the first line, Dogen uses the word "practice," but he doesn't mention it subsequently. Why?

What is practice? What does it mean to practice Zen? What does it mean to practice the Way of Everyday Life? In the West many people who come in contact with the teachings suffer from a sickness called "anything-goes Zen." The same phenomenon occurred in China and in Japan when Zen migrated there. It is logical that such a problem should arise. Because the teachings proclaim that each one of us is inherently enlightened—each one of us is perfect and complete right from the beginning—there is a tendency to conclude that we don't have to do anything. If we are enlightened as we are, why do we have to do zazen or work with a teacher?

The fact is that we are, indeed, already enlightened. It is true that each one of us, right from the very beginning, is perfect and complete, but unless this truth is realized it cannot impart strength to you or to others. Realization is not a matter of intellectual understanding; it is not an idea or a belief; it is not mouthing words someone else has said. It is a direct and personal experience.

In Zen training we distinguish between what we call "experiential" and "intrinsic" truth. Intrinsically, all beings are buddhas from the very beginning, but until this truth is manifested experientially in the world, it is not the actualized Buddhadharma. The word "Buddha" in Buddhadharma points to the intrinsic truth, the absolute; "Dharma" points to the experiential truth, the world of differentiation. To link these words together is to integrate them. This is what we do through practice; we bridge the gap between absolute and relative.

To practice the Way is to practice one's life but, mistakingly, this statement can be taken to mean that everything we do is the Way. Although intrinsically the Dharma is everywhere and we're already enlightened, experientially this is not so if we haven't realized it and manifested it in our lives. This is where it counts, where we reveal ourselves, where all the masks come off. Until the teachings are manifested in our lives, they don't mean anything. They're just a lot of words.

But again, what is practice? What does it mean to practice the Way? Webster's dictionary defines "practice" as "to do." It's interesting that the words used to define "practice" are also the words used to define "commitment." Commitment means "to do"; practice means "to do." How does this relate to Zen? What is Zen? What makes zazen practice? What makes *Genjokoan*, the Koan of Everyday Life, practice?

STUDENT: Five o'clock, sitting; six o'clock, service; seven o'clock, breakfast; eight o'clock, work; nine o'clock, one client; ten o'clock, another client; but I don't know what I'm doing.
TEACHER: Is that practice?
STUDENT: I don't know.
TEACHER: Are you saying that practice is not knowing what you're doing?
STUDENT: No. Practice is five o'clock, sitting; six o'clock, service; seven o'clock, breakfast; eight o'clock, work.
TEACHER: Is that practice?
STUDENT: I don't know.
TEACHER: Not knowing is very intimate. But my son says the very same thing to me. I say, "How was school today?" He says, "I don't know." Is that practice?
STUDENT: I don't know.
TEACHER: Were you doing these things before you began Zen training?
STUDENT: Yeah, the same things.

TEACHER: Was it practice then?

STUDENT: No.

TEACHER: How is it different?

STUDENT: Now it's five o'clock, sitting; six o'clock, service; seven o'clock, breakfast.

TEACHER: Thank you for your answer.

∞

STUDENT: [Makes motion of cleaning bowl.]

TEACHER: Is that any different than this? [Raises hand.]

STUDENT: Yes.

TEACHER: What's the difference?

STUDENT: I clean my bowl, you raise your hand.

TEACHER: Is it the same or different?

STUDENT: I clean the bowl, you raise your hand. This is practice, that is practice.

TEACHER: I clean the bowl, you raise your hand. Period. Everything else is extra. The minute you go beyond that, you've lost it.

STUDENT: Thank you for your answer.

TEACHER: May your life go well.

∞

STUDENT: I have nothing to say.

TEACHER: Is "I have nothing to say" nothing to say? "I have nothing to say" is saying a lot.

STUDENT: If you say so.

TEACHER: Yeah, I say so. What do *you* say?

STUDENT: I have nothing to say.

TEACHER: How do you practice?

STUDENT: [Chants.] "Sentient beings are numberless, I vow to save them."

TEACHER: And in the world, how do you save them?

STUDENT: "Zen Mountain Monastery, this is Karen."

TEACHER: Putting aside "How do you practice?" and "What is practice?" Master Dogen says that practice and enlightenment are one. How do you understand that?

STUDENT: [Emits ear-splitting yell.]

TEACHER: What is that—enlightenment?

STUDENT: I don't know.

TEACHER: Not-knowing is stupidity on the one hand and intimacy on the other. What kind of not-knowing are you presenting to me?

STUDENT: [Silence.]

TEACHER: Find out!

STUDENT: Where should I look?

TEACHER: Don't turn to Daido or Zhaozhou; don't look up to the Buddha, and don't search in the sutras. There's only one place.

STUDENT: I don't find anything.

TEACHER: Then you should continue looking. This gigantic body contains the whole universe. There is no place for you to stand. That's where you should look.

STUDENT: Thank you for your answer.

TEACHER: May your life go well.

STUDENT: [Bows.]

TEACHER: Do you have anything to add?

STUDENT: [Bows.]

TEACHER: Anything else?

STUDENT: [Bows.]

TEACHER: I understood the first bow, and I got the second and the third. After four, five, six bows, how will you answer the question, "Do you have anything to add?"

STUDENT: [Bows again.]

TEACHER: Oh, what's happening to my Dharma?!

STUDENT: Thank you for your answer.

TEACHER: May your life go well.

STUDENT: In the portion of the *Genjokoan* that you quoted, why *does* Master Dogen use the word "practice" only in the first line?

TEACHER: My question is, why does Dogen omit the word "practice" in the second and the third line? Was it purposeful? Did he forget? I am not aware if anybody has addressed this question in depth but I'm sure Dogen didn't simply forget. One way of understanding it is this: In the beginning there are mountains, rivers, and the great earth; after many years of training, and deepening practice, I realize there are no mountains, no rivers, and no great earth; then, as my training continues, I further realize that there are mountains, rivers, and the great earth. In other words, the same things exist in the beginning as in the end. In the middle, in experiencing *shunyata,* there is only emptiness, with no buddhas, no enlightenment, no delusion, no life, no death. But why not include "no practice?"

STUDENT: [Silence.]

TEACHER: How do you practice?

STUDENT: I practice sitting zazen and I practice during the day.

TEACHER: How is "during the day" different from zazen?

STUDENT: I don't think it is different. Eating, walking, and sleeping are all practice.

TEACHER: How is that different from a random visitor who strolls through the doors of this monastery? She eats, walks, and sleeps. Does she see her life as practice?

STUDENT: She doesn't have a conscious desire or wish for enlightenment.

TEACHER: That is true. A goal is a part of the definition of practice. Practice is headed somewhere. Even though Zen doesn't have any goals, we don't need to think of having a goal as delusive. It is both true and not true. There is a goal. You will never get anywhere if you don't have a sense of direction. You will wander around endlessly, bumping into obstacles and encountering dead ends, but the process of arriving at that goal and the goal itself are not two separate things. That's the key. The goal of practice is enlightenment. The process is zazen, or practice. Yet, practice and enlightenment are one. The fundamental basis of the *Genjokoan,* and the revolution of Master Dogen's teachings, is the idea that even a rank beginner doing zazen is manifesting the enlightenment of the Buddha. By saying that there is a certain direction, an intent, you are pointing to the heart of practice. It takes a certain attitude of mind, a particular kind of consciousness, to see the activity as the manifestation of the goal. For a musician, practice is the performance. If you practice that way, with the attitude that practice is the performance, you will have the attitude of mind that Master Dogen was talking about. You will see that practice and enlightenment are one.

STUDENT: Thank you for your answer.

TEACHER: May your life go well.

STUDENT: How would you teach me to practice?

TEACHER: Practice begins and ends with yourself. Until you raise the *bodhi* mind, there is no practice. Bodhi mind is essentially the mind of enlightenment, but unless there is some sense of direction, there can be no practice. The difference between someone chopping wood and carrying water who is doing Zen practice, and someone chopping wood and carrying water who is not doing Zen practice is that in the first case the activities are directed in a specific way. In the intrinsic sense, there is no teaching. Once the bodhi mind has been raised, once you have the aspiration for enlightenment, then virtually everything you do within the teacher-student relationship—which is what you're asking about—is pointing to practice. The teacher's responsibility is to refrain from giving the student anything to lean on. If your practice in life has been to do it "whatever way I want," the teacher will pull the rug out from under you to get you to deal with things with a different attitude.

STUDENT: Why?

TEACHER: Because that's where you stick. Master Dogen says it this way: "Flowers fall with our attachment and weeds spring up with our aversion." Attachment and aversion are manifestations of delusion, and they characterize self-styled Zen practice. A person who says, "I do whatever I want" is not free if they can only do whatever they want. If you can do what must be done, *then* you're really free. Whatever we hold on to—whether it's emptiness, the Dharma, "This is it!"—needs to be thrown away. If that seems abhorrent, that attitude needs to be thrown away, too. Whatever our likes and dislikes are, when we attach to them they become a cage. The only way to solve the dilemma is to get rid of the cage. Nobody put it there except ourselves. Practice is about letting go, making yourself empty. You look at whatever comes up, acknowledge it, and throw it away. When a delusion arises—"I like this, I hate that,"—you look at it, acknowledge it, and throw it away. When enlightenment comes up, you look at it, acknowledge it, and throw it away.

STUDENT: Where does it end?

TEACHER: Practice does not end. When there is nothing left, you throw that away too, because nothing is just another thing to get rid of.

STUDENT: Can we hold on to anything?

TEACHER: There's nothing to hold on to. In order to hold on to something, it has to be outside of you. Outside and inside are the basis of delusion. How can you hold on to what you are? When there is nothing else in the universe except you, when "you" contains everything and is so vast and boundless that you encompass everything, not only in the present but also in the past and future, what is there outside of you and who will do the holding? When you are the object itself, how do you hold on to it? You're the whole thing. Do you understand?

STUDENT: I understand that I have to understand. I understand it in a general sense, not deeply.

TEACHER: To experience the universe in that way is what we call enlightenment. It's possible to talk about enlightenment, it's possible to understand it, it's possible to believe it. Indeed, it's a wonderful and very religious thing to believe in. It is not that difficult to understand. It has a logic of its own, but it's just made up of more profound or entertaining ideas. Believing makes you dependent on a belief system and the minute that system collapses, you crumble with it. Understanding enlightenment fails because understanding it places you outside of it. There's a knower and a thing that is known, and this is a very vulnerable position. Suppose somebody says, "What do you know! Shakyamuni never existed! They've just found out it was all a political hoax." If your appreciation depends on the reference system that was just undermined, your position falters. On the other hand, if you experience enlightenment directly, nobody can take it away from you. If you've cast off body and mind and forgotten the self; if you've experienced the ten thousand things returning to the self—then how can anybody say anything about it? What is there to say? You have the confidence and the strength that comes from your own direct experience. Nothing short of that will do.

STUDENT: But I've heard that the little glimpses of insight experienced in Zen training are part of a benign conspiracy to keep people practicing.

TEACHER: If it's anybody else's glimpse, it's a benign conspiracy; but if it's your glimpse, it's as real as your glimpse is. You know what a thing tastes like by tasting it. In practice, sometimes that taste, that glimpse, is not enough. It makes you want to see more and more—the whole thing. Your experience can be the same mystical experience as that of Shakyamuni Buddha. Why not? You have everything he had, so why shouldn't it be? Why shouldn't your experience be the same as that of Christ or Moses or any of the great spiritual leaders? Who singled them out, after all? Why were they special? They were special because of the practice and perseverance that led them to their realization. These days everybody runs around trying to imitate them, but in Buddhism imitation doesn't cut it, believing doesn't cut it, understanding doesn't cut it. Only when you make practice your own is it valid, and it's very clear when that happens. There's no way to hide it and there's no way to fake your way when you don't have it.

STUDENT: Thank you for your answer.

TEACHER: May your life go well.

STUDENT: I may need a little help with the quote, "When all dharmas are Buddhadharma." Michael, I told you for three days in a row to stack that wood and now I'm going to stand here and watch you do it. That's my practice. The second line?

TEACHER: "When the ten thousand things are without self..."

STUDENT: I can't find anything. The third line…
TEACHER: "Buddha Way is beyond being and non-being…"
STUDENT: Michael, I told you for three days in a row to stack that wood.
TEACHER: How does that differ from the first line?
STUDENT: Michael, I want you to stack that wood. That is my practice.
TEACHER: And in the last?
STUDENT: Michael, I want you to stack that wood.
TEACHER: That seems clear. And in the middle one?
STUDENT: I look and I can't find.
TEACHER: What happened to Michael?
STUDENT: I can't find him.
TEACHER: What happened to you?
STUDENT: I can't find her.
TEACHER: Thank you for your answer.

STUDENT: A phrase you used earlier really stuck in my mind, "What must be done." Please elaborate on what you meant by it.
TEACHER: It is the other side of "I do what I want." To be able to function freely in either doing or not doing is what I'm talking about—to do what must be done. You've made a commitment and you have a responsibility. You have a child, let's say, and it gets in the way. You want to paint. To be a good artist you have to devote yourself wholeheartedly to your art. To be a good Zen practitioner you have to devote yourself wholeheartedly to your practice, but this kid keeps annoying you, getting in your way. To be able to see that child as your practice is doing what has to be done. That's freedom.
STUDENT: Thank you, but I was thinking more about what must be done in the world.
TEACHER: You mean social responsibility?
STUDENT: Yes.
TEACHER: Social responsibility is directly associated with the depth of one's understanding. Some people ignore problems through trivial preoccupations or outright denial. Others become relentless professional activists. Between the two extremes there's a middle way. There are many things that can be done, but what we choose depends on one's understanding. Problems or crises are not outside of ourselves; they are all our responsibility. The President is my responsibility. The Middle East is my responsibility. When I realize that, I empower myself to do something about them. You will look at today's social,

psychological, or environmental difficulties very differently if you place your-self outside of them rather than being intimate with them. For example, suppose you are unjustly sentenced to life imprisonment. It's one thing to be happy and full of equanimity when everything is going smoothly, but what if you end up in jail because of a mistake, how do you respond then? Or suppose a physician tells you that you have two months to live. How do you deal with life and its responsibilities in that situation? You perceive your life very differently if you live in the moment-to-moment awareness of existence, being intimate with each moment, as opposed to seeing yourself as a separate entity, closed off from everything else.

STUDENT: So, one must really practice being one with the President?

TEACHER: Acknowledge your responsibility for the President and for any problems that you may encounter.

STUDENT: Thank you for your answer.

TEACHER: May your life go well.

STUDENT: If I encompass everything, how will I cross the street?

TEACHER: "If I encompass everything" is an idea. You don't encompass a damn thing unless you are convinced of that.

STUDENT: Everything is an idea.

TEACHER: If you say so.

STUDENT: How do I get it out of the realm of ideas?

TEACHER: Move a little closer. [Pinches her cheek.]

STUDENT: [Yelps.]

TEACHER: Is that an idea? There's a big difference between the experience and the words that describe it. I could have said, "I pinch your cheek," and that would have communicated something, but it's very different from the experience itself. Do you know what I mean?

STUDENT: I know what you mean.

TEACHER: Now you have to go from this understanding into the whole body and mind experience of your life.

STUDENT: When I gave birth to my daughter, there was no problem; it was whole body and mind. I don't do that every day, though. Life gets stuck.

TEACHER: Now we turn full circle to the original question of "What is practice?" How do you practice your life? What is the Way of Everyday Life? It suddenly takes on a spiritual dimension. It's no longer just "everyday life." It's the heart of what Master Dogen was talking about when he said, "Those that regard mundane life as a hindrance to practice only understand that in the secular there is nothing sacred. What they don't understand is that in the sacred, there is nothing secular." If all activities are practice, then everything we do is the sacred teaching of the Buddha. In this very moment, you're dressed in the clothes of the Buddha, you eat the food of the Buddha, sleep in the Buddha's bed, think the thoughts of the Buddha. Easy to say, hard to do.

STUDENT: Thank you for your answer.

TEACHER: May your life go well.

STUDENT: You said that we're all intrinsically buddhas, therefore why practice? Then you said that, although we are all intrinsically buddhas, it doesn't "cut it" if you don't realize it. Are you saying that the reason we practice is to enable us to realize that fact?

TEACHER: Do you want me to speak for everybody?

STUDENT: Why should "one" practice?

TEACHER: Beats me. If "one" doesn't know that, I sure as hell can't help.

STUDENT: Why do you practice? Do you practice?

TEACHER: Practice? I never heard of it. What's practice?

STUDENT: I was just going to ask *you* that.

TEACHER: I don't know. Somebody asked me that question a long time ago and, after years of zazen, study, interview, and dharma encounter, I still haven't figured it out. I still don't have an answer.

STUDENT: Is that intimacy or stupidity?

TEACHER: I think it's stupid.

STUDENT: Thank you for your answer.

TEACHER: May your life go well.

3 TEACHINGS OF THE INSENTIENT

Master Dogen said:

> The way insentient beings expound the Dharma should not be understood to be necessarily the way sentient beings expound the Dharma. The voices of sentient beings should follow the principle of their discourse on Dharma. Even so, it's contrary to the Buddha Way to usurp the voices of the living and conjecture about those of the non-living in terms of them. Even though human judgment now tries to recognize grasses, trees, and the like, and to liken them to non-living things, they too, cannot be measured by the ordinary mind.

Although some of the more romantic among us unwittingly anthropomorphize nature, our tendency is to think that mountains, rivers, and rocks are, after all, lifeless. The Dharma of insentient beings now being expounded is not an anthropomorphized Dharma; this is not what Dogen was talking about. Dogen said: "Mountains, rivers, and the great earth are not sentient, nor are they insentient. The self is neither sentient nor insentient." He also told a story of the poet who, when sitting in the silence of the night, heard the sound of the brook and experienced a deep enlightenment. The poet wrote:

> The sounds of the brook are nothing
> but the gigantic tongue of the Buddha.
> Figures of the mountains are none other
> than the Buddha's body of purity—

Eighty-four thousand gathas since last night:
how can I explain it to others?

Dogen commented:

That night when this poet was enlightened, can we say that the poet was enlightened
by the stream, or was it the stream that was enlightened by the poet? Dare anyone
say that this is a pint of water, or an ocean into which all rivers enter? Ultimately
speaking, is it the poet who has been enlightened, or is it the mountains and rivers
that are enlightened? He who has discerning eyes should apprehend the gigantic
tongue of the Buddha and the body of purity.

Mountains and rivers are neither sentient nor insentient. The self is neither
sentient nor insentient. When this is realized, the ten thousand things are the
teacher, the teachings, and the student. The ten thousand things are realized as the
Three Treasures: the Buddha, the Dharma, and the Sangha. Earth and living beings
expound the Dharma. Water, birds, and trees teach the Dharma. "These mountains
and rivers of the present are the actualization of the life of ancient buddhas."

We should understand, though, that insentient does not only mean trees, birds,
and rocks, but also cars, cement buildings, and the Brooklyn Bridge. The Dharma
is constantly expounded by all of them. What, then, is the teaching of the nuclear
bomb? What can genetic programming teach us? What can the environment teach
us? What do the dying, the unborn, expound?

The mountains, the rivers, the great earth, the ten thousand things—they do
speak. Can you hear them? Master Dongshan said: "If you hear it with the ear and
see it with the eye, you'll never get it. Only when you hear with the eye and see with
the ear will you truly understand it. How do you hear with the eye? How do you see
with the ear?" In the Mountains and Rivers Sutra Dogen talked of the mountain's
walk, of a mountain giving birth to a mountain child, of a stone woman giving
birth to a child in the night. He also said, "Water speaks water." How does water
speak water? What does it say?

The teachings are continuously expounded by the insentient. When the teacher
disappears, and teacher and student merge, the ten thousand things become the
teachings. So, tell me, how do you understand the teachings of the insentient?

STUDENT: Walls, tiles, rubble, raindrops, purple robes, black robes. It's a good
thing, but it's not as good as nothing.

TEACHER: Nothing doesn't function.

STUDENT: Blankets of rain cover the whole earth.

TEACHER: How will you step outside of that to feed the hungry baby? When blankets of rain consume the whole universe, how will we prepare our holiday dinner to feed the homeless?

STUDENT: "Waaaaaa! Here, little one." [Extends her hand.]

TEACHER: "Here" reaches it, crying doesn't. Crying is very intimate, but it doesn't serve. Extending a hand separates, but it serves.

STUDENT: "Separating and serving" doesn't reach it either.

TEACHER: What reaches it?

STUDENT: Reaching not reaching.

TEACHER: What is that—"reaching not reaching?"

STUDENT: "Waaaaaa! Here, little one." [Extends her hand.]

TEACHER: Which is it—the crying or the reaching?

STUDENT: How do you separate them?

TEACHER: "Waaaaaa!" [Extends his hand.] Heaven and earth are separated in those two. How do you unify them?

STUDENT: When it's time for dharma encounter, I do dharma encounter. When I'm hungry, I eat; when I'm cold, I get goosebumps. [Laughs.] When I don't know, I keep talking.

TEACHER: Keep talking, keep talking. May your life go well.

STUDENT: Thank you for your answer.

STUDENT: The teachings of the insentient are very seductive for people who are trained in science. Yet science is not enough. Being trained as a scientist, I know that I must learn a new way of looking at things, trying to see with my ears and hear with my eyes.

TEACHER: Some of the greatest discoveries made in science—Kekule's discovery of the benzene ring, for example—had to do with the teachings of the insentient.

STUDENT: But was that discovery enough?

TEACHER: He discovered the benzene ring. He began the study of molecular structure—a wonderful field of science. Einstein rode a light beam into outer space. To me that seems no different than riding the clouds and following the wind.

STUDENT: So is Mu sentient or insentient?

TEACHER: You're neither sentient nor insentient. The mountains and rivers are neither sentient nor insentient, so how could Mu be one or the other of those two? Is Mu any different than the mountains and rivers, any different than you, me, or the ten thousand things?

STUDENT: I don't know.

TEACHER: Find out!

STUDENT: Thank you for your answer.

TEACHER: May your life go well.

STUDENT: "A stone woman giving birth to a child in the night"—what is this teaching telling us?

TEACHER: A stone woman is a barren woman. By definition, a barren woman can't give birth, yet here she is bearing a child. Empty, yet inconceivably existing; that's what the ten thousand things are. You are empty but inconceivably existing. The ten thousand things, the Buddhadharma itself, enlightenment, delusion: all of it is empty but inconceivably existing, and because it is empty, it can manifest itself in a myriad forms. It's that manifesting in a myriad forms that allows the blue mountain to walk, East Mountain to move over water, the stone woman to give birth to a child in the night. That "empty" is the falling away of body and mind. When that's experienced, you're no longer locked in the bag of skin, and there's no separation between the self and the ten thousand things.

STUDENT: Thank you for your answer.

TEACHER: May your life go well.

STUDENT: I can be intimate but now, when talking, I'm not intimate. What if I want not to be intimate so that I might picture, describe, celebrate?

TEACHER: Picturing, describing, celebrating without intimacy is picturing, describing, and celebrating that has no life. With intimacy the spirit of the picture, of the celebration, is present.

STUDENT: But I don't have the need to celebrate when I'm intimate. When I'm not intimate, I have a great need.

TEACHER: In intimacy with the painting you don't need to be there: the brush paints. In intimacy with the dance, you don't need to be the dancer: the dance dances itself. In intimacy there's no separation, and it's a different kind of creativity. There is also the creativity of separation, but there is a big difference between the two results.

STUDENT: Until I bring myself to the point of being intimate, there is separation and then—let's say with the dance—there's letting go and the dance dances itself. But somehow, in this practice, that never comes to pass and when I'm separate I miss it.

TEACHER: What you're really asking is how to transcend the unity and the separation, absolute and relative, sentient and insentient. We say all the time that the truth is in none of those extremes. Where is the truth to be found? That's the unity of this very life itself.

STUDENT: And that unity has no choice, right?

TEACHER: Picking and choosing are not in that unity.

STUDENT: So, that unity is: when dance is there, dance happens?

TEACHER: When the clouds gather, rain falls.

STUDENT: And that demands total trust?

TEACHER: Trust in yourself.

STUDENT: In myself?

TEACHER: Trusting your life; just as the clouds and the rain trust the manifesting of their existence.

STUDENT: Thank you for your answer.

TEACHER: May your life go well.

∞

STUDENT: [Holds both arms up and, fluttering her fingers, slowly moves them downward from side to side, making delicate rain noises.]

TEACHER: There is no separation in that. There's no eye, ear, nose, tongue, body, or mind. There's no color, smell, sound, taste, touch, or phenomena. How will you take care of your child?

STUDENT: "Come here little one. Sit on my lap for a moment."

TEACHER: Is that the same as what you just presented to me?

STUDENT: Yes.

TEACHER: Is it?

STUDENT: When I'm a mother, I'm a mother. When I'm the rain, I'm the rain.

TEACHER: How does the rain function?

STUDENT: [Repeats earlier movements and sounds.]

TEACHER: That's the truth of the rain; that's not its functioning. How does it function?

STUDENT: Its functioning is washing away dirt and watering the earth.

TEACHER: After your brilliant presentation, don't explain it. You've got the motions down pat, and you even say the words, but you're not convinced, and because you're not convinced, I'm not convinced. Make it your own.

STUDENT: Thank you for your answer.
TEACHER: May your life go well.

STUDENT: Do the insentient have desires, and do their teachings spring from delusion if they're not enlightened?
TEACHER: If insentient beings didn't have desires, how could they walk? How could East Mountain walk over water? How could the stone woman give birth to a child in the night?
STUDENT: What if that wasn't their desires but just what they had to do?
TEACHER: Isn't that what desire is?
STUDENT: I don't know. You told a story about the teacher who, when he heard the bell ring, came into the zendo to teach; and when he heard it ring again, he left. Did he desire to do that?
TEACHER: If that's not desire, give me an example of something that is desire.
STUDENT: I'd really like to have a beer. That's desire.
TEACHER: Is that any different from coming into the zendo to teach?
STUDENT: Doesn't it depend on the mind with which you come into the zendo?
TEACHER: Is the mind that comes into the zendo any different from the mind that wants to have a beer?
STUDENT: I don't know.
TEACHER: Do you have two minds?
STUDENT: I think I do. Maybe more.
TEACHER: Well, there's the problem. Collect them; bring them together.
STUDENT: What if they start an argument with one another?
TEACHER: When they are one, there is no arguing.
STUDENT: Let me guess. Do I do this by doing zazen?
TEACHER: You do it by bringing those minds together. You are the one who has separated them; now just reverse the process.
STUDENT: Thank you for your answer.
TEACHER: May your life go well.

STUDENT: Recently I saw a documentary about the rainforests being destroyed in Borneo. There were big tractors and other machines that knocked down trees like matchsticks, and one activist said that the iron the machines were made of spoke to him and said it didn't like being manifested in that form. So he took it upon himself to destroy the machinery so that it could return to the earth. Do you think that was necessary?

TEACHER: Was he the owner of the tractors?

STUDENT: No.

TEACHER: He's got a problem and there are consequences to what he did. I would say that while his heart may be in the right place, his understanding is definitely in the wrong place. It's very unskillful. Buddhism offers us *upaya*, skillful means. What is the Buddhist teaching on saving the forest? Don't separate. This man may be intimate with the machinery, but he's separated himself from the manufacturers and owners of the machines.

STUDENT: In the same documentary twenty people signed up to go on a Greenpeace mission to stop whale killing. A Greenpeace worker told them, "It's going to be life or death. We want to stop them," and he quoted a Sioux Indian saying: "Today is a good day to die." Three of the people decided to do it and seventeen dropped out. This film presented alternative ways for people to save the environment.

TEACHER: Sure, but it was based on the Judeo-Christian ethic. We have yet to really see the Buddhist ethic in action. The examples you gave me are really no different than the action of a very deranged woman who planted a bomb in an attempt to kill the head of a pharmaceutical company that experimented on animals. She loved animals and she wanted to kill this guy because of the work he was doing.

STUDENT: Isn't it true that the Buddhist teachings on non-killing say that the only time it is permissible to kill is when somebody is on their way to death, or when an animal is in pain and it's going to die, or if a person chooses euthanasia?

TEACHER: I wish it was as simple as that. I wish I could give you a set of rules, but I can't. If I did, it would be misleading. The Buddhist teaching on non-killing is incredibly profound; it goes beyond killing and non-killing. It's not just a matter of "kill this" and "don't kill that," this is okay and that's not okay. The teaching must take into account time, place, your position in the context of the circumstances, and the degree of action necessary.

STUDENT: Thank you for your answer.

TEACHER: May your life go well.

∞

STUDENT: Do you really want to know what the bomb would say?

TEACHER: Yes.

STUDENT: Too bad! I brought one with me. Daido, you're toast!

TEACHER: Anything else?

STUDENT: Yeah. It also says, "Michael, you'd better stop screwing around, get your ass in gear, and start practicing twice as hard."

TEACHER: Anything else?

STUDENT: It says, "I don't want to die."

TEACHER: What will you do about it?

STUDENT: [Lets out a tremendous growling, groaning yell.]

TEACHER: Well, that's a beginning. May your life go well.

STUDENT: Thank you for your answer.

STUDENT: When it comes to the falling away of body and mind, what am I holding back?

TEACHER: It's more like holding on to something. Whatever we hold on to separates us from the falling away of body and mind. The things we hold on to continually reinforce the illusion, "I exist, I exist, I exist." Every thought does that because the thought and the thinker reflect off each other. When you work with Mu, or the breath, give yourself up to the breath. *Be* the breath, *be* Mu. You can't do that as long as you're holding on to something.

STUDENT: I give myself up to my practice and let go as much as I'm able. I think I'm working hard, so is it just a question of time?

TEACHER: It takes time. It takes time to even be aware that we're holding on to something. In the practice of sitting zazen, sooner or later, everything that we carry around comes up to the surface. When your superficial internal dialogue stops, deeper "stuff" pops up, and you are able to see what you hold on to. Then you can let it go.

STUDENT: Does that mean that the stuff that has come up so far isn't deep?

TEACHER: Let's say it isn't all of it. We have a lifetime of patterns, conflicts, and tensions that we carry around; all of our baggage. Put down the baggage; take off the blinders. Be Mu with the whole body and mind; be the breath with the whole body and mind; be the sound of the stream with the whole body and mind.

STUDENT: A lot of things that have come up have been very painful. They feel like big stuff to me. I wonder if it gets progressively worse as my capacity to let go grows. [Laughs.] I wonder if the fear of what I think is coming holds me back.

TEACHER: I don't know, but I wouldn't worry about it, because the more you worry, the more you separate yourself from the very thing you're trying to do. Just take it as it comes. If a feeling comes up, acknowledge it, take responsibility for it, and let it go. Go back to the breath, go back to Mu. If the same thing comes up repeatedly, then experience it fully. Let it exhaust itself, then let it go. Someone said to me recently, "I'm losing my grip," and I said, "Wonderful!" Having a grip means holding on; to let go is frightening because we're used to equating what we hold on to with our identity; it's our reference system. At the same time, letting go is incredibly liberating. You can't really love, you can't really care, until you've lost your grip on the things you love and care about.

STUDENT: Okay, I'm going to lose my grip. Thank you for your answer.

TEACHER: May your life go well.

STUDENT: A rock is a rock, and sentient beings are complicated and messy. How do I move toward being more like a rock?

TEACHER: You want to be a rock?

STUDENT: Well, yes. There are many fine qualities in a rock which I envy.

TEACHER: [Laughs] I wonder what your husband thinks about that.

STUDENT: Just leave him aside for now. Let's think of the rock-like qualities: strong, quiet, safe, dependable.

TEACHER: They can't dance, though. What makes you think that you don't have those qualities?

STUDENT: Because...

TEACHER: Because you've identified with this bag of skin as being who you are. When you realize that this bag of skin is not what contains you, then you're free of it. That's what Dogen calls, "to be enlightened by the ten thousand things." The ten thousand things are that rock, the rain, the great ocean, these mountains. Once you realize emptiness, all of the possibilities are there. To be Mu with the whole body and mind is to forget the self. To be the rock with the whole body and mind is to forget the self. There are no limits. May your life go well.

STUDENT: Thank you for your answer.

STUDENT: BOOOM!!!

TEACHER: Yasutani Roshi once said that.

STUDENT: But did he also say, "I am Vishnu?"

TEACHER: You are Vishnu?

STUDENT: The bomb is Vishnu.

TEACHER: I don't understand "Vishnu."

STUDENT: Vishnu, the destroyer of worlds, the beginning and end of time in Hindu tradition.

TEACHER: I see. Radioactivity in that bomb can also be very healing.

STUDENT: It depends on how skillful we are in using it.

TEACHER: Does the lesson go any further than complete annihilation?

STUDENT: Yet to be seen.

TEACHER: How do we take it in that direction?

STUDENT: Action, talking, consciousness, our deeds.

TEACHER: And always remembering the teachings of...

STUDENT: BOOOM!!!

TEACHER: Right. The teaching is, as Yasutani Roshi said, "Be one with the bomb." In fact, after he said that, he paused for a few seconds and then said, "Whether you do or don't, sooner or later, if you don't do something about it, you *will* be one with the bomb."

STUDENT: Thank you for your answer.

TEACHER: May your life go well.

STUDENT: In attempting to be a mirror in zazen, I keep trying to catch some image of the true thing and it won't stick. Nothing will stay, and I get frustrated. Is it better to just not try?

TEACHER: Mirrors by their very nature don't catch, they reflect. Why are you trying to catch something?

STUDENT: I want to see it, and to know that it's there, that something is there.

TEACHER: When you really see that mirror, you see that the mirror and the image it reflects see each other. But catching—that's another story.

STUDENT: It's hard to understand that.

TEACHER: Well, catching is getting a grip on it and reflecting is losing your grip.

STUDENT: But I keep wanting to see something, know something, and yet...

TEACHER: You're not going to do it with a mirror.

STUDENT: So my practice is just to be the mirror and don't try to see anything.

TEACHER: If you really are the mirror—with the whole body and mind—the ten thousand things come home. The self is forgotten. The mirror fills the entire universe, reaching everywhere, and there's nothing remaining to reflect in it. That's Master Dongshan's first rank of the relationship between the relative and the absolute. Implicit in that first rank are the other four ranks. So we need to take the next steps. Coming out of that realization of oneness is Dongshan's second rank; manifesting that as compassion in the world is Dongshan's third rank. Integrating "mirror filling the whole universe" and "mirror separate from the whole universe" is Dongshan's fourth rank. The fifth rank is: neither mirror nor the ten thousand things, neither sentient nor insentient, neither being nor non-being, self or other. In Dongshan's Five Ranks is the life of each one of us—my life, your life.

STUDENT: Thank you for your answer.

TEACHER: May your life go well.

STUDENT: I worked with the peace movement for a while and got very discouraged because there was so much infighting. People were fueled by their anger, so they got into head trips and clashed. It was always such a bind to know what to do in situations like that; know how to respond without adding more gasoline.

TEACHER: It's more than just anger; it's also greed. We think of greed as being greedy for bad things. But you can be greedy for the Dharma, greedy for peace. So greed, anger, and ignorance always cause conflict. When you turn them over, on the other side you find wisdom, compassion, and enlightenment. With wisdom and compassion, one's way of approaching peace and conflict is very different. There is no self and the work is not self-serving anymore. One of the things that we constantly try to do is to make the other person wrong and ourselves right; we blame the rest of the world. There's no way you can resolve conflicts by doing that. So, how do you go to the other side? How do you turn greed, anger, and ignorance and reveal the three virtues of wisdom, compassion, and enlightenment?

STUDENT: It's not just a matter of small peace groups doing it. I thought the Twin Cities Project was very right-on, trying as much as possible to identify with the Russians, but—

TEACHER: Aside from yesterday and aside from thinking about it, what will you do now?

STUDENT: I suppose if there are petitions to sign, people need to sign them and carry them around. But I've even seen people mess up with that. I saw a lady...

TEACHER: Wait, wait, wait! Never mind what's wrong. What will you do?

STUDENT: [Sighing.] I really have no idea.

TEACHER: Then find out! Otherwise you're doing the same thing you're complaining about.

STUDENT: I haven't done anything about it in a while because I can't. . .

TEACHER: Why?!

STUDENT: I don't know why!

TEACHER: Find out! You have to find out. You have to empower yourself to do something.

STUDENT: But that doesn't mean going out and telling everybody...

TEACHER: I don't know what it means. It has to be what you can do, what you are willing to do, what your understanding says you can do. Do you understand?

STUDENT: Not really. It will happen.

TEACHER: It won't happen like that. It won't happen until you're ready to commit. Are you ready to commit? Are you ready to vow to put an end to war? To put an end to the destruction that's imminent in the nuclear holocaust? That's where it starts.

STUDENT: Thank you for your answer.

TEACHER: May your life go well.

STUDENT: The clouds that come together and make rain aren't necessarily going to help someone. They could possibly hurt thousands of people by causing floods. I'm afraid that when I forget the self my actions will be like that. I'm afraid that I'll mess up.

TEACHER: That's why you need to trust yourself. Trusting yourself doesn't mean that it's all going to happen the way your preconceived ideas say it should happen. Trusting yourself has nothing to do with expectations, or with the idea that if you trust yourself everything's going to be wonderful. Trusting yourself means that whatever you do is okay; that it's okay to fall and it's okay not to fall. The key is knowing how to fall and how to get up—not not-falling, not not-failing, not not-making mistakes. Seven times falling, eight times get up.

STUDENT: That means when other people fall around me, I should view them with the same compassion that I should view myself.

TEACHER: You should view them not as other people falling, but as you yourself falling. Then there's no question about what to do.

STUDENT: But I can't; I get so self-righteous.

TEACHER: Don't separate yourself. That's the key. As long as there's a self locked in the bag of skin, there's always that separation. That's what has caused the problems we have. We have a culture, a philosophy, a medicine, a political system all based on the separation of self and other. When you start with that premise, everything is dualistic, but when the self is forgotten and the ten thousand things merge, what kind of world is that? We call it the Diamond Net of Indra. What kind of philosophy does the Diamond Net manifest? What kind of sociology? What kind of medicine and healing, government and people? It's a very different world, yet everything remains the same.

STUDENT: To me that means I have to give up everything I now understand and everything good and happy and enjoyable; everything I look forward to in the whole world, saying, "Okay, I don't need that anymore."

TEACHER: No, it doesn't mean that. It means get rid of everything, not just the good things, the joyful things, but everything—every thought, every idea, every position. There's nothing to compare it to when you do that. There's no place to put this gigantic body. When the world collapses, *It* is indestructible. Do you understand?

STUDENT: [Silence.]

TEACHER: Any questions?

STUDENT: Thank you for your answer.

TEACHER: May your life go well.

∞

Student: A child is born and nothing is added. We can blow up the planet and nothing is lost. What is the truth?

Teacher: How do we keep from destroying this beautiful earth, with all its mountains, rivers, and people? That's where the truth is to be found. This very life is the life of the Buddha. Please, don't destroy it. Do you understand?

Student: But if we do destroy it, then what's the truth?

Teacher: You know. May your life go well.

Student: Thank you for your answer.

∞

This Dharma is boundless. It touches every aspect of life and has staggering potential consequences for the West at the turn of the twenty-first century, yet only a handful of people are aware of this. Those of you who hear the teachings are among those people. How do you manifest the Dharma? How do you avoid manifesting it? Each one of us takes it into our life and into everything we do. How you live your life, how you raise your children, drive your car, do your work: all of it is an opportunity for the actualization of the life of the ancient buddhas.

It's one thing to sit zazen together, pat each other on the back and say, "Isn't it wonderful what we're doing? Isn't the Dharma great?!" It's quite another thing to take it into our lives—not by running around preaching and trying to get converts; that's not what Zen is about. Zen is about manifesting wisdom and compassion in our lives. Every gesture, every action is a potential moment of practice. Every question, every barrier is a chance to realize ourselves. We have in our hands the opportunity to really make a difference in this world. Whether we realize it or not, we have the opportunity to do it. The teachings of the Buddhadharma are profound, subtle, and boundless. They reach everywhere. They're in your hands. What will you do with them? How will you use them? *When* will you do it?

PEARLS, PERILS, AND THE PATH

We should understand right from the outset that, in terms of our spiritual journey, the path itself is a peril when we give it edges. When we realize that it has no edges, it fills the universe and is one bright pearl. Fear is a peril when it happens to us; when we're intimate with it, it reaches everywhere, and it's one bright pearl. The teacher and student are each perils; when they become each other, one bright pearl is revealed. This great universe is both perils and pearls, co-dependent, mutually arising, intermingling, each reflecting the other in function and in identity. This too, is just one bright pearl.

The following koan, extracted from Master Dogen's *Three Hundred Koan Shobogenzo*, addresses the reality of the "one bright pearl." The prologue to this koan says:

> If your life is not free of a fixed position, you will drown in a sea of poison. Following after another's words, mimicking others' actions is the practice of monkeys. Zen practitioners should be able to shed some fresh light of their own. After all, if all the waves of Sokei were the same, this great earth would be populated by zombies.

The main case focuses on an encounter between Master Yantou and one of his students:

> A monastic asked the great Master Yantou, "An old monastic has said, 'The entire universe in the ten directions is a bright pearl.' How can I understand the meaning

of that?" The master said, "The entire universe in the ten directions is a bright pearl; what do you keep looking for?" Later the master asked the monastic, "The entire universe in the ten directions is a bright pearl; how do you understand it?" The monastic replied, "The entire universe in the ten directions is a bright pearl; what do you keep looking for?" The master said, "I knew you'd been making your living in the black mountain ghost cave."

I added footnotes to each line in order to clarify them: "A monastic asked Master Yantou, 'An old monastic has said the entire universe in the ten directions is a bright pearl.'" The footnote says: "Tens of thousands know it, but how many have realized it?"

Then the monastic said, "How can I understand the meaning of that?" The footnote says: "This monastic deserves a beating; there's no avoiding it."

"The master said, 'The entire universe in the ten directions is a bright pearl, what do you keep looking for?'" The footnote to that says: "There's no place to take hold of this. Still, he deserves to have his meditation seat overturned."

"Later the master asked the monastic . . ." The footnote says: "When he raises his head, I can see horns." The next line is "The entire universe in the ten directions is one bright pearl; how do you understand this?" The footnote says: "Ka! He first inflicted a flesh wound; now he goes for the gut."

"The monastic replied, 'The entire universe in the ten directions is a bright pearl, what do you keep looking for?'" The footnote says: "This monastic is not very alert; again he is defeated."

"Then the master said, 'I knew you'd been making your living in the black mountain ghost cave.'" The footnote says: "Master Yantou is a competent teacher of our school. Why does he talk so much?"

The poem to this koan reads:

> Words cannot reach it,
> understanding misses it.
> To direct yourself toward it is to move away from it.
> This one bright pearl—
> when the world is destroyed,
> It remains indestructible.

Master Dogen once said that all the buddhas and ancestors for countless generations have only transmitted spiritual entanglements. He also said that a gourd is made up of vines, which are nothing but entanglements. A big, plump, round, continuous gourd—nothing but entanglements transmitted from generation to generation. So too, is this one bright pearl—nothing but the perils themselves.

Using this koan as a starting point, let's investigate the nature of the spiritual journey. How do you realize the perils of the path as one bright pearl? How do you realize it without moving towards or away from it? Most importantly, how do you manifest your own perfection?

STUDENT: You say that the path is a peril. I say that to even think that there's a self is a peril.

TEACHER: I agree. But what about the path?

STUDENT: [Moans.] Ughhh. I feel like shit today.

TEACHER: That may be so. But what about the path? How do you transform the path—which in itself is a peril—into one bright pearl?

STUDENT: [Enthusiastically.] Oh, I feel like shit today.

TEACHER: That's not going to do it. You'll just go on feeling like shit for the rest of your life. How do you transform the peril of the path into one bright pearl?

STUDENT: [Hits teacher's wooden platform.]

TEACHER: That's not going to reach it either. Where is the path? What is the path? How big is it? How long is it? Should you direct yourself toward it or not? Say something.

STUDENT: [Shouts.]

TEACHER: Say something on behalf of all the new students here who don't understand what we're talking about.

STUDENT: I can't possibly say a thing. What could I say?

TEACHER: Say something about the path.

STUDENT: Zazen.

TEACHER: You just put edges on it. How do you get rid of the edges?

STUDENT: I'm so glad that Jeff is the bookkeeper now, and I can be a programmer.

TEACHER: That isn't going to get you out of here.

STUDENT: Can you help me out?

TEACHER: What are you looking for?

STUDENT: I don't know.

TEACHER: May your life go well.

STUDENT: Thank you for your answer.

STUDENT: Pearls, p-e-a-r-l-s; perils, p-e-r-i-l-s; bullshit, b-u-l-l-s-h-i-t .

TEACHER: It sounds good, but the perils are undeniable. There is anger, fear, anxiety. They don't go away when you deny them. Calling them bullshit only deepens the problem. People frequently say to me, "Oh, everything's fine," as they stand in shit up to their nostrils.

STUDENT: It all depends on how you use it.

TEACHER: What are you going to use it for?

STUDENT: Use what for?

TEACHER: Whatever you're talking about.

STUDENT: Depends on how you use it.

TEACHER: Use what?

STUDENT: Let's use an example. When I'm angry, I use it however I need it. If I need to yell at someone, "Stop!" I yell, "Stop!" If I need to hold it in, and grin and bear it, I grin and bear it. It depends on the situation.

TEACHER: Where does anger come from? We say that greed, anger, and ignorance are the three poisons, but when one realizes them they are transformed into wisdom, compassion, and enlightenment. How do you transform them?

STUDENT: You don't. They're happening.

TEACHER: According to what you are saying, when the Buddha and the ancient masters said that the other side of greed, anger, and ignorance is wisdom, compassion, and enlightenment, they were just kidding.

STUDENT: Yes, from the kidding perspective.

TEACHER: That's the problem. What is it from the perspective of one bright pearl?

STUDENT: Great day, and I'm almost out of here!

TEACHER: Not quite. Denying it won't do it.

STUDENT: You've got a stick in your hand.

TEACHER: [Laughs.] If I thought it would help, I'd use it. From what I've seen, you do a fine job dealing with anger. Look at that.

STUDENT: So?

TEACHER: How do you do it?

STUDENT: [Takes a deep breath and growls.]

TEACHER: May your life go well.

STUDENT: Thank you for your answer.

STUDENT: [Yells.] I can't hear the question!

TEACHER: How do you transform the perils of the path into one bright pearl?

STUDENT: [Yells.] I can't hear!

TEACHER: Come closer.

STUDENT: [Leans forward.]

TEACHER: You can hear.

STUDENT: [Laughs.] No, I can't.

TEACHER: Cut out the crap.

STUDENT: There's nothing in my head.

TEACHER: What moves your mouth?

STUDENT: I don't know.

TEACHER: Not knowing is blank consciousness. Say a word on manifesting one bright pearl.

STUDENT: One word. It's the universe.

TEACHER: You said it, and then you said too much. Do you understand?

STUDENT: [Nods.]

TEACHER: May your life go well.

STUDENT: Thank you for your answer.

STUDENT: No questions are coming up right now. It's kind of refreshing.

TEACHER: I'll give you one.

STUDENT: Go right ahead. Make waves.

TEACHER: How do you manifest one bright pearl?

STUDENT: [Snaps his fingers.]

TEACHER: Snapping your fingers? Are you a magician?

STUDENT: [Snaps his fingers.]

TEACHER: How do you transform the perils of the path into one bright pearl? How do you transform the peril of the path itself into one bright pearl? The peril of the teacher-student dichotomy into one bright pearl?

STUDENT: Is there one right here right now?

TEACHER: Is there?

STUDENT: Asked you first.

TEACHER: I don't know, do you?

STUDENT: I don't know either.

TEACHER: I'll buy that. May your life go well.

STUDENT: Thank you for your answer.

STUDENT: The path is messy. I constantly want to clean it up and organize it. Just as I had gotten my path together for the next three-month intensive, the phone rang and someone at the Drug Treatment Center asked me to teach a video class on Thursday nights, time that I set aside for coming to the Monastery. What do I do?

TEACHER: Take a guess.

STUDENT: That's what it's always like. The path for me is always filled with clocks and calendars, and I feel like I have to travel all the way across China to come to see you.

TEACHER: Nonetheless it's the same far-reaching, all-inclusive path of the buddhas and ancestors, isn't it?

STUDENT: It's hard to see that when the path looks so messy.

TEACHER: That's because when you regard the mundane as being something separate from the path, then there's no path in the mundane. When you realize that the path reaches everywhere, then there is nothing that is mundane. That's one bright pearl.

STUDENT: Thank you for your answer.

TEACHER: May your life go well.

STUDENT: The teacher is a peril. I like that.

TEACHER: Liking is a peril too. It is just the other side of hating. How do you transcend them both?

STUDENT: Don't tell me what to do!

TEACHER: No, that won't do it.

STUDENT: But I'll do it nonetheless.

TEACHER: A little better, but I would say, "It's all my fault, Julie. I'm sorry." Do you understand?

STUDENT: Is it always your fault?

TEACHER: Always. The whole catastrophe is my fault.

STUDENT: And what's my responsibility?

TEACHER: That's for you to see.

STUDENT: Will I ever stop fighting?

TEACHER: Do you fight?

STUDENT: Perhaps not enough.

TEACHER: Will you ever stop?

STUDENT: I don't know.

TEACHER: Do you want to?

STUDENT: Well, sometimes it seems nice to be in the position of some of the people around here who seem to trust you without reservation.

TEACHER: I do my best to deceive them.

STUDENT: Could that be a perilous place to be?

TEACHER: Which place, mine or theirs?

STUDENT: Trusting the teacher.

TEACHER: It can be a peril. In fact, as long as there's a teacher, you'll have perils.

When you kill the teacher, perils are pearls. One bright pearl. How do you kill the teacher?

STUDENT: Becoming one with the teacher.

TEACHER: That's an explanation.

STUDENT: It's all my fault, Daido.

TEACHER: May your life go well.

STUDENT: Thank you for your answer.

STUDENT: You said the path doesn't have any edges. [Unties her student robe and takes it off.]

TEACHER: Is your robe the path?

STUDENT: No, but?

TEACHER: That's the problem. You are just following after a form. Responding to bells.

STUDENT: Or not responding to them on purpose.

TEACHER: Not responding to them on purpose is also following after form. Master Yunmen said, "This world is vast and boundless." What he meant was, this world is one bright pearl. Why then, when the bell rings, do you put on your robes?

STUDENT: I always put them on.

TEACHER: That's the problem.

STUDENT: How do I live spontaneously then, without doing something on purpose?

TEACHER: One of the basic teachings in Zen is not to follow after sound or run after form. So why do you put on your practitioner's robes?

STUDENT: If I don't, you may not let me in the zendo.

TEACHER: That's the reason?

STUDENT: Yes.

TEACHER: Get rid of the reason. Why do you eat? Why do you sleep? Why are you sitting here annoying this old monastic with your questions?

STUDENT: A whim?

TEACHER: You can do better than that.

STUDENT: If I think about it.

TEACHER: Don't think about it.

STUDENT: Here I am.

TEACHER: Why do you do it?

STUDENT: It just happens.

TEACHER: Do you know why you do it?

STUDENT: Sometimes.
TEACHER: Get rid of that.
STUDENT: I know. I know.
TEACHER: What's left then?
STUDENT: Just now.
TEACHER: That's an explanation. What does "just now" mean? What does it mean in terms of your student's robe being or not being the path?
STUDENT: If I try to answer, will my cup be too full?
TEACHER: If you open your mouth it will.
STUDENT: I thought so.
TEACHER: How do you tell me without opening your mouth?
STUDENT: [Picks up her robe.]
TEACHER: Ten percent. May your life go well.
STUDENT: Thank you for your answer. [Puts on her robe as she goes back to her seat.]
TEACHER: [Yells.] THAT'S IT! THAT'S IT!

STUDENT: I have a horrible problem. It may have been a dream, but a couple of years ago in the zendo, the wooden buddha popped down from the altar, came up to me and said, "Excuse me." I said, "What?" And he said, "Would you hold this water cup for me?" It was the water cup from the altar, and suddenly it was in my hands and he said, "You're the only one I can ask to do this. Don't say anything." He started back to the altar, then turned around and said, "Please be careful; don't spill it. This is the only water there is, and I get really thirsty." As he turned to go I said, "Wait a minute! Water of the Buddha is one bright pearl. You can't spill it. What are you talking about?" He flashed around and roared, "You're spilling it!" I've been stuck with this cup of water ever since.
TEACHER: He's right. You're spilling it.
STUDENT: [Sighs.] Nice and wet.
TEACHER: May your life go well.
STUDENT: Thank you for your answer.

STUDENT: As one who believes that the main peril is the path, I'm reminded of something that Henry Miller wrote; he said that there are only two kinds of people in the world, the quick and the dead. To which group do you belong?
TEACHER: Obviously the walking dead.

STUDENT: Well, how can you prove that? You look alive to me.

TEACHER: Between heaven and earth there is only this body and mind.

STUDENT: Is that dead?

TEACHER: Dead.

STUDENT: Well, I'm sorry to hear that. My condolences.

TEACHER: May your life go well.

STUDENT: Thank you for your answer.

STUDENT: A pearl is a wonderful image. An oyster starts with a grain of sand and wraps layer after layer of nacre on top of it; then we peer in and see a gem. What peril is there in that?

TEACHER: The peering in.

STUDENT: Rather than peering out?

TEACHER: Peering is the peril.

STUDENT: Peering rather than making a pearl?

TEACHER: There's no making.

STUDENT: Then how is there a pearl?

TEACHER: How is there not?

STUDENT: Thank you for your answer.

TEACHER: May your life go well.

STUDENT: I feel a separation between the pearl and my life. It looks to me like there's the pearl, and then there's me. In that space, I tell myself I'm not good enough, even though I know it's bullshit.

TEACHER: How can you transform it?

STUDENT: [Does not respond.]

TEACHER: Intimacy is the key. Really be intimate with yourself. Really be intimate with your life. That intimacy is one bright pearl. Nothing other than that. [Pause.] Do you know how to be intimate?

STUDENT: Not exactly. I'm working on it.

TEACHER: It's not so complicated. When you sit, just sit. When you walk, just walk.

STUDENT: When I sit I'm falling asleep. Dogen said that zazen is actualization, but how is sleep actualization?

TEACHER: Buddhas don't sleep?

STUDENT: [Laughs.]

TEACHER: Also, don't believe Dogen. Don't believe a word I say, either. We're all a bunch of swindlers. Make this your own. Find out for yourself. Don't do what the monastic did in the koan, following Yantou's words, getting entangled.

STUDENT: When I try to make it my own, I want to be different from everybody; I want to be special.

TEACHER: When you make it your own, there's nobody else. There's no inside, no outside. The ten thousand things return to the self, where they've always been. That's what "Between heaven and earth I alone am the honored one," means. Alone means "all one," to contain everything, to not be separate from anything.

STUDENT: I don't believe you.

TEACHER: Don't believe me.

STUDENT: Thank you for your answer.

TEACHER: May your life go well.

STUDENT: I keep working very hard at sculpting perfect little pearls that I can plop on the floor in front of you, but by the time I get in to see you they've turned to mud and sand in my hands. What's the story?

TEACHER: Why are you bringing me mud and sand?!

STUDENT: It's pretty stupid, isn't it?

TEACHER: Any questions?

STUDENT: Where's the pearl?

TEACHER: Why are you bringing me mud and sand?!

STUDENT: I'll stop.

TEACHER: Stopping's not going to do it.

STUDENT: I'll go then.

TEACHER: Going is not going to do it.

STUDENT: I'll be content.

TEACHER: Turning into a believer won't do it either; neither will moving forward nor backward. When you move forward you move away from it. When you move back you're denying it. If you neither move forward nor backward, you're a dead man, eyes glowing in the coffin. How do you leap free of all this?

STUDENT: When the bell rings, I get up.

TEACHER: What about the mud and sand?

STUDENT: I've got to sit through anything.

TEACHER: That's an explanation.

STUDENT: [Pause.] Can I go now?

TEACHER: Hit him with a mud ball! [Mimics throwing mud balls at the student.] BOCK! BOCK! Hit him with a mud ball! May your life go well.

STUDENT: Thank you for your answer.

STUDENT: When my son was born it was obvious that he was perfect and complete, lacking nothing. Now he's four and a half, and it's getting so complicated that the only time he's perfect and complete, lacking nothing, is when he's sleeping. During the day I get very angry and frustrated with him. This is the peril. How do I deal with it?

TEACHER: Are you perfect and complete, lacking nothing?

STUDENT: Oh, no.

TEACHER: That's why he's not.

STUDENT: I have to start with me?

TEACHER: No, you have to realize that you're perfect and complete, lacking nothing, and then you'll see the perfection and completeness that encompass everything.

STUDENT: But I feel that I have to teach him things, like, "Don't hurt people's feelings."

TEACHER: Yes. Perfect and complete, lacking nothing.

STUDENT: Even when he's hitting his aunt?

TEACHER: DON'T HIT!

STUDENT: Well, how about the anger then?

TEACHER: What anger?

STUDENT: In me.

TEACHER: What anger?

STUDENT: [Laughs.]

TEACHER: Why are you laughing. Is that anger?

STUDENT: No.

TEACHER: Where is it? Where does it come from? Where does it go? Who is the master? May your life go well.

STUDENT: Thank you for your answer.

STUDENT: All of my questions evaporated.

TEACHER: So, no questions. Are you alive?

STUDENT: I don't know.

TEACHER: If you don't know, then you're dead.

STUDENT: That makes two of us.

TEACHER: What can you do for someone who's dead?

STUDENT: Nothing.

TEACHER: Wrong! Wisdom's sword has two sides to it. One kills and one gives life.

STUDENT: Am I on the wrong side?

TEACHER: Being dead you're on the wrong side.

STUDENT: Can I just walk around to the other side?

TEACHER: As long as you do it in the bright light of day. Don't try to do it in the dark.

STUDENT: Why?

TEACHER: In the dark there is no eye, ear, nose, tongue, body, mind. There's no color, sound, smell, taste, touch, phenomena. Just darkness.

STUDENT: No sword.

TEACHER: Right. You've got to do it in the bright light of day.

STUDENT: Thank you for your answer.

TEACHER: May your life go well.

STUDENT: Listening to the koan it sounds to me like there are rules to the game. Rule one is don't parrot. I'm wondering what game are we playing?

TEACHER: What would you like to call it?

STUDENT: Maybe it's form versus emptiness.

TEACHER: No, it's called life and death.

STUDENT: Funny you should say that because I used to think I was interested in losing the self, but now I'm interested in dying.

TEACHER: Is there a difference?

STUDENT: I guess it depends on whether I'm looking at it from Mu's eyes or somebody else's.

TEACHER: There's only one eye.

STUDENT: This one? [Points to his forehead.]

TEACHER: This one! [Points to his eyes.]

STUDENT: Ah, you have two and I have one.

TEACHER: Maybe that's the problem. Anything else?

STUDENT: That's enough.

TEACHER: May your life go well.

STUDENT: Thank you for your answer.

STUDENT: I can't help but think that working and discussing the truth of these matters within the parameters of the relative is just co-signing each other's delusions.

TEACHER: Yes. Discussing it, definitely, but work is not necessarily in the realm of the relative. Work, the activity, is neither absolute nor relative. You're neither absolute nor relative. The ten thousand things are neither absolute nor relative. To say it's absolute is just blank consciousness—no life. To say it's relative is being caught up in words. It's neither of those. How is it neither of those?

STUDENT: Absolutely relative?

TEACHER: [Laughs.] That's not going to do it.

STUDENT: I told you I'd come wielding the sword of ignorance.

TEACHER: You got me. [Holds his gut.] Uhk. . . May you life go well.

STUDENT: Thank you for your answer.

STUDENT: [Pointing to himself.] This is one bright pearl. Robert is a peril.

TEACHER: That's an excellent definition. Now show me.

STUDENT: [Falls off his cushion onto the floor. Laughs as he gets up.] Well, I tried.

TEACHER: That's a peril. May your life go well.

STUDENT: Thank you for your answer.

STUDENT: I've been reading about diamonds and jewel palaces and clouds dropping precious gems. [Teacher plugs his ears. Student raises his voice.] All kinds of stuff like this. How do all of these things measure up to one bright pearl?

TEACHER: [Unplugs his ears.] What? I don't understand you.

STUDENT: Actually, I have another question.

TEACHER: Thank you.

STUDENT: An expression that really struck me: entering into the ocean of vows. What does that mean?

TEACHER: The liturgist shouldn't be asking a question like that.

STUDENT: Why not?

TEACHER: [Chants.] Sentient beings are numberless, I vow to save them.

STUDENT: Is that an ocean of vows or just one vow?

TEACHER: An ocean: that's all there is. Just one vow: that's all there is. An ocean of vows.

STUDENT: How do we enter into that?

TEACHER: How do you get out of it?

STUDENT: Yeah!

TEACHER: May your life go well.

STUDENT: Thank you for your answer.

STUDENT: Here I am.
TEACHER: Nice to see you. Do you want me to do something?
STUDENT: No. Yes. Stop my heart from beating so fast.
TEACHER: I know what you mean. Do you understand?
STUDENT: [Shakes her head. Bows as if to leave.]
TEACHER: Stop my heart from beating so fast.
[Pause. Tense silence. A watch beeps. Student laughs and points toward the sound.]
TEACHER: May your life go well.
STUDENT: Thank you for your answer.
TEACHER: Can't top that.

STUDENT: About those perils that were mentioned before, the way I see it, they can all be reduced to one cause.
TEACHER: Okay, I'll play along.
STUDENT: About those perils, the way I see it, they can all be reduced to one cause.
TEACHER: I agree. Now what will we do?
STUDENT: We could go have lunch.
TEACHER: Good idea. May your life go well.
STUDENT: Thank you for your answer.

We should realize that Zen training is not about putting yourself in front of a teacher who will either mold you into a buddha, or uncover from deep within you a hidden perfection. The truth of this incredible Dharma is that neither of those approaches is true. We are fully equipped, just as Shakyamuni Buddha was. There is nothing that anyone can give you.

Don't say there's no practice. There is definitely practice, but it's not going to lead you along the path that ends in enlightenment. Practice is enlightenment: one bright pearl. The path reaches everywhere; it has no boundaries: one bright pearl. Each one of us wears the clothes of a buddha; eats the food of a buddha; lives the life of a Buddha: one bright pearl. Whether we realize it or not: one bright pearl. May your life go well.

5
MORAL AND ETHICAL TEACHINGS

There is a common misunderstanding of the Zen teachings on ethics and morality. Many people think that Zen is amoral, that it is beyond good and bad. That is simply not so. From an intrinsic point of view it appears that way, but we live our lives not as some absolute distillation of reality but as the manifestation of the absolute in the world of phenomena, in the world of good and bad.

The precepts, the moral and ethical teachings, arose from Shakyamuni's own enlightenment experience. In Zen we have the *vinaya*, the monastic rules; and the *shila*, the moral teachings. The latter are the sixteen precepts of the Buddha, the manifestation of the ethical conduct of a realized being.

The first three of these sixteen precepts are the Three Refuges. First we have the Unified Three Treasures. We say, "I take refuge in the Buddha. I take refuge in the Dharma. I take refuge in the Sangha. I take refuge in the Buddha, the Incomparably Honored One. I take refuge in the Dharma, honorable for its purity. I take refuge in the Sangha, honorable for its harmony." The Unified Buddha Treasure is *anuttara-samyaksambodhi*, or perfect enlightenment. The Unified Dharma Treasure is purity and undefilement. The Unified Sangha Treasure is the virtue of harmony.

Then there's the Manifested Three Treasures. Direct realization of enlightenment is called the Buddha Treasure. The Buddha's realization is called the Dharma Treasure. The practice of the Buddha's Dharma is called the Sangha Treasure.

Last we have the Abiding Three Treasures. The teachings on these Three Treasures say, "Converting *devas* and liberating humans, appearing in vast space or in a speck of dust: this is the Buddha Treasure. Transformed into the sutras and converted into the Oceanic Storehouse, delivering the inanimate and animate: this is the Dharma Treasure. Saving beings from suffering: this is the Sangha Treasure."

This way of understanding the Three Treasures was presented to Master Dogen by his teacher, Jujing, when he received the mind-to-mind transmission in China, and it forms the basis of the Three Pure Precepts that, in turn, are the basis of the Ten Grave Precepts.

All of these teachings have an absolute basis, an absolute truth. We call it wisdom. They also have a worldly truth that we call compassion. Together, these teachings form what we call the precepts, what we call the Three Treasures.

So, what is perfect enlightenment? Why do we say that the Dharma is pure and undefiled? Why do we associate harmony with the Sangha? What are the Three Treasures? What does "abiding," "manifested," or "unified" mean?

STUDENT: I see the Three Treasures when I'm on the subway in New York City and a group of teenagers get on. They're shouting and screaming, and I see the clarity of the Buddha, the purity of the Dharma, and the harmony of the Sangha.

TEACHER: How is that any different from the days before you began Zen practice?

STUDENT: It's exactly the same.

TEACHER: Was it there before you started Zen practice?

STUDENT: Yes.

TEACHER: And it's there after you started Zen practice?

STUDENT: Yes.

TEACHER: Then why practice?

STUDENT: For the Buddha, the Dharma, and the Sangha.

TEACHER: That's copping out. What are those Three Treasures?

STUDENT: Right now they're sitting here in front of you.

TEACHER: May your life go well.

STUDENT: Last week when I was driving to Boston, there was a car on the turnpike that had crashed into the guardrail. It was on fire and filled with smoke. There were a couple of people standing a few hundred yards away who might have been the passengers, or they may have just been bystanders. I drove by without stopping. If there were people in that car who died, I broke the precept "Do not kill." I defiled the Three Treasures.

TEACHER: What will you do about it?

STUDENT: My legs are sore from all this sitting.

TEACHER: That doesn't solve the problem of people burning in the car.

STUDENT: What car?

TEACHER: That's exactly the problem of misunderstanding the precepts.

STUDENT: What can I do now but wonder about what you're saying, and why my legs hurt so much?

TEACHER: Atonement. If it didn't exist you wouldn't have brought up this story. You carry it with you. At-one-ment: that's what you do when you notice that you have moved away from the precepts. You acknowledge the fact that you moved away, you take responsibility, and then return to the precepts. Anything else?

STUDENT: No.

TEACHER: May your life go well.

STUDENT: Thank you for your answer.

STUDENT: I noticed that whenever anybody with a rakusu goes to the bathroom here at the Monastery, they take it off and leave it outside. I've always had a problem with that because I don't want to leave anything outside when I'm doing something fully, so I bring my rakusu inside and go to the bathroom. Is that defiling the precepts?

TEACHER: It's not defiling the precepts; it's defiling the vinaya, the monastic rule.

STUDENT: Why is that?

TEACHER: It's the same reason that you bow to your shit before you flush it down the toilet. You are treating each thing in an appropriate way, with due respect.

STUDENT: What if I feel that it's more respectful not to leave what I really love outside?

TEACHER: Try to practice what's been transmitted for two thousand five hundred years. Let go of your ideas; realize the teachings, and *then* you can flush them down the toilet.

STUDENT: Do you feel it's wrong to want to know the reasoning behind the rules?

TEACHER: In order to get us to make the moral and ethical teachings our own, the ancestral teachers ritualized them. They ritualized the precepts. There's a morality of washing the face, of cleaning the teeth, of cooking a meal, of using the bathroom. All of these are the vinaya, or in case of Master Dogen's teachings, the *shingi*. The spirit of the "rules" is not authoritarian, hierarchical, institutional, or legal. They are a definition of the Way, and it's through practicing them that we come to realize the Way. It's through defiling or defying them that we separate ourselves from the Way. The first thing we need to do is to bow and be humble. We need to practice, to realize, and to actualize. Then and only then are we in a position to throw the teachings away. Our journey starts with raising the bodhi mind. Raising the bodhi mind is the aspiration for enlightenment that leads to practice of the vinaya and the shila. Practice leads to realization, and once you reach that point, you've made it your own. It's no longer a rule; it's your life. The next step is actualization, where you manifest wisdom for all sentient beings. Then you throw it all away.

STUDENT: Have you thrown most of it away?

TEACHER: No, I'm a teacher. I need to constantly attend to it because what I do communicates most directly to my students.

STUDENT: You shave your head just for us?

TEACHER: I do it because I'm a teacher and a monastic.

STUDENT: Yesterday you said that it reminds you of why you're teaching.

TEACHER: Yes. It's like any other ritual. Ritual is a restatement of the common experience of a congregation. In a congregation of monastics, shaving the head is a restatement of having taken the vows of a monastic.

STUDENT: That's where I have a problem. If you're restating your vows and need to remind yourself of why you're here, then it seems like it's not important enough for it to exist on it's own.

TEACHER: It's called practice. Among many of my functions, I'm a teacher of monastics. I practice that.

STUDENT: When does practice not have to be practice anymore?

TEACHER: It goes on endlessly. The practice of the buddhas and ancestors is ceaseless; it's beginningless and it's endless. When you practice or I practice, we affirm the realization of all buddhas that preceded us and will follow us.

STUDENT: So what is the relationship of intimacy to practice? Is practice an expression of separation, or is practice intimacy?

TEACHER: It's a continuum.

STUDENT: Where do the reminders come in?

TEACHER: Practice is reminding. Practice means to do.

STUDENT: But reminding is not intimacy. Reminding takes two, right?

TEACHER: You practice intimacy.

STUDENT: But then I'm not intimate.

TEACHER: When you're practicing it, you're practicing intimacy.

STUDENT: That's what I'm trying to say.

TEACHER: What you're saying is an idea. When there's intimacy, there are no questions, there is no defilement, there is no opposition...

STUDENT: ...and no practice.

TEACHER: Right! There's no practice, but as long as you're resisting, there will always be a place for practice. That's what you're doing now; you're resisting it. You're giving me a lot of "absolute" horseshit, but what you're doing is resisting. You've got a good rap, but not a good practice. When you can take that rakusu off and treat it with deep respect, when you follow the vinaya, you will do everything else with the same kind of respect. That's what practice is.

STUDENT: Thank you for your answer.

TEACHER: May your life go well.

STUDENT: In harmony with the Sangha and respecting her buddha nature, this Tuesday I will go to a patient's house and give her a shot of a drug called Prolixin, so her ego shell can close down and she can feel separate and know where she begins and where the rest of the world ends.

TEACHER: And?

STUDENT: I see a potential contradiction.

TEACHER: What's the contradiction?

STUDENT: That there needs to be a separation.

TEACHER: Of course. That's what it means to come down off the mountain, back into the world. It's important to know that you have done that. When you do come back into the world, you can manifest wisdom in a variety of ways. That's what "appearing in vast space or in a speck of dust" means; that's what "converting devas and humans" means—to be able to manifest in the myriad forms, not for one's own benefit, but for the benefit of all beings. That's very different than not knowing where the edges are. You know quite clearly where the edges are. Right now they're here. It's important to know the difference between break*through*—that is, realizing the unity of all beings—and break*down*, not knowing where the edges are and where to go or what to do.

STUDENT: When I offer that shot, am I in harmony with the Three Treasures?

TEACHER: In the West, at this time in history, you are. Maybe a hundred years from now we'll find out there's a much better way to accomplish what you're trying to accomplish. What's important is the intent of your practice. Your intent is to nourish and to heal, and you're doing the best you can, which is all we can do. You absorb the knowledge of your field that's available in this day and age. You may do it differently when you've absorbed the Buddhadharma.

STUDENT: It doesn't feel like it's the best way. I want something else out of you. I want something else out of this moment, right now.

TEACHER: That's the problem: wanting it out of me. I don't have it. I'm sorry. I wish I had something to give you. It's for that reason—having nothing to give—that each one of us is the Buddha, the Enlightened One. Each one of us has what we seek. It doesn't come from the outside. May your life go well.

∞

STUDENT: There's a scene in a play about Hank Williams' life in which he's talking to his manager about a song. He had been listening to a whippoorwill in the woods, and so in the song he wrote, "It sounds so all alone. I'm so lonesome I could die." He gave the song to his manager and said, "Do you think they'll understand?" Hearing the sound of the whippoorwill is the Three Treasures abiding endlessly. Naming it "sounding so all alone" is manifesting the pain and joy of the Three Treasures as they burst forth. Saying "I feel so lonesome I could die" is unifying the Three Treasures in this body, this mind. Saying "Do you think they'll understand?" defiles the precepts and the Way and the mind of all buddhas. I live constantly on that cusp of "Do you think they'll understand?" and I don't know how not to ask that. What should I do?

TEACHER: Realize that what you've said is good, but it's still only eighty percent. Work on the twenty percent.

STUDENT: Do you understand?

TEACHER: No, I don't.

STUDENT: Do you care?

TEACHER: I care very, very, very much.

STUDENT: Thank you for your answer.

TEACHER: May your life go well.

∞

STUDENT: I come before you as a killer, the blood in my veins running cold. Do I kill? What do I kill if I should kill?

TEACHER: Affirm life; do not kill.

STUDENT: Doesn't that turn me into a coward, running away from it?

TEACHER: Far from it. Affirming life is not the activity of cowards, it's the activity of buddhas.

STUDENT: If I find the Buddha on the road, I shouldn't kill him?

TEACHER: What are you calling Buddha?

STUDENT: I don't understand.

TEACHER: What are you calling Buddha? What is Buddha?

STUDENT: I don't know.

TEACHER: Then how will you kill it?

STUDENT: I said "if."

TEACHER: Are you looking for Buddha?

STUDENT: I think I am.

TEACHER: Throw away the looking.
STUDENT: Thank you for your answer.
TEACHER: May your life go well.

∞

STUDENT: If I move forward in life, I hurt people. Doing one thing, I leave another thing undone. Trying to act rightly in one way, something else goes wrong. Is there any help for that?
TEACHER: Sure, there's help. Practice your life like the mountain practices its life. Blue mountain walks neither forward nor backward. Moving forward manifests in the world; moving backward is the absolute basis. What does it mean to move neither forward nor backward? That's the realization of all buddhas.
STUDENT: Thank you for your answer.
TEACHER: May your life go well.

∞

STUDENT: Sangha is harmony, but frequently I feel disharmony due to my likes and dislikes. There are some people whom I really don't like. How can I find harmony in not wanting to be around them?
TEACHER: The very language that you use to present this puts you on one side and the sangha on the other. When there is no separation between you and the sangha, you will manifest the virtue of harmony.
STUDENT: That's enough work for a lifetime.
TEACHER: Yes. May your life go well.
STUDENT: Thank you for your answer.

∞

STUDENT: I've caught some people taking things that were given to me for my care. I think they should be killed and I'm not averse to doing it. I don't see a morality and I don't see an ethic. I just feel society out there is getting more and more evil. I've tried rational means, only to be turned down and turned away and ignored.
TEACHER: Do you have a question?
STUDENT: Where's the morality or ethic for me?
TEACHER: You said you don't have it.
STUDENT: I'm not saying I don't think I should have some.

TEACHER: Do you know the story of Ryokan, the poet?

STUDENT: No.

TEACHER: He lived on a mountain in a little hut. One day he was away begging. He was very poor; didn't own much. When he returned home he surprised a thief who was in his hut looking for something to steal, but there was nothing there. Ryokan felt so bad for this thief that he took off his robe and gave it to him. The thief left with the robe while Ryokan sat shivering by the window of the hut. He looked out at the full moon and said, "Oh, if I could only give this beautiful moon to him!" Learn something from that. May your life go well.

STUDENT: That's a beautiful story, and the precepts are beautiful, and so is the idea of harmony and purity, but when I look at the world I see a very different reality. Most people who have taken these precepts and who supposedly should be living by them, don't. That reality is much more powerful and convincing than the beautiful ideas that the precepts express.

TEACHER: So, you've got a good excuse not to follow them.

STUDENT: That's right. Do you follow the precepts?

TEACHER: Yes. I practice them day and night to the best of my ability.

STUDENT: Do you need the precepts to live a moral life?

TEACHER: Realized buddhas don't, because at the point of realization there is intimacy with the precepts; there's no separation.

STUDENT: Is it possible to not have any separation with everything and live a moral life?

TEACHER: That's exactly what I'm taking about.

STUDENT: But what do the precepts have to do with that?

TEACHER: Before realization, you practice the life of a buddha by following the precepts.

STUDENT: Did Buddha follow the precepts?

TEACHER: Yes.

STUDENT: Where did they come from?

TEACHER: His realization. Buddha's realization is the basis of the precepts. The Buddha Treasure *is* the realization of anuttara-samyaksambodhi; that's where it started. For students coming into practice, and particularly once sitting begins, a feeling of compassion arises, and they think to themselves, "I really want to do this. How can I do it?" Well, that's the purpose of the precepts. They are guidelines for the practice of a moral and compassionate life. You practice the breath the same way you practice the precepts, and each time that you're in accord with a precept, you're manifesting enlightenment. Each time you go off it, you acknowledge it, take responsibility, and return to the precept. So in that way, practice remains actively conscious and little by little you bring it into your life. Ultimately, this process needs to be realized, and when that realization occurs, there are no precepts, no buddhas.

STUDENT: Thank you for your answer.

TEACHER: May your life go well.

STUDENT: Can you say a few words about what it really means to be an attendant and to serve the teacher?

TEACHER: To be the teacher's attendant is probably the most powerful training opportunity. Practicing as an attendant is the closest thing to being able to manifest the moral and ethical teachings with the whole body and mind. I remember when my teacher's teacher would come to the Zen Center of Los Angeles, Roshi wouldn't let anybody else attend him. He was the head of the monastery, but when his teacher came, he became his teacher's attendant. He felt that none of us had really learned to do it the right way. Attendants must give up their own personal life. Their whole identity merges with that of the teacher. They must constantly see to what is needed, and so they begin to develop an incredible amount of awareness. After a while, a good attendant knows what to do before the thought even arises in the teacher's head.

STUDENT: When I look back over the last couple of months, my approach has been "get in, get out, don't get into trouble." It's not even a conscious attitude on my part. Growing up, my sister and I were forced to give up our ego, our humanity, just to survive. In a lot of situations with you, I feel I'm going through this again. I'm just dimly aware of my reactions.

TEACHER: This is also giving up your ego in order to survive.

STUDENT: I don't understand.

TEACHER: What you realize in that merging with the teacher is the unification with the ten thousand things. If you can be one with the teacher, you can be one with the ten thousand things, and that's about survival of the individual, it's about survival of the species, of the planet, of the ten thousand things. That's what we call the buddha nature.

STUDENT: It's not easy for me, because I can only see my reactions after the fact, and often I don't catch them at all.

TEACHER: Why?

STUDENT: Much of this stuff is held physically.

TEACHER: At the most basic level, it has to do with the movement of your mind. That's why you cannot catch it; there's no room, no place in which to catch it. It's like playing softball with a ball already in your glove; you can't catch another one.

STUDENT: Yes. I'm fond of filling my mind with good stuff so that I don't feel the bad stuff. Thank you for your answer.

TEACHER: May your life go well.

STUDENT: I need to make peace with my parents. You suggested that I face them and atone. I don't know where the will comes from to do that, but I will do it.

TEACHER: You shouldn't do it because I told you to do it. It's just a practice I suggest. The reason it's important to do it is because you and they are not two separate things, and if you can't accept them, you can't accept yourself. If you can't be at one with them, you can't be at one with yourself, or with the ten thousand things. Whatever you separate yourself from, be it a speck of dust or the ten thousand things, that is how much heaven and earth are separated, how much you isolate yourself, and pain and suffering continue.

STUDENT: I see it come up again and again.

TEACHER: So where are they right now? You say they're dead. I say where are they right now?!

STUDENT: They're here before you.

TEACHER: You bet they're here before me! You've been carrying them on your back all your life. It's about time you unload the baggage. Make yourself free. Nobody can do it for you.

STUDENT: I know, I know.

TEACHER: May your life go well.

STUDENT: Thank you for your answer.

STUDENT: Recently someone tried to give me some advice. They suggested that I lie to the monastics here to get out of a difficult situation. I said, "I can't do that here at the Monastery." Then I caught myself. Why am I making these distinctions? Why am I saying, "I can't do it here, but I can do it out there; I can't do it to the monastics, but I can do it to someone else?"

TEACHER: Yes. Any questions?

STUDENT: No. That's all.

TEACHER: We create that dichotomy. We bow to each other here in the meditation hall and push each other on the subway; we do a holy dance here and then go outside and trample over anyone who gets in our way. We hold the illusion of the sanctuary versus the world, as if they were two different things. They're not. The sooner we realize that the sooner we'll get real about spiritual practice. May your life go well.

STUDENT: At the moment when I'm acting I feel very harmonious. I don't feel my actions are premeditated. I don't feel like I'm going to express my ideas. I often seem to respond to the situation, and it seems very clear; it comes out and I find it very free and open. Once I'm removed from the situation, however, I often feel very differently. Perhaps I feel I was very egocentric, and I get terribly confused. I don't know where the confusion comes from, because most of the time I can't even see that I acted egocentrically.

TEACHER: One is the action and the other is the reflection on the action. Reflection always causes complications. That's why that great mirror of samadhi that reflects whatever is in front of it is so important. When the image is gone, nothing is in the mirror; you've let it go. But if the object leaves and the image still sticks there, then the next image is reflected on top of the last image and the next image on top of that, and so on. That's where all the complications come in. Samadhi always happens in the moment. When nothing happens, there is no action. When something happens, you respond—always in accord with circumstances, always spontaneously.

STUDENT: So, after I've left a situation, I've got to get into the...

TEACHER: Just let it go!

STUDENT: I know what you're saying, but I'm still not very good at it.

TEACHER: Well, thank God for practice. May your life go well.

STUDENT: I think everybody is buddha; everybody is perfect all the time. So why is there karma?

TEACHER: Is there karma?

STUDENT: I think there is karma if you think there is karma; if you think karma is nothing, karma is nothing.

TEACHER: I think what you're saying is that when you think there is karma, there is karma, and that when there is no thinking, there is no karma. That's true. So when all beings are perfect and complete—no karma. All beings are perfect and complete, but not realizing that, being moved by the activities in the world—there is karma. Action, karma. Doing, karma. No doing, no karma. Both doing and not doing, perfect and complete, like all buddhas.

STUDENT: Thank you for your answer.

TEACHER: May your life go well.

STUDENT: Yesterday I went down to Philadelphia to try to persuade my mother to commit herself to a psychiatric ward. She's very paranoid and her husband and doctor couldn't get her to do it. She thinks they are plotting together, so they couldn't persuade her. I went down to try to do it with love and patience. None of it worked, so I bullied her and I made her sign the papers. She was sure she was going to be killed in that ward and knew that I was leaving her to her death. How am I going to deal with this kind of damage I've done to her and to me, even though I accomplished what was needed?

TEACHER: First of all you need to be very clear that you were doing this entirely for her benefit and that it was the best route; that it needed to be done. Then you have to do it. There are times that you have to break somebody's legs to keep them from killing themselves. On the surface compassion isn't always beautiful and lovely. You say you went there and did it with love and harmony and it didn't work. If you're looking for something to work or not work, there's no love or harmony, there's just working and not working. Once you're clear that what you are doing is not self-serving, you do the best you can. I had to do the same thing with my mother. She said, "You're telling me I have no choice?" And I said, "Right. If you won't make the decision, I'll make it for you, just like you used to make them for me."

STUDENT: That's what I said, except more violently. It made us all feel pretty sick, including her.

TEACHER: So, you're not over it; it's not finished. That's why we say that this is a continuous practice. You need to work with her while she's in the hospital to help her understand what's going on. Otherwise, she's not going to heal herself; she'll be there under protest. There have been situations here at the Monastery where we've been able to act in a loving and compassionate way; other times we've had to do it by force—and incidentally, we create karma any way that we do it.

STUDENT: That's what I'm worried about. She believes that we're all under control of people who are plotting against her.

TEACHER: Of course. That's part of why she's in the hospital. It's not easy.

STUDENT: Thank you for your answer.

TEACHER: May your life go well... and may her life go well.

STUDENT: When I got on line I had a question that seemed very important. Now I really don't feel like asking my question anymore. I think I already know the answer.

TEACHER: That's the value of getting on line, of committing oneself. If it weren't for these waiting periods, my job would be really tough. Everybody takes care of it when they're on line. Then they come in feeling stupid because they don't really have anything great to ask or say.

STUDENT: Or they ask it, but it's not really authentic anymore.

TEACHER: I would say, "Thank you for not having a question." May your life go well.

STUDENT: Thank you for your answer.

TEACHER: I will only take that once, so don't anybody else try it as an excuse.

STUDENT: I'm feeling pretty overwhelmed. All this pain! For me personally...

TEACHER: Oh, wasn't that for you personally?

STUDENT: Right.

TEACHER: So.

STUDENT: Personally, very personally.

TEACHER: So. Today the whole room is pain. What's the other side? Personally? Whole room?

STUDENT: There's no other side.

TEACHER: That's the problem. Try to see both sides, then realize that the truth is in neither of those two. A lot of pain in this room; no pain in this room—neither is it. Where is it? Anything else?

STUDENT: It really hurts to not take responsibility and it really hurts to close one's eyes knowingly. I know that there's something I can do to take responsibility, to open my eyes.

TEACHER: What if that hurts, too?

STUDENT: Tough.

TEACHER: Is it a matter of which hurts the least that will determine what you'll do?

STUDENT: That's a good question, and a big part of my problem.

TEACHER: These precepts and this practice are not about guilt. It's not about saying to yourself, "Now that I know what the precepts are, I'll feel like a bastard if I don't observe them; therefore I will observe them." That's not the Buddhadharma. That's not even half-assed morality. It has to come out of your own life and practice. It's got to come out of the raising of the bodhi mind. The precepts are not meant to be a chore; they're not meant to restrict you. They're meant to help you realize your freedom.

STUDENT: I'm beginning to see that. I've talked to you before about the problems that my brother is having and how it just came to a real head. I realize that it's been a year since I found out all this stuff, and that I'm responsible for the fact that he was thrown out on the street, that he couldn't pay for his rent. I'm responsible for the fact that he got himself thrown into jail and his life is completely falling apart. I could have helped in some way, and I didn't do it. Now, I'm beginning to see just how much pain he is experiencing. He's saying, "My God, I have nothing; I have no one and I have nothing." I'm responsible for that.

TEACHER: Not only for your brother getting thrown out of his house and being on the street, but for all who have been thrown out of houses and are on the streets, for all who have ended up in jail, for all who are suffering. Your responsibility is not just for your brother. How will you practice this? It seems so overwhelming. There's so much pain. It feels so hopeless. So what will you do? Nothing? That hurts. Trying to do it? That hurts, too. It's impossible. What will you do?

STUDENT: The first thing that I haven't really done yet is to try to completely identify with what is happening to him. I've been afraid and separated myself. I don't want to feel the pain. I think the first thing is to really feel him and communicate with him.

TEACHER: That's a good first step. Don't forget the rest of your brothers and sisters. The world is filled with them. When you took the vows of a monastic, you increased your family size by the world's population. May your life go well.

STUDENT: Thank you for your answer.

When we realize absolute truth, we realize the wisdom of all buddhas and ancestors. The eye of wisdom is the eye of Manjushri Bodhisattva, and compassion is the eye of Avalokiteshvara Bodhisattva. Compassion arises out of wisdom, because wisdom is the realization that there is no separation between the self and the ten thousand things, so there's no way not to take responsibility once having realized it.

All sentient beings have both eyes, all buddhas have both eyes. It's just a matter of opening them and seeing with them. That's what our practice is about. When we've realized this absolute truth, Buddha is no longer an abstraction, but our very life itself. Realization means giving life to the Buddha, giving life to wisdom and compassion. It's no small thing. Being born human we have the opportunity to realize ourselves. It's part of what comes with the package called human life. It's up to you whether you do it or you don't. It's your choice.

6

PAINTED CAKES SATISFY HUNGER

In Zen teaching and in our training we use all kinds of imagery: the buddha statue on the altar, the sutras that we chant, the poetry used as capping phrases for koans or as dharma words during a memorial service. There is a constant use of images in liturgy, art, and academic studies. And there is a general understanding among spiritual practitioners that the images and the reality that they represent are not the same. The phrase "painted cakes do not satisfy hunger" refers to that way of understanding. Master Dogen has this to say about painted cakes:

An ancient buddha said, "The painting of a rice cake does not satisfy hunger." This statement has been studied by ancient buddhas and present buddhas. Nevertheless, it has become the mere chatter of seekers in grass-roof huts and under trees. When they transmit their teaching they say this statement means that studying the sutras and commentaries does not nourish true wisdom. Or they suppose that it means that the study of sutras of the three vehicles or the one vehicle is not the way of perfect enlightenment. To say a painting of a rice cake does not satisfy hunger is like saying to refrain from all unwholesome actions and to respectfully practice wholesome actions. It is like saying, "What is it that thus comes?" It is like saying, "I am always intimate with this." You should investigate it in this way. Know that a painting of a rice cake is your face after your parents were born, your face before your parents were born. Thus a painted rice cake made of rice flour is neither born nor unborn. Since this is so, it is the moment of realization of the Way. This cannot be understood by the limited view that a painted rice cake comes and goes.

The paints for painting rice cakes are the same as those used for painting mountains and rivers. For painting mountains and rivers, blue and red paints are used. As for painting rice cakes, flour is used. Thus, they are painted in the same way and they are examined in the same way. The phrase "does not satisfy hunger" means this hunger, not the ordinary matter of twenty-four hours. Even if you were to eat a painted rice cake, you would never put an end to this hunger. Rice cakes are not separate from hunger. Rice cakes are not separate from rice cakes. Thus, the activities and teachings cannot be given away.

When you try to paint mountains and rivers, you use paints, strange cliffs, grotesque boulders, seven rare gems, and the four treasures—a brush, ink, paper, and inkstone. The manner to draw cakes is like this also. In order to portray a person, you make use of the four elements and the five *skandhas*. To delineate a buddha, you utilize not only mud and plaster but the distinguishing marks—a stem of grass from which the golden body of the Buddha is manifested, the bodhisattva's practice of the three kalpas and the hundred kalpas and so on. Inasmuch as one draws a scroll picture of a buddha in such a manner, all the buddhas are the pictured buddhas. All the pictured buddhas are all the buddhas. Examine carefully the pictured buddhas and the pictured cakes. You should understand thoroughly which is a guardian lion and which is the iron staff, which is form and which is mind. All are nothing but pictures. Thus viewed, birth and death, coming and going are pictures without exception. Supreme enlightenment is nothing but a picture. As a rule, in the phenomenal world and the empty sky there is nothing that is not a picture. If you say that a picture is not real, all things are not real. If all things are not real, Dharma is not real either. If Dharma is real, then pictured cakes are real.

Dogen is saying that the image of the truth and the truth itself are completely interpenetrated, interdependent, mutually arising, and non-hindering. All of his teachings manifest this level of appreciation of the nature of dualities and oneness. All of his teachings are phrased within the matrix of the Five Ranks of Master Dongshan. Whether we are talking about the dualities of absolute and relative, heaven and earth, good and evil, man and woman, monastery and world, stillness and activity, or zazen and enlightenment, the same applies. The picture is reality, reality is the picture. Dogen presents very clearly the non-dual conception of picture and reality.

The conclusion he draws is contrary to the traditional interpretation of "painted cakes do not satisfy hunger." He says that the pictured cakes alone satisfy hunger. Or, to put it differently, unless we eat the pictured cakes, we can never satisfy our hunger.

Dogen goes on to say,

Therefore, except for the pictured cakes there is no medicine for satisfying hunger. You do not encounter a person unless your hunger is the pictured hunger, nor do you gain energy unless your satisfaction is the pictured satisfaction. Indeed, you are filled in hunger and feel sufficient in no hunger. You do not satisfy hunger nor feel sufficient in no hunger. You do not satisfy hunger nor do you gratify no hunger. This truth cannot be understood as spoken of except in terms of the pictured hunger.

An ancient buddha said, "Attaining the Way, a thousand snowflakes disappear. Painting blue mountains, several scrolls appear." This is the utterance of great enlightenment—actualized practice in the endeavor of the Way. Accordingly, at the moment of attaining the Way, blue mountains and white snow are painted on countless scrolls. Motion and stillness are nothing but a painting. Our endeavor at this moment is brought forward entirely from a painting. The ten names and the three cognitions are a painting on a scroll. The virtues, the powers, the methods, the Noble Path are also a painting on a scroll. If you say a painting is not real, then the myriad things are not real. If the myriad things are not real, then Buddhadharma is not real. As Buddhadharma is real, a painted rice cake is real.

The great Master Yunmen was asked by a monastic, "What is your statement about going beyond the buddhas and surpassing the ancestors?" The master said, "A rice cake."

Dogen says you should quietly examine these words:

When this rice cake is actualized, an ancient teacher gives expression to going beyond buddhas and surpassing ancestors. An iron person asks this question and students understand. Thus this expression is complete. Opening the matter and hurling it back as a rice cake is itself two or three painted rice cakes. Yunmen's is a statement that goes beyond buddhas and surpasses ancestors, an activity that enters buddhas and enters demons.

There is no remedy for satisfying hunger other than a painted rice cake. Without painted hunger you can never become a true person. There is no understanding other than painted satisfaction. In fact, satisfying hunger, satisfying no hunger, not satisfying hunger, and not satisfying no hunger cannot be attained as spoken of without painted hunger. For some time, study all of these as a painted rice cake. When you understand this meaning with your body and mind, you will thoroughly master the ability to turn things and be turned by things. If this is not done, the power of the study of the Way is not realized. To enact this ability is to actualize the painting of enlightenment.

So what is the medicine for satisfying hunger? If the image is reality and the reality the image, is there any reality outside of images? Are the buddhas of stone and wood and clay the same as the real buddhas of flesh and bones and marrow? Are the words that define reality and the reality they are defining the same or are they different? How do you turn things? How do you allow yourself to be turned by things? How are birth and death, coming and going, all pictures without exception?

∞

STUDENT: I'm full.
TEACHER: What are you telling me?
STUDENT: I'm very full. [Grunts.]
TEACHER: "Very full" excludes the whole universe. I would say, "Wash your dishes."
STUDENT: [Belches.]
TEACHER: How do you turn that around?
STUDENT: [Makes washing motion with her hands.]
TEACHER: May your life go well.
STUDENT: Thank you for your answer.

∞

STUDENT: Though it seems that a painted rice cake is real, I've never eaten one and I don't want to, either. What are we talking about?
TEACHER: With the painted rice cake?
STUDENT: Yes.
TEACHER: Painted rice cake is a reference to a classic image found in Zen literature. In the Linji school it is said that painted cakes do not satisfy hunger; that is, if someone is hungry, a painting of a cake will not help them. Dogen says that painted cakes do satisfy hunger. It all depends on how you understand painted cakes, hunger, and satisfaction. What you can say about painted cakes, hunger and satisfaction, you can say about all imagery—liturgy, music, sculpture, painting, dance, calligraphy, gardening, flower arranging, tea ceremony. Whether or not it satisfies depends on how you understand it, how you understand not satisfying; what is satisfaction; what is not satisfaction; how you understand an image; how you understand self and other. That is basically what we are talking about. Anything else?
STUDENT: No.
TEACHER: May your life go well.
STUDENT: Thank you for your answer.

∞

STUDENT: There is this one rice cake. To paint it, I've got a rowing machine. [Works hard at rowing movements.]

TEACHER: There is this one rice cake. To paint it I've got a rowing machine?

STUDENT: It's what I use to paint it with.

TEACHER: What is the rice cake?

STUDENT: I've never seen it.

TEACHER: And what does it mean to paint it?

STUDENT: [Laughs.]

TEACHER: May your life go well.

STUDENT: Thank you for your answer.

TEACHER: Those of you who are witnessing dharma encounter for the first time need to listen a little differently. If you try to make sense of these exchanges from your own reference system, it is not going to work. You need to listen with the eye, to see with the ear; that is, with the whole body and mind.

STUDENT: After we have eaten our fill of rice cakes and painted rice cakes, then what?

TEACHER: Go straight ahead. How do you go straight ahead?

STUDENT: [Silence.]

TEACHER: To eat your fill is to have the landscape strewn with skulls; to crush the mountains level with the plain. You are a dead man. The only thing you can do with a dead man is to bury him. The question is how do you come back to life? One edge of the sword of Manjushri, bodhisattva of wisdom, kills. That is being completely satisfied, filled with rice cakes. The other edge gives life. That is the painting of the rice cakes, manifestation of wisdom in the ten directions. Do you understand?

STUDENT: [Sighs.]

TEACHER: May your life go well.

STUDENT: Can the painter ever be resting from painting pictures?

TEACHER: Who is the painter?

STUDENT: I don't know. That was going to be another question.

TEACHER: What is the subject? What is the picture? What is the rice cake?

STUDENT: I'm tired now. It's been a long day and I'm trying to paint a picture of being awake, but I keep falling asleep. Am I being a good painter by falling asleep?

TEACHER: What is a good painter? Who is a painter? What is a painting?

STUDENT: The teacher is a painting.

TEACHER: Why do you insist on going outside of yourself? Find out about that painting and the painter and the thing that the painter is painting. That is the key to all art and Dharma. Photographer, subject, image, and audience are not separate entities. When they are separate, all things are separated. When they are realized, the camera photographs by itself, the brush paints by itself, the music plays by itself. It's not "no music, no painting, no hunger"—all of it is very much there. Any questions?

STUDENT: Does the painter ever wake up to the fact that he is painting?

TEACHER: I refuse to get involved in your abstract discussion. Who is the painter? Who are we talking about?

STUDENT: Me.

TEACHER: And what is your painting? Am I your painting?

STUDENT: Right now, yes.

TEACHER: And what is your question?

STUDENT: [Long silence] I don't know. [Laughs.]

TEACHER: If you don't know, I don't know. Do you understand?

STUDENT: I'll sit with it.

TEACHER: You don't know, I don't know. Does this help you with your painting of me?

STUDENT: No. [Laughs nervously.]

TEACHER: May your life go well.

STUDENT: Thank you for your answer.

∽

STUDENT: Do rice cakes have different tastes?

TEACHER: Of course.

STUDENT: Can one choose the taste and the colors?

TEACHER: Sure. It's the same with buddhas. They are all different. Some are male buddhas, some are female buddhas, some are tall, some are short, some are fat, and some are skinny.

STUDENT: Is there a possibility of limiting oneself to sweet rice cake only and, when savory rice cake is presented, pushing it away?

TEACHER: What is your question?

STUDENT: About choosing the flavor and taste of one's rice cakes.

TEACHER: When you intimately realize sweet rice cake, you realize all rice cakes—past, present, and future. When you realize one buddha, you realize all at once the ten thousand buddhas—past, present, and future.

STUDENT: When you don't like the taste of a rice cake and want to spit it out, then have you also realized all rice cakes?

TEACHER: No, that is not realizing; that is spitting out rice cakes.

STUDENT: So, I swallow a rice cake and don't like the taste.

TEACHER: That is swallowing a rice cake and not liking it. It is not realizing rice cake. How do you realize rice cake?

STUDENT: Being the rice cake.

TEACHER: What does that mean?

STUDENT: Digesting it, making it my blood.

TEACHER: That is an explanation. Does it satisfy you?

STUDENT: When it is digested.

TEACHER: How do you realize you?

STUDENT: She is still too busy picking and choosing and not really eating.

TEACHER: Picking and choosing is itself the entry gate to the non-dual Dharma. That is what we call using entanglements to cut entanglements. That is what we call transmitting entanglements. That is one of the views Master Dogen is pointing to. When one realizes Buddha, there is nothing outside of it in the whole universe—past, present, and future.

STUDENT: So my movie is real.

TEACHER: If painted rice cakes are real and reality is painted rice cakes, then your movie is real. And at the same time it is a dream, just like enlightenment is a dream.

STUDENT: But I can't go anywhere with it. You don't walk home with a movie.

TEACHER: What do you mean, "You don't walk home with a movie?"

STUDENT: It is gone after you have seen it.

TEACHER: You came here with a movie. Why won't you walk home with one? Enlightenment is a movie; delusion is a movie; the buddhas and ancestors are movies. Do you understand?

STUDENT: And I'm making it.

TEACHER: You make everything. Why not the movie? If everything is a movie, life is a movie, death is a movie. May your life go well.

STUDENT: Thank you for your answer.

∞

STUDENT: The world is full of painted rice cakes and no one is hungry.

TEACHER: That's too bad.

STUDENT: When they think about it, they will get hungry.

TEACHER: They?

STUDENT: The world.

TEACHER: What is the world?

STUDENT: Painted rice cakes.

TEACHER: Where is it?

STUDENT: [Touches the microphone which emits a groan.] Also, the buddha image on the altar is the Buddha.

TEACHER: What is not?
STUDENT: The buddha image on the altar.
TEACHER: May your life go well.
STUDENT: Thank you for your answer.

STUDENT: I'm not content.
TEACHER: What are you looking for?
STUDENT: I am missing something.
TEACHER: Where? When? What do you seek? What have you missed? What do you want? Those are critical questions. If you don't engage those questions, your energy gets dispersed in the ten directions.
STUDENT: If I don't have the questions, my energy is dispersed?
TEACHER: Right. Life becomes vague and diffuse. The questions create a straight-ahead mind. Intent gets clarified. Now, what is your question?
STUDENT: Why don't I hear?
TEACHER: It seems like you hear. When I ask questions, you nod your head.
STUDENT: Why do I sleep?
TEACHER: Are you asleep now?
STUDENT: Yes, in a way.
TEACHER: Why shouldn't you sleep? Why shouldn't you be deluded? Why shouldn't you suffer? Why shouldn't you be confused? Why shouldn't you be enlightened?
STUDENT: It's our sleep.
TEACHER: Good night. May your life go well.
STUDENT: Thank you for your answer.

STUDENT: The rice cake rice-caked up to the rice cake and rice-caked, "Why are you painting?"
TEACHER: I'm not understanding what you are saying.
STUDENT: The rice cake rice-caked up to the rice cake and rice-caked, "Why are you painting?"
TEACHER: You are talking as if the rice cake was action, name of a subject, and name of an object. Do you take rice cake to be all those things?
STUDENT: I can't even find the rice cake.
TEACHER: With all that you just said, it doesn't sound like that. There is only one rice cake.
STUDENT: So why paint?

TEACHER: I have no idea why paint. Beats me.

STUDENT: Thank you.

TEACHER: Will you go around being a rice cake for the rest of your life?

STUDENT: I don't know how to help it.

TEACHER: You need to see the other side. A rice cake fills the whole universe.

STUDENT: I really hate rice cakes!

TEACHER: That's better.

STUDENT: And they are tastier with jam.

TEACHER: That's better still. Just don't get stuck in a rice cake.

STUDENT: Jam is very sticky. Have to be always on our guard.

TEACHER: Please take good care not to get stuck—jam or otherwise.

STUDENT: Thank you for your answer.

STUDENT: May your life go well.

STUDENT: You talked about the other side of painting. Would that be the canvas?

TEACHER: Being the rice cake with the whole body and mind is one side. There is nothing but rice cake. It fills the universe. There is no eye, ear, nose, tongue, body, or mind. There is nothing you can do with no eye, ear, nose, tongue, body, or mind. There is no way you can get across the street, no way you can practice your karate. There is no way that you can love, hate, feel, laugh, dance, or cry. There is no enlightenment; there are no buddhas, no ancestors. So, you need to see the other side. And the other side is laughing, crying, dancing, buddhas, enlightenment, delusion, pain, suffering. Still, the truth of the Buddhadharma is to be found in neither of those two extremes; in neither the rice cake itself nor in the painting of the rice cake, in neither absolute nor in relative. When I say "the other side," I mean the other side of absolute—"rice cake fills the whole universe." Or when I say "the other side," I mean the other side of the relative—"a painting of a rice cake." Do you understand what I am saying?

STUDENT: The middle way.

TEACHER: Right.

STUDENT: Thank you for your answer.

TEACHER: May your life go well.

STUDENT: I'm very hungry. Do you have anything for me to eat?

TEACHER: I'm sorry. There's nothing I can do to help you.

STUDENT: What am I going to do?

TEACHER: Feed yourself.

STUDENT: I don't have any money.

TEACHER: You have been living in this monastery, drinking the wine of these teachings, and you come here trying to act like a poor person.

STUDENT: I'm selfish.

TEACHER: How will you feed yourself, cook?

STUDENT: [Silence.]

TEACHER: By taking a cabbage leaf and manifesting the ten-thousand-foot golden body of the Buddha.

STUDENT: But I'm tired.

TEACHER: Be tired then, with the whole body and mind. Don't separate yourself from being tired. Then there is no tired.

STUDENT: What is there?

TEACHER: [Yawns.] Can't stay awake.

STUDENT: I'm tired of being tired.

TEACHER: Be tired and then you won't be tired of being tired. Be completely tired. Don't analyze it, judge it, compare it, categorize it, systematize it, understand it, not understand it, evaluate it. Just be it.

STUDENT: OK. [Flops down on the floor.]

TEACHER: It's not like an image reflected in the mirror, where you have the image, the thing, and the reflection. No separation. No self-consciousness. Do you understand?

STUDENT: No.

TEACHER: Then find out. When you sit on your cushion, get rid of everything. A single thought separates heaven and earth, you and the ten thousand things. When a thought comes up, throw it away, get back to your practice. Be your practice with your whole body and mind. That is what your practice is—being it with your whole body and mind; whether it's cooking, cleaning, working with a koan, sitting, laughing, dancing, crying. It doesn't matter which of those things you do; when you do it with the whole body and mind, the ten thousand things return to the self where they have always been. With Master Yunmen it was a scream when his foot got caught in the door. He realized himself through excruciating pain.

STUDENT: And then no more pain?

TEACHER: Then no eye, ear, nose, tongue, body, or mind. No color, sound, smell, taste, touch, phenomena. No world of sight. No world of consciousness. I think, but I'm not sure, that includes no pain.

STUDENT: For how long? Just for a moment?

TEACHER: For ten billion kalpas.

STUDENT: And then the next day?

TEACHER: Ten billion kalpas.

STUDENT: Sounds terribly overwhelming.

TEACHER: Don't be overwhelmed. Stick your head in the garbage pail and suffer. Either way is okay. Enlightenment is okay. Delusion is okay.

STUDENT: You have a lot of patience.

TEACHER: I have none at all.

STUDENT: Okay. Thank you.

TEACHER: Anything else?

STUDENT: Thank you.

TEACHER: You want to leave now?

STUDENT: What do you mean?

TEACHER: Do you want to leave? Is that what you are telling me by bowing and saying "Thank you," and squirming around?

STUDENT: It doesn't seem like there is much more to say. You can hit me on the head.

TEACHER: [Taps her on the head.] Your head makes a remarkable sound.

STUDENT: Thank you for your answer.

TEACHER: May your life go well.

∞

STUDENT: This rice cake is very hungry.

TEACHER: I know that and I think it is wonderful.

STUDENT: [Makes a motion of eating her arm.]

TEACHER: That is another way to do it.

STUDENT: It's not doing anything.

TEACHER: That is because you are not doing it.

STUDENT: [Lets out a loud yell.]

TEACHER: Feel better?

STUDENT: Not really.

TEACHER: That's what it means to be really intimate with the self—a complete gesture. To be really intimate with the self is to be intimate with the ten thousand things. It doesn't matter if we are talking about the breath, the koan Mu, fear, joy. To really be intimate with it is to be intimate with the self. To forget the self is to be intimate with the self. Do you understand?

STUDENT: I wish I didn't.

TEACHER: You wish you didn't. I wish you didn't. How will you not understand? How do you get rid of understanding?

STUDENT: [Points to herself.]

TEACHER: Just do it. And then keep in mind that it is not enough. What you really need to see is where that comes from, the origin of all of that. Before that, what is it like?

STUDENT: Who made the rice cake?

TEACHER: [Laughs.]

STUDENT: It's very frustrating.

TEACHER: For now. That is your active edge.

STUDENT: I hate it.

TEACHER: You will learn to love it.

STUDENT: What do I do?

TEACHER: Keep practicing and go deeper.

STUDENT: I just hurt when I go deeper.

TEACHER: Beyond that there is more—much, much more. It is endless and boundless. That hurting is separating yourself from it. Be the hurting. In order to appreciate a painted rice cake, you have to have painted hunger, painted satisfaction, the whole thing.

STUDENT: Painted pain?

TEACHER: That pain is another thing—it's using entanglements to cut entanglements. Entanglements are not something that we should push away. We should welcome them. They are the gates. The senses are the creation of delusion but they are also the gates to enlightenment. They are enlightenment. To hear is enlightenment. Anything else?

STUDENT: No.

TEACHER: May your life go well.

STUDENT: Thank you for your answer.

∞

STUDENT: Is the image of myself the same as the reality of myself?

TEACHER: How do you see it?

STUDENT: I see the image changing.

TEACHER: When you say image of myself, where is that? And when you say reality of myself, where is that?

STUDENT: In my mind and more than my mind.

TEACHER: What is "more than your mind?"

STUDENT: The true substance of who I am.

TEACHER: Where do you find that? In a book in God's library under your name, which says, "This is who Nell really is. It's not what she thinks or what people think. This is what she really is?" What is truth?

STUDENT: I think that this true substance of who I really am is the perfection that I am trying to uncover, and the image I have is not complete now.

TEACHER: When you say, "the perfection that I am trying to uncover," implicit in that statement is that it is there.

STUDENT: Yes.

TEACHER: So that is what you are.

STUDENT: That is what I am.

TEACHER: But you want to see that.

STUDENT: Yes.

TEACHER: Is that any different from what you see?

STUDENT: Sometimes I see the imperfection.

TEACHER: Is the imperfection any less perfect than perfection? You have an idea that the perfection of the ten-thousand-foot golden body of the Buddha is some kind of a hundred percent perfect Wonder Woman image. But that excludes so many people. Does that mean someone without legs is less than perfect? That someone handicapped isn't a buddha? What is the image of perfection? Where do we get it from? Hollywood? Madison Avenue? Each thing, just as it is, is perfect and complete, lacking nothing; whether it is a person, a mountain, or a car. Inherent perfection includes everything just as it is. That's what has to be realized. And how does all of this happen? Mind. You create the universe. You create yourself. You create time and being. You create me. That is why we can say it is like a dream. Mind is Buddha. Do you understand?

STUDENT: Some.

TEACHER: Anything else?

STUDENT: How do you cultivate an eye that hears and an ear that sees? By sitting?

TEACHER: I wouldn't say cultivate; I'd say realize. It's not something that you are growing, it's something that you have. It's a faculty that you are born with. The eye that hears is to see form with the whole body and mind; the ear that sees is to hear intimately, with no separation between yourself and the universe. You start by being intimate with the breath. To be intimate with your breath is to be intimate with yourself. May your life go well.

STUDENT: Thank you for your answer.

I think we pretty much took care of the rice cakes. We boiled them, fried them, baked them, cooked them, and ate them. This teaching of Master Dogen is key in appreciating how the imagery, symbols, and metaphors function in our practice, and what it means to really understand how entanglements are transmitted; how to take entanglements—the very hindrances that block our progress in practice, the barriers of our lives—and use them as a way of understanding, use them as a place of realization.

BEING BORN AS THE EARTH

Being born as the earth is not the same as being born into the world. It is not a matter of simply occupying space on this great planet. To be born as the earth is to realize the earth—to realize mountains, rivers, and the great earth as the body and mind of the Tathagata, as one's own body and mind. Master Dogen taught:

> From the beginning, spring and fall, mountains and rivers, have never been separated. It is not possible to perceive them independently. Time cannot be separated from the mountains and rivers. Seekers of the Buddhist Way should study the verse, "The mountain flows, the river is still." It is a pity that from ancient times up to the present there are people who do not realize that the universe is proclaiming the actual body of the Buddha. These people are miserable. What do they see when they look at a mountain, what do they hear when they listen to a mountain stream? Do they hear only one sound instead of the eighty-four thousand hymns? It is regrettable that many only appreciate the superficial aspects of sound or color. They can neither perceive nor experience Buddha's shape, form, and voice in a landscape. They have never had the opportunity to see the wonderful Buddhist Way. Mountains and rivers ceaselessly proclaiming the law, the color of the mountains manifesting his pure body. This is limitless life.
>
> A monastic once asked Zen Master Changsha, "How can we possess the mountains, rivers, and the earth as our own?" In reply the master said, "How can we return to the mountains, rivers, and the earth?" What is it that separates us from mountains, rivers, and the great earth?
>
> Another monastic asked Master Langye, "How can our original nature be

mountains, rivers, and the earth?" Langye replied with this question, "How do you interpret 'mountains, rivers, and the earth?'"

My question is, what are you calling your original nature? The green foliage of the pine tree in spring or the beauty of a chrysanthemum in autumn are the real form of truth. When a true master attains this level of enlightenment, they are a teacher of humans and gods. But if you try to direct people without attaining enlightenment first, there will be nothing but opposition. If you do not know the real form of the spring pine or the autumn chrysanthemum, how can you find the real meaning of their existence, how can you penetrate your own being?

Dogen goes on to say,

It's natural to listen with your ear, but it is also possible to hear through the eye. When you meet with Buddha you will see Buddha in yourself and in others. Do not be amazed or frightened at the appearance of a great buddha, or doubt the appearance of a small one. These diverse forms of the Buddha are in the sound of a valley stream and the color of the mountains. When you realize this, there will be a great proclamation of the eighty-four thousand hymns, complete freedom will be attained, and great enlightenment achieved. When you look up, your vision extends limitlessly. As Master Jujing said, "Endless sky is filled endlessly."

And so, I ask you, how can we return to, rather than possess, mountains and rivers and the great earth? How can we hear the eighty-four thousand hymns of the valley stream? What does it mean to study the verse, "Mountains flow, the river is still?" How can you find the real meaning of the true form of the spring pine and the autumn chrysanthemum? How do you understand, "These mountains and rivers of the present are themselves wise ones and sages?" These are important questions, very important questions. If all sentient beings would realize the truth of these teachings, then there would be no need for an Environmental Protection Agency, there would be no need for environmental protection legislation, there would be no hole in the ozone layer, or oil in the harbors. There would be no endangered species, pollution in the air and in the water, no greenhouse effect, no depletion of natural resources. These problems are the self-inflicted wounds of the human race—human cause, human effect—and they can only be realized by humans. They can only be healed by humans.

STUDENT: This spring breeze cools no body except this one.

TEACHER: And in winter?
STUDENT: [Shivers.]
TEACHER: How do you hear the eighty-four thousand hymns?
STUDENT: [Whistles a bird call.]
TEACHER: May your life go well.
STUDENT: Thank you for your answer.

STUDENT: In New York City, I'm carrying a banner that says, "Save the Earth." In Phoenicia I'm drunk as a skunk, sittin' at the bar watching TV, complaining about all this damn environmental consciousness. Why don't they have the game on? Up on the mountain I'm scurrying around looking for nuts. In the class I'm complaining about the government and teaching kids how to save the Earth.
TEACHER: How will you save it?
STUDENT: [Points.] Pick up that piece of paper. [Shrugs.] Okay, I'll pick it up myself.
TEACHER: That separates you from it.
STUDENT: I'm not picking up that paper, you pick it up yourself!
TEACHER: That doesn't function.
STUDENT: [Picks up the imaginary piece of paper.] I'll put it in my pocket, I guess.
TEACHER: Damn right. May your life go well.
STUDENT: Thank you for your answer.

STUDENT: I don't even know how to ask the question. [Starts to cry.] This is my whole life question.
TEACHER: Those are the only kind of questions—whole life questions. What is your whole life question?
STUDENT: [Crying.] How do I take my life and give it back without any traces?
TEACHER: Give it back to what?
STUDENT: Give it back to what it is, give it back to where it came from.
TEACHER: Where did it come from?
STUDENT: I don't know, it's always just coming and coming.
TEACHER: From where? Going to where? All of that coming and going always takes place right here, right now. Giving and receiving is always right here, right now. Cause and effect is always right here, right now. What is that coming and going?

STUDENT: What is that? How do I get rid of that? How do I manifest the sixteen-foot golden Buddha in a pile of shit? Tell me!

TEACHER: There is neither coming nor going.

STUDENT: Why don't I live that?

TEACHER: Stop coming and going. Stop trying. Just be Angie.

STUDENT: I'm scared.

TEACHER: Of what? All there is is Angie.

STUDENT: To me it seems like there's this and that.

TEACHER: That's the mind. A single thought arises and there is this and that; coming from someplace and going to someplace else. There is birth and death, there's Angie and the earth, and there's a question and there's an answer. When the ten thousand things return to the self, where they have always been, there is no Angie and no earth.

STUDENT: How does that happen?

TEACHER: Let go.

STUDENT: [Weeping.] I don't know how to let go.

TEACHER: [Holding the stick up.] How do I let go? Tell me how to let go of this.

STUDENT: Just open your fingers.

TEACHER: I don't understand; that's an explanation. How do I let go? Don't tell me, show me.

STUDENT: [Continues crying.]

TEACHER: Help me! Show me how to let go! Reach out and show me!

STUDENT: [Sobs.]

TEACHER: Take it and show me!

STUDENT: [Reaches out and holds onto the stick. Teacher lets go. Student keeps holding the stick.]

TEACHER: Now let go. LET GO!

STUDENT: [Sob.] I can't.

TEACHER: TEACH ME HOW TO LET GO!

STUDENT: I can't. [Teacher takes the stick back.]

TEACHER: Everyday get yourself a stick, go sit by the river, and learn how to do this. [Drops the stick.] When you can do that, come back to me, and ask me again, "How can I let go?" When you let go, LET GO! Anything else?

STUDENT: [Shakes her head.]

TEACHER: Do you understand practicing letting go?

STUDENT: No.

TEACHER: No one can make it happen. No one can do it for you. No one can save you but yourself. And if you're not willing to do it, it won't happen. Un-fortu-nately, that's the way it is. You have to trust yourself. Teachers can't do it. Buddhas can't do it. There is only one person in this entire universe who can do it, and her name is Angie. Empower yourself; let go of the hold. Trust yourself—give yourself permission to either fail or succeed. Either way is okay. May your life go well.

STUDENT: Thank you for your answer.

STUDENT: I can't really enjoy this because I am stuck and still choking on this thing in my throat. Help!

TEACHER: Well, you know what the solution to that is, don't you?

STUDENT: Yeah. You tell me all the time.

TEACHER: How do you take care of choking in the throat?

STUDENT: Be it.

TEACHER: "Be it" is an explanation. I can get away with saying "be it." You can't. How do you take care of it, Kim?!

STUDENT: Swallow.

TEACHER: NO! There is only one way. Do you understand?

STUDENT: [Laughter.] No.

TEACHER: [Leans forward, and puts his hands around student's neck and shakes her.] Ha, ha, ha! Thank you, thank you for this opportunity. May your life go well.

STUDENT: Hey!

TEACHER: There is nothing more than that. [Makes retching, choking noises.] Uuaaagghhhhh!

STUDENT: [Hopeless sigh.] Ughhh. [Whines.] That doesn't help.

TEACHER: That's because you're not doing it; you're thinking about it.

STUDENT: How do I do it?

TEACHER: [Leans forward and makes louder retching noises.] Bluuuuaagghh! Blaaaughghgh!

STUDENT: Aughghghgh! [Finally, with energy.]

TEACHER: Good.

STUDENT: That doesn't help; I still feel awful.

TEACHER: Keep doing it.

STUDENT: [Laughs.]

TEACHER: I'm serious! This is not some philosophical problem. You just find yourself a nice corner and Uuaaaghghghgh! And you'll see after a while how wonderful it feels. Now, go away!

STUDENT: Wait a minute!

TEACHER: Go away! There is no more!

STUDENT: But that doesn't help!

TEACHER: You haven't done it. Do it!

STUDENT: I don't know what that means.

TEACHER: Uaghgh uaghgh uaghgh. Uagh!

STUDENT: Go around making barfing noises?

TEACHER: No, don't go around! Go into a room by yourself so you don't disturb anyone else. Right now. And choke on what's stuck in your throat. Be it! With the whole body and mind.

STUDENT: What does that mean, be it? Just be miserable?

TEACHER: Be choking on what's in your throat. Or is that an idea, something you made up?

STUDENT: No!

TEACHER: Is there something really that you're choking on? Or is it all in your head?

STUDENT: It hurts in my body.

TEACHER: Then choke. Go choke.

STUDENT: [Begins to cry.]

TEACHER: I'm serious.

STUDENT: [Cries.]

TEACHER: Not cry, choke!

STUDENT: [Laughs.] I don't understand.

TEACHER: Because you can't understand it. You have to do it!

STUDENT: How will that help?

TEACHER: You want to talk about it. You want a neat intellectual answer. Why not do it?

STUDENT: It's silly.

TEACHER: It's not silly. When you choke, just choke.

STUDENT: And then it doesn't hurt?

TEACHER: Try it.

STUDENT: Aauuaagkkkkh.

TEACHER: No, no, no. Practice it. Practice it. Give it an hour. And call me in the morning. [Laughter.]

STUDENT: So then I'll choke and I'll gag, and maybe I'll finally swallow the goddamn thing.

TEACHER: Or maybe you'll spit it out. Either way is okay.

STUDENT: Okay, or maybe I'll spit it out. And then there's still going to be more pain.

TEACHER: Oh, you've got it all figured out.

STUDENT: Yeah, I've got it all figured out.

TEACHER: If you've got it all figured out, guaranteed there will be more pain. No question about it.

STUDENT: Isn't that true?

TEACHER: Maybe for you, but not for me.

STUDENT: So, you saw it, and then there was no more pain in your life?

TEACHER: There is always pain. But I know what to do when it happens. When it's stuck in my throat, uuuaaghgh! Uuuaaghgh! That's what I do. When I hurt, [Holds his gut.] Ooouuchh! I hurt. When I laugh, I laugh. HA HA HA HAHAHAHA! HAAA HA HA HA! What else is there, Kim? Are you going to float off into the sublime cosmos? Take a magic pill and the sun will shine all the time, and it will never rain?

STUDENT: I just don't understand.

TEACHER: Stop trying to understand. Practice it.

STUDENT: [Sighs.] It just makes me want to curl up into a little ball in despair when I think, my God, there is just going to be more pain and more pain and more pain.

TEACHER: There doesn't have to be. But as long as you keep creating it that way, there will always be pain and more pain and more pain. That will indeed happen and you can curl up into a ball.

STUDENT: I don't want to. I'm sick of that.

TEACHER: Okay. Then there is another side to it. You stand up, take responsibility for it, and be it. You can't run away from it. Do you know why you can't run away from it? Because it is not something that's happening to you. It is you. It is not coming from the outside; there is no outside. You create it, and you can put an end to it. That's what you've got over me; I can't end it for you. There is nothing I can do for you.

STUDENT: I know.

TEACHER: Except drive you to despair until you finally do it. Make you crazy. Push you off the edge. If I could do it for you, I would.

STUDENT: So far, the only way I know to be my pain is to cry. I feel better when I cry, when I just let it happen and feel it and let it go. If I did that every time I was in pain, I would spend most of my time crying.

TEACHER: Maybe you have to do that for a while until you take care of it all. There is nothing wrong with crying. It is a wonderful practice.

STUDENT: I'll disturb everyone in the zendo.

TEACHER: I don't think anybody minds. We've all had our share of crying in the zendo. People do it all the time.

STUDENT: [Crying and trying to catch her breath.]

TEACHER: Give yourself a break.

STUDENT: How? What does that mean?

TEACHER: Trust yourself. Empower yourself.

STUDENT: On some level I know I can do it. I just am so impatient and I hurt and I want it NOW!

TEACHER: I believe you can do it, too. I trust you. But that doesn't help, does it?

STUDENT: Not really.

TEACHER: You have to trust yourself. Okay?

STUDENT: Okay.

TEACHER: May your life go well.

STUDENT: Thank you for your answer.

STUDENT: I wanted to see what it feels like to come up here and face you. So far, so good. I don't have anything to say about being born as the earth, but I thought I'd let you know that I'd like to become a formal student here at the Monastery. I can't seem to talk myself out of it; maybe you can.

TEACHER: That's a good way to do it. The time to become a student is when it's already happened for you. The time to become a Buddhist is when you're already a Buddhist. The time to become a monastic is when you're already a monastic. The time to get married is when you're already married. The ceremony is just about "making visible the invisible." Because, again, you're the only one who can do it. You're the only one who can really take that step. That rite of passage is totally within your domain.

STUDENT: Still, it seems like it is important to formally say it.

TEACHER: That is commitment. Commitment is the challenge. It's one thing to silently say to yourself, "I'm doing it," and it's quite another to say to the people whom you respect or love, "I vow to attain the Way."

STUDENT: I do, everybody. [Student and teacher laugh.]

TEACHER: Say it louder.

STUDENT: I really do!

TEACHER: They can't hear you in the back.

STUDENT: [In a singing yell.] I'm gonna do it! [Laughter.]

TEACHER: Do what?

STUDENT: I don't know.

TEACHER: Attain the Way.

STUDENT: Okay.

TEACHER: Don't miss the point of it.

STUDENT: Well I know it's unattainable.

TEACHER: Show me.

STUDENT: It's already done.

TEACHER: Show me.

STUDENT: [Hesitates.]

TEACHER: In your way, show me.

STUDENT: What am I showing you?

TEACHER: That it's already done.

STUDENT: Thank you for your answer.

TEACHER: That takes care of the dialogue, but not the Way. Work on it.

STUDENT: I give up.

TEACHER: Work on it. Don't give up! Do it! You just took a vow that you're going to do it.

STUDENT: Yikes! [Laughter.]

TEACHER: What kind of a commitment is that? This much. [Signals "very little bit" with thumb and finger.] This is BIG commitment.

STUDENT: I'll work on it.

TEACHER: May your life go well.

STUDENT: Thank you for your answer.

STUDENT: I planted a garden and things started growing. There were some flowers and vegetables; some weeds. I thought maybe I should go in there and do some weeding. I started pulling out the weeds, but then I didn't really know the difference between baby weeds and flowers and vegetables, and I started pulling out some of those. Then, after a while, I got lazy and just let everything grow. Later, I went out there and looked at it again, and thought maybe I should take some weeds out. But the weeds were kind of interesting plants too, and I thought, they have as much right to be there as the flowers and the vegetables. But somehow I feel like there's this pressure on me to get rid of the weeds and pick up the litter that the wind blew into the garden, and I'm not really sure where to go at this point. That's why it took me a long time to become a student. I felt like I didn't want to become a student until all my motivations were absolutely pure and there were no weeds. The same with wanting to become a Buddhist. Although I felt like I was a Buddhist and I tried to observe the precepts, I didn't want to ask for *jukai* until there were no weeds in my garden. And it looks like there are always going to be weeds and trash in my garden.

TEACHER: So, what will you do? Are you going to keep waiting for the perfect garden?

STUDENT: No. It is perfect, right now. I just have to keep reminding myself of that.

TEACHER: There are different ways of cultivating a garden. First of all, keep in mind that you planted the garden, so you started the whole problem.

STUDENT: Right. It's my fault.

TEACHER: Secondly, you're impatient. Very few people can identify the tiny plants when they spring up; it's hard to tell whether they're weeds or plants. Give them a chance to grow. I've seen some healthy, robust plants that have come out of weedy gardens—some plants just tough it out and overtake the weeds. Also, if you like weeds, make a little weed garden. Give the other plants a break. Or, if you think they should get along together, use the weeds to fertilize the flowers. Then use the flowers and plants to fertilize yourself.

STUDENT: Is that what you mean when you say, "the lotus blooms because of the fire?"

TEACHER: Yes. The fire is the fertile soil for lotuses.

STUDENT: Thank you for your answer.

TEACHER: May your life go well.

STUDENT: You said that when everyone realizes themselves, there will be no holes in the ozone layer, no need for the Environmental Protection Agency. I think people who will realize themselves will drive their cars as much as they do right now, and the hole in the ozone layer will persist.

TEACHER: It depends on how you understand "realizing." It is like you sitting down and making an agreement with yourself: "I agree that I won't take an ice pick and poke out my eye. And I agree that I won't take a cleaver and chop off my hand. And I agree that I won't take a sword and stick it down my throat."

STUDENT: But even with such an agreement, you could fall down and accidentally break your arm.

TEACHER: Of course. There will be forest fires, there will be earthquakes. There will be lions killing lambs.

STUDENT: What about pressure-treated lumber in the Esopus River? What about darkroom chemicals being poured down the drain?

TEACHER: I don't think you will find those problems.

STUDENT: No?

TEACHER: No. The only reason we develop photographs the way we do is that we're using a process that was invented hundreds of years before anyone understood its effect on the environment. It doesn't need to be done that way. Look at the wonderful electronic photographs you get without using chemicals.

STUDENT: I like the old one's better. They look a lot nicer.

TEACHER: Well, there are lots of ways of doing it. They used to employ mercury, then they found out that it was killing people, so they went to silver. It just takes a little longer with silver, that's all.

STUDENT: Right.

TEACHER: I just saw a report about the American Wilderness Society giving an award to the 3M Company for their environmental activity. It's incredible what they've done. They've worked out ways to completely recycle scotch tape, and developed glues that no longer pollute. They have smoke stacks that no smoke comes out of—the scrubbers really work. It is all possible within the range of technology that exists today. And the only thing that keeps us from doing it is we don't really care. We don't understand that it's like cutting off our own arm.

STUDENT: So how is my practice going to change what politicians and big companies do? How am I going to be able to get these people to see that what they're doing is cutting off their own arm?

TEACHER: You want all the solutions right now. Just do it. Find out for yourself. Do you want promises from me, a guarantee?

STUDENT: I don't want promises from you, but it is easy for me to sit here and listen to you.

TEACHER: I'm telling you to do it. Don't listen to me; don't believe me. Prove me wrong. Realize yourself, then destroy the environment and come back and say, "Look at what I did."

STUDENT: Okay.

TEACHER: May your life go well.

STUDENT: Thank you for your answer.

STUDENT: I've been practicing letting go of all these thoughts about dharma encounter and what I was supposed to do here only to realize that I don't know any words of truth. What words of truth do you know?

TEACHER: I don't know any either.

STUDENT: I would sing you a song, but I forgot the words to it.

TEACHER: [Laughs.] That's okay, you don't have to. Anything else?

STUDENT: I'm still here.

TEACHER: Yes. Do you have a question?

STUDENT: Not right now.

TEACHER: Do you have an answer?

STUDENT: No answers.

TEACHER: Just don't know.

STUDENT: Just don't know.

TEACHER: Just like Bodhidharma! Congratulations, may your life go well.

STUDENT: [Hesitates.] All of the sudden I feel stuck.

TEACHER: [Laughs.] What you need to do is roll back on your heels, stand up, and move over there.

STUDENT: Thank you for your answer.

TEACHER: May your life go well.

STUDENT: When I dump on the world, I really am dumping on myself. That seems shortsighted.

TEACHER: Yes, no question about it. So what will you do about it?

STUDENT: Stop dumping.

TEACHER: What are you going to do with all the stuff?

STUDENT: I don't know. Just let go of it.

TEACHER: Aside from realizing yourself, there are actually technological solutions for our environmental problems. For example, there are millions upon millions of used tires accumulating around the world. They just sit in dumps, and never decay. Water collects in them, mosquitoes make nests in them and spread malaria. If you burn them you pollute the atmosphere. Well, some guy created a company that burns tires with no effluent coming out. He completely reclaims the oils from it, all of the toxins are absorbed out, and energy is produced; and he's making millions of dollars. He's planning to set up factories all over the country. Tough independent environmental groups, not the EPA, checked him out, and it's true. The process is working. Of course it's working! If we can make a tire, we can take it apart—we have the technology.

STUDENT: We can't all become scientists, but we can support these people.

TEACHER: Exactly. We can make it so that you absolutely must, by law, solve the problem of disposal before you put a product on the market. In other words, development needs to include the responsibility of not poisoning people.

STUDENT: We have to be really aware of what's going on.

TEACHER: Very much aware. And take it personally.

STUDENT: See it like this arm; it's part of us.

TEACHER: Not us. You!

STUDENT: Me.

TEACHER: Right. It's got nothing to do with me or anyone else; it's only you. Anything else?

STUDENT: No.

TEACHER: May your life go well.

STUDENT: Thank you for your answer.

STUDENT: When I was sitting zazen late last night with what you had said, "Have the watcher be Mu," for some reason I thought I knew what it meant.

TEACHER: How do you think you will know when that happens?

STUDENT: Probably because I'll scratch my face and it'll be an hour later? I don't think I know how I'll know.

TEACHER: You won't know. As long as you're knowing as you go along, the witness is still there. When you stop knowing, there is no longer anybody witnessing the whole process.

STUDENT: [Nods his head.]

TEACHER: This is a hell of a thing to tell someone who's about to go into college: "Don't know." [Laughs.]

STUDENT: I'm not so sure about going to college. [Laughter.] It doesn't make a whole lot of sense to me, leaving this place of life training, not having my questions settled, to go off and do what? What's the point of it?

TEACHER: There is a point. Don't get me wrong. I don't want to give the impression that I'm opposed to knowledge. Knowledge is important. I love to study, to read, to find out about new things. But we need to recognize that that's only one half of being human. The other half is the stillness out of which all of the activity arises. Both of them, together, make the whole. They're not separate. Our cultural tendency is to get an academic education, which brings us only to one side. Or, we suddenly become fanatical, like you're sounding, and we reject that and want to withdraw to a Zen monastery. That's making a living in a ghost cave. It's just as bad.

STUDENT: Well, I couldn't stay here any longer, anyway. It's nothing against anything, it's just that this place is an inferno. This last month especially has been an endless edge. I wake up in the morning and I can't believe how intense my life is. But I know that it's just my own stuff.

TEACHER: The inferno is fine. This monastery is definitely an inferno. The problem is that you're wearing an asbestos suit. Get rid of it. Get rid of the fire-retardant stuff and let it burn you up.

STUDENT: I think I've done that a few times; maybe not enough.

TEACHER: Burn the self until it's no longer there. Forget the self. Then there is nothing to separate you from the great earth or the mountains and rivers.

STUDENT: Okay.

TEACHER: [With a silly smile.] Isn't that nice?

STUDENT: [Laughs.] Yeah.

TEACHER: May your life go well.

STUDENT: Thank you for your answer.

STUDENT: I have this vision: on the river bank, there is Angie holding her ladle, and there is Kim going "Uaaakkk!" and maybe Mark's there waddling around the bank making honking sounds. What am I supposed to be doing?

TEACHER: What's your question? Do you want to be one of them?

STUDENT: No, I don't want their questions. I think I have my own, somewhere.

TEACHER: What is it?

STUDENT: Actually, I'd just like to take a swim.

TEACHER: You didn't have to come up here for that.

STUDENT: Sometimes I wonder how to make my practice more specific.

TEACHER: More specific than what? What is your practice?

STUDENT: I constantly try to let go, always be in the moment, not have expectations, not get caught up in the past.

TEACHER: That sounds like a lot of stuff. Maybe just be the breath. Being the breath, you're in the moment. When you are the breath, there are no expectations. You don't have to think about anything else. If you do think of anything else, acknowledge it, let it go, and come back to the breath. That's a start. Of course you can't just do that for the rest of your life. Sooner or later, it has to manifest in everything. But it starts there.

STUDENT: You just get bored of watching what you're doing, and then let go? That's what I do when I'm sitting.

TEACHER: If you're really with each moment, there is no opportunity to get bored. Boredom has to do with thinking ahead, or thinking of the past, or getting caught up in the passage of time, or the illusion of the passage of time, or continuity. But when each moment is the first moment and the last moment of your life, there is nothing to bore you. Then when the moment is complete, you let it go; moment to moment to moment to moment. Very exciting. Even this "boring" conversation. [Laughter.]

STUDENT: I think what I'm hoping will get boring is watching myself trying to stay in the moment. I'm aware that I'm always trying to be in the moment.

TEACHER: That's not being in the moment; that's trying to be in the moment.

STUDENT: Right. Do you get bored with that?

TEACHER: You always get bored with trying. Don't try. Do it. Whenever someone says, "I'll try," I get the sense that they've already struck themselves out.

STUDENT: For sure.

TEACHER: Anything else?

STUDENT: I'll do it.

TEACHER: May your life go well.

STUDENT: Thank you for your answer.

STUDENT: I've been up here before, but I feel I've never done dharma encounter with you. It's mainly been a bunch of bullshit that I've presented to you. I was up in my cabin this morning, trying to empty my mind so I could start fresh, and it didn't work too well because all kinds of questions, ideas, ways of putting you down, or ways of building myself up kept coming into my mind. And I realized as you were talking about the earth, that I use the earth just to cover my ass, to protect myself from any kind of risk. I want to end that.

TEACHER: I don't understand what you mean. How do you use it to cover yourself?

STUDENT: I preplan everything; I think everything out in advance—if you go this way, I'll go that way. This way my whole life is taken care of for the most part, and much of the time I feel a lack of spontaneity, especially when I'm in situations where I might be at risk of being found out.

TEACHER: The secret to resolving that tension is in giving yourself permission to fail. People who come to Zen practice tend to be high achievers. Let's face it, "Shakyamuni Buddha did it, I can do it!" [Laughter.] So they take up this big challenge to realize oneself and struggle, making themselves sick and tense. Some of the people who are stuck on Mu look like they are dying. They haven't given themselves permission to fail. Once you fail you find out that it's not quite so bad. That's one of the kind ways that my teacher always helped me—at every opportunity, he showed me up as an asshole in public. Privately, he was always supportive and encouraging to me. He respected and treated me like an equal. But publicly he would puncture the balloon, particularly when I was being a wise ass. And it took a long time for me to see that there was no way out of it, except to be able to adjust to his pulling the rug out from under me. It's a matter of trusting yourself. Trusting yourself really means giving yourself permission to fail. To be an asshole, or to be successful—either way has to be okay. If success is something that's very important; "Oh, I'm wonderful, I succeeded," or if failure is important; "Oh, I'm horrible. What would my parents think of me. I failed," then you're caught between two iron mountains that will squeeze your guts out. The only way to practice that is to throw yourself completely into whatever you are doing, with no expectations.

STUDENT: I know that. I just have to do it.

TEACHER: I'll help you practice. You dumb bastard, get out of here! You don't know anything! Why don't you do some sitting? Don't give me your intellectual crap!

STUDENT: [Surprised.] Oh, yeah? Well you're a dumb bastard yourself! You don't know anything.

TEACHER: Stop fighting! I know I'm a dumb bastard. [Laughter.]

STUDENT: I just wanted to make sure you knew it.

TEACHER: May your life go well.

STUDENT: Thank you for your answer.

STUDENT: How is it that trees torn down off this mountain to make condominiums are a defilement, but those trees never leave this body?

TEACHER: Who said they're a defilement?

STUDENT: Isn't there an association trying to stop this destruction?

TEACHER: Yes. The destruction that's being fought is a particular way certain developers use to clear land, devastating it like strip miners do, taking everything down so that bulldozers can get in there, then putting up plastic houses.

Strip the land and take the trees away and the land leaches out down into the river. Put a hundred houses up on a mountain slope that drains into a stream, and the leakage from the septic tanks ends up in the water. It is possible to develop land another way. I would like to see us with a waste treatment plant on this mountain that is so efficient that by the time the treatment is finished you could drink the water that comes out. It is possible. It was possible twenty-five years ago. I worked with an engineering company that did that for a small town. The chief engineer took me to the effluent pipe. I saw all the sludge from the toilets coming into the plant, and now it was coming out the other end through this plastic pipe as clear water. He said, "Feel it." It was ice cold. He said, "Smell it." It smelled clean. He said, "Taste it." I said, "No, thank you." [Laughter.] He filled a glass with that water and drank it. He was the chief engineer. So, it is possible.

STUDENT: How do you know when to trust yourself in situations like this? How do you know that you haven't made a mistake in taking something from nature and creating some new problem?

TEACHER: There is enough knowledge of the environment and natural resources today to know when we're doing that.

STUDENT: Are you saying that we simply need to use our heads?

TEACHER: Basically. And remember that just because we are "natural," that doesn't mean that everything is fine. Everybody wants to be natural and heat with wood. But wood is an awful pollutant. There are other ways of producing heat that are significantly less polluting to the environment. Just because a substance is natural, doesn't make it innocuous, and just because it's synthetic doesn't make it dangerous. There's a context within which everything functions, and we have gained knowledge in the last decades of the twentieth century to know when we're hurting and when we're not. And if you take the whole matter of the life of this planet very personally, it gets really clear, real quickly. I just remembered the statement I made at the beginning of this gathering; if we realize ourselves there will be no need for environmental legislation. I guess that would put you out of a job, huh?

STUDENT: That's what I was thinking. [Laughter.]

TEACHER: Sorry.

STUDENT: Then I won't be able to afford to come here anymore. Thank you for your answer.

TEACHER: May your life go well.

STUDENT: A little over a year ago when I began this practice, I discovered that I have very bad legs. I am unable to get into any of the cross-legged sitting positions. I was able to do zazen in the kneeling posture, so I thought, "At least I can do that; at least I don't have to sit in a chair." Well, after about six months I blew a cartilage in my knee, and here I am with the chair. I'm doing what I wanted least to do. Masters in the past have put a lot of emphasis on getting into the proper position to sit. I can't say that I notice any difference myself. Could you give me some perspective on the various positions?

TEACHER: Yes. There is no esoteric significance to whether you cross your legs, kneel, or sit in a chair. Zazen has nothing to do with what you do with your legs. Zazen has to do with what you do with your mind. The rest of it is ego.

STUDENT: So, it's basically a waste of time to worry about looking dorky sitting in a chair.

TEACHER: Yes, but this is a symptom of a much more pervasive disease. I remember hurting my knee once in the middle of a sesshin. It had swollen up, but because I was the head monk for the sesshin I wasn't going to sit in a chair. So, I kept sitting cross-legged and it kept getting more and more swollen, until I could barely walk. Luckily, my friend who was an emergency room specialist was participating in that sesshin, and he insisted on looking at my leg. At first I resisted but then I showed it to him and he put this rap on me like they would have to amputate my leg the next day. He scared the hell out of me. I went into a chair, but I felt really silly sitting up there in charge of the zendo, encouraging everyone to "Sit strong!" It was really tough on my ego.

STUDENT: It's like wearing clothes that are out of fashion. I guess you get used to it.

TEACHER: There was also an ancient master who, because there was something wrong with his legs, never sat cross-legged. He was a monastic who became an abbot, one of the great teachers. But his legs just refused to bend properly. When it came time to die, he wrote his death poem, forced his legs into a lotus position, breaking them, and died. So you always have that to look forward to. [Laughter.]

STUDENT: Different strokes for different folks. Thank you for your answer.

TEACHER: May your life go well.

STUDENT: I'm interested in a good spiritual upbringing for my children. There is very little religious exposure at all in our home life. We used to go to church but then that stopped. I think we were doing it for a show. But I'm interested in being a good father.

TEACHER: The best advice I can give you on how to raise your children in a spiritual way is to really be yourself. It's got nothing to do with prayers or chants or proper social milieu. It's got to do with you; with how you live your life. That's how you teach them. The way you pick up a cup of coffee, the way you treat the environment, the way you speak with your wife. Your kids are watching you, and they see and feel, very intensely and very precisely. They won't do what you tell them they should do. They will do what you do. They are amazing mirrors. My three sons were the greatest help in my practice, because I saw that my practice was and is the biggest influence in their lives. That may not be clearly apparent along the way. But as they grow up you begin to see the accumulated effects of the interface of your life and theirs. Ultimately, your values are going to be their values, as long as you don't try to force feed them. Just be yourself. You can't legislate it; you can't proclaim it; you can't demand it. You have to do it. You have to treat them with respect in order for them to treat you with respect. And let that attitude extend to other people and environments. I once asked Trungpa Rinpoche the same question many years ago. I figured that he must have the ultimate solution to my children's spiritual life. I asked, "What can I do to help my children be spiritual beings?" He smiled and said, "Really be yourself." There is nothing more effective and powerful than that. When you're aware that every action, word, and thought affects another life and the generations to follow, you become a lot more responsible for what you do. Don't take it lightly.

STUDENT: Thank you for your answer.

TEACHER: May your life go well.

STUDENT: The only blemish on this Earth Day is this bright, cool, spring morning.

TEACHER: Yes. But how do you keep it from being a bright, cool, spring morning?

STUDENT: Ahhhhh...

TEACHER: Feels good, doesn't it? Ahhhhh... We should have a liturgy that includes that, "Ahhhhh, ahhhhh." A new Zen cult. [Laughter.] Anything else?

STUDENT: No.

TEACHER: May your life go well.

STUDENT: Thank you for your answer.

 INSTRUCTIONS TO THE COOK

Master Dogen's "Instructions to the Chief Cook" is a collection of regulations and advice for a monastery cook on how to prepare the food for a community. Dogen took ordinary circumstances of daily life and used them to reveal the most profound Dharma imaginable. The instructions are as practical as guidelines on how to drive a car, yet they also reveal the most subtle dimensions of Zen teachings—the interpenetration of principle and phenomena, the non-obstruction of the absolute and the relative.

Dogen says,

> Since ancient times, the position of the chief cook has been held by accomplished monastics who have raised the Way-seeking mind or by senior disciples with an aspiration for enlightenment. This is so because the position requires wholehearted practice. Those without a Way-seeking mind will not have good results despite their efforts.

Great masters such as Dongshan, Guishan, and Xuefeng held this position. A chief cook (*tenzo*) is usually one of the most senior positions at a monastery:

> When you wash rice and prepare vegetables, you must do it with your own hands, your own eyes. Make sincere effort. Don't be idle even for a moment. Do not be careful about one thing and careless about another. Do not give away your opportunity, even if it is merely a drop in an ocean of merit. Do not fail to place even a particle of earth at the summit of the mountain of wholesome deeds.

Xuefeng was once the chief cook at the monastery of Master Dongshan. One day, when Xuefeng was washing rice, Dongshan asked him, "Do you wash the sand away from the rice or the rice away from the sand?"

Xuefeng replied, "I wash both sand and rice away at the same time."

"What will the assembly eat?" asked Dongshan.

Xuefeng overturned the rice washing bowl.

Dongshan said, "One day you will meet a true master who will be your teacher."

That master was Deshan and, at Dongshan's suggestion, Xuefeng went and studied with him and later succeeded him.

When you prepare food, do not see with ordinary eyes. Do not think with ordinary mind. Take up a blade of grass and construct a Treasure King's land. Enter into a particle of dust and turn the great Dharma wheel.

Dogen is being very practical in one sense and very profound in another sense. How do you enter into a particle of dust? What does it mean to take a blade of grass and construct a Treasure King's land? Remember that throughout all of his works, Dogen presents both the absolute and the relative, presents neither absolute nor relative, presents mutual, non-hindering interpenetration of absolute and relative. The absolute is the ground of being—having no eye, ear, nose, tongue, body, or mind. The relative is eye, ear, nose, tongue, body, and mind. But the truth of this incredible dharma life can be found in neither absolute nor relative, in neither good nor bad, in neither heaven nor earth, in neither self nor other. Where will you find it?

Keep yourself harmonious and wholehearted in this way. Do not lose one eye, or two eyes. Take up a green vegetable and turn it into a sixteen-foot golden body of the Buddha. Take the sixteen-foot golden body of the Buddha and turn it into a vegetable leaf. This is a miraculous transformation, a work of a buddha that benefits sentient beings.

When the Assembly eats even one grain of rice from Lo Lin [a special province in China that made the best rice], they will feel the monastic Guishan in the chief cook. When the chief cook serves this delicious rice, he will see Guishan's water buffalo in the heart of the assembly.

The water buffalo swallows Guishan and Guishan herds the water buffalo. Guishan used to say to his monastics, "Many years from now, I will be reborn at the front gates of this monastery as a water buffalo, and on the side of that water buffalo will be written the words, 'Monastic Guishan, such and such.' If you call it Guishan, you miss it. If you call it a water buffalo, you miss it. What will you call it?"

Guishan was trying to tie up the tongues of the monastics so that they wouldn't fall into absolute or relative, but go for the real truth itself. What is that real truth that is neither absolute nor relative?

In Dogen's conversation with the chief cook of one of the monasteries in China, Dogen asked about the nature of words and practice. The chief cook said, "To study words you must know the origin of words. To endeavor in practice you must know the origin of practice."

Dogen asked what words were. The chief cook said, "One, two, three, four, five."

Dogen asked what practice was.

The chief cook answered, "Nothing in the entire universe is hidden."

Through one word or seven words, or three times five, if you thoroughly investigate the myriad forms, nothing can be depended upon. Night advances, the moon glows and falls into the ocean. The black dragon jewel you have been searching for is everywhere.

Finally, toward the end of "Instructions to the Chief Cook," he says, "The cook" —and the cook is each and every one of us. To be the cook means to cook one's life, to practice one's life. Don't think that to be the cook means to prepare vegetables or rice. To be the cook means to manifest one's life as the Buddhadharma—"should manifest three kinds of minds: a joyful mind, a kind mind, and a great mind."

To penetrate the joyful mind, even if you become a wheel-turning king, there will be no merit if the meal you cook is not an offering to the Three Treasures; your efforts will be like bubbles or vanishing flames. Kind mind is parental mind. Just as parents care for their children, you should bear in mind the Three Treasures. Even the poor suffering people raise their children with deep love. Their hearts cannot be understood by others. This can be known only when you become a father or a mother. They do not care whether they themselves are poor or rich; their only concern is that their children grow up. They pay no attention to whether they themselves are cold or hot, but cover their children to protect them from the cold and shield them from the sun. This is extreme kindness. Only those who have aroused this mind can know it and only those who practice this mind can understand it. Therefore you should look after water and grain with great compassion and care, as though tending your own children.

The Great Master Shakyamuni gave the final twenty-five years of his life to protect us in this age of declining learning. What was his intention? He offered his parental mind to us without expecting any result or gain. Great mind is a mind like a great ocean. It doesn't have any partiality or exclusivity. You should not regard a pound as light or a ton as heavy. Do not be attracted to the sounds of spring or take pleasure in seeing a spring garden. When you see autumn colors, do not be partial to them. You should allow the four seasons to advance in one single viewing and see an ounce and a pound with an equal eye. In this way you should study and understand the meaning of "great."

If the chief cook at Mount Ju had not studied the word "great," he would not have awakened Senior Fu by laughing at him. If the great Master Isan had not understood the word "great," he would not have blown on the unlit firewood three times. If the priest Dongshan had not known the word "great," he would not have taught the monastic by saying, "Three pounds of hemp." You should know that these great masters all study the word 'great' over hundreds of matters. They brought forth the great shadow freedom, expounded the great principle, penetrated the great question, trained the great student, and in this way completed a single great matter. The abbot, officers, staff, and other practitioners of this monastery should not forget about these three kinds of mind.

In taking up any of the points presented by Dogen and engaging in a dharma encounter, keep in mind that what Dogen is speaking about is beyond shouts, beyond pointing, beyond banging on the floor, beyond holding up and putting down. It transcends this and that. It is not, "Hello, this is Zen Mountain Monastery," and it is not, "Mary, pick up your toys." It's not absolute and it's not relative. It's not both absolute and relative, and it's not neither absolute nor relative. But it is about your life.

STUDENT: That was a really nice meal Dogen just prepared.
TEACHER: How about the three minds of Dogen? How do you see them?
STUDENT: Dogen is so amazing!
TEACHER: That won't reach it. What are the joyful mind, kind mind, great mind?
STUDENT: The joyful mind is, "Thank you Dogen."
TEACHER: How about a parental mind?
STUDENT: "Alex, I told you to clean up your room and I really mean it."
TEACHER: Not in this case. Parental mind is a kind, compassionate mind.
STUDENT: [Firmly.] "Alex, clean up your room."
TEACHER: That's not compassion of the Great Avalokiteshvara Bodhisattva. I wasn't kidding when I said that shouts, hits, bangs, "Alex, clean up your

room," "Mary pick up your toys," "Hello this is Zen Mountain Monastery," and all the rest of the Zen bullshit is out. What is the subtle Dharma?

STUDENT: I really don't know.

TEACHER: To really not know is the absolute and the absolute doesn't reach it. "Alex, pick up your stuff," is relative and relative doesn't reach it. Banging on the floor is neither and that doesn't reach it. When will you put it to rest?

STUDENT: [Laughs.]

TEACHER: Thank you for your answer.

STUDENT: When the sand and the rice are washed away, look at the incense smoke rising. Incredible!

TEACHER: What is the sand? What is the rice? What was Dongshan saying to Xuefeng with that question? Xuefeng was actually washing the rice.

STUDENT: If you clean the mirror, that's not it. If you throw away the mirror and the cleaning, that's not it. What is it?

TEACHER: The mirror? What's the impurity, the dirt, and what's the rice?

STUDENT: I can't get our journal out on time. I don't know what to do.

TEACHER: What's that: the rice or the impurity?

STUDENT: Sandy, sandy beach.

TEACHER: And what's the rice?

STUDENT: It's no problem.

TEACHER: "No problem" doesn't reach it. That's a cop-out.

STUDENT: It's finished and done with.

TEACHER: That's better. Thank you for your answer.

STUDENT: I can't work on the sand. I'm thinking about that blade of grass and a sixteen-foot golden body of the Buddha. It's taken me right in and is confusing me.

TEACHER: Taking the sixteen-foot golden body of the Buddha and manifesting it as a blade of grass is saying exactly the same thing as the rice and the sand. That blade of grass has the power to kill or to give life. The giving of life is its manifestation in the world; killing is taking away everything: no eye, ear, nose, tongue, body, mind. It can be used that way. It can be manifested as the body of the Buddha, the absolute body of reality, or it can be manifested as the ten thousand things. It is the lotus blooming in the fire.

STUDENT: Thank you for your answer.

TEACHER: May your life go well.

STUDENT: What is the parental mind of compassion when the parent is inattentive to the children, or worse yet, abuses them?

TEACHER: When Dogen spoke about parental mind, he didn't mean that just because you're a parent you have a parental mind. He was referring to a specific activity of compassion, compassion that may call for the parent to swat a child on the behind if that is the appropriate action. There are parents who don't have parental mind and there are parents who do. And he's asking people who aren't parents to have parental minds in dealing with all beings. He himself wasn't a parent. His teachings obviously have nothing to do with procreating in the conventional sense. There are all kinds of offspring. I'm producing Dharma offspring here. Maezumi Roshi is my father; Yasutani Roshi is my grandfather.

STUDENT: Thank you for your answer.

TEACHER: May your life go well.

STUDENT: I sure am glad that I took care of that cold this week.

TEACHER: What cold?

STUDENT: I have a very bad cold.

TEACHER: How do I feel?

STUDENT: Much better. [Laughs.]

TEACHER: How's your son?

STUDENT: Mommy! Mommy! Mommy!

TEACHER: And how do you practice and take care of raising a child?

STUDENT: Here I am!

TEACHER: Thank you for your answer.

STUDENT: In the exchange between Xuefeng and Dongshan, Xuefeng answered, "I'm separating these things." Isn't that differentiating?

TEACHER: No. Dongshan asked him, "Do you separate the dirt from the rice or do you separate the rice from the dirt?" Xuefeng said, "I remove them both." Dongshan said, "If you remove them both, how will you feed the monastics?" Xuefeng turned over the big basin full of rice. And Dongshan acknowledged him by saying, "Some day you will realize yourself." That didn't mean that what Xuefeng did was a demonstration of complete realization, but he was on the right path.

STUDENT: I think he's saying he simply separates things.
TEACHER: He's saying just the opposite.
STUDENT: How so?
TEACHER: You remove both extremes. It's neither rice nor dirt. It's neither absolute nor relative.
STUDENT: Thank you for your answer.
TEACHER: May your life go well.

STUDENT: I'm grateful to be the cook here and happy to hear that I could go on being the cook. I've become very attached to this position. I could be a cook for the rest of my life...
TEACHER: Not if you're attached to it.
STUDENT: I'm getting to that. I meant the other kind of cook, one who doesn't just cook in a kitchen.
TEACHER: That's the same kind.
STUDENT: Still, I'm having a lot of trouble with attachment. I stood on the front doorstep this morning and looked at the wonderful grey, damp, misty November morning. I loved it. And I know I have to let go of the pleasure of being chief cook, let go of the pleasure of a grey, misty November morning.
TEACHER: Non-attachment doesn't mean not appreciating or not enjoying. We have a difficult time in the West differentiating between attaching and appreciating. People think that if you're not attached, you can't love somebody. The only way you can love is not to be attached. If you're attached, that's manipulation. It's not love. If you're holding onto something, you're smothering it, not allowing it to be. This applies to people, ideas, anything and everything. You're not putting yourself into it and being it. You're controlling it. It's like having a puppet on strings. It doesn't nourish, it doesn't heal. It's deadly. So cut away all attachments and then loving can exist with no restrictions. That's why in Zen training we move people around and let them engage different positions and occupations. Don't say you're attached to cooking, or tomorrow you will be cleaning bathrooms.
STUDENT: Thank you for your answer.
TEACHER: May your life go well.

STUDENT: I love cleaning bathrooms. [Laughter.]
TEACHER: In Japan that would be understood by everyone. One of the ways a

chief seminarian expresses his practice and virtue is by getting up in the middle of the night and secretly cleaning all of the bathrooms and going back to bed, not taking any responsibility for it. I understand what you mean.

STUDENT: My question is about what Dogen asked the Chinese cook on the origin of words, and the origin of practice. The origin of practice is what prompts me to practice, what makes practice possible. And origin makes it possible for words to be authentic.

TEACHER: Origin means source. Dogen asked what the source of words is and the cook said, "One, two, three, four, five." Then Dogen asked, "What's the origin of practice?" And the cook responded, "Nothing in the world is hidden." Those two responses to two different questions are pointing to the same place. The answer is not to be found in the words, "One, two, three, four, five." And it's not to be found in the idea or concept that nothing is hidden.

STUDENT: It's somewhere in between.

TEACHER: No, it's not in between.

STUDENT: Then where?

TEACHER: Where indeed?

STUDENT: Where shall I look? In the bathroom? [Laughter.]

TEACHER: Definitely. [Laughter.]

STUDENT: Thank you for your answer.

TEACHER: May your life go well.

STUDENT: When Xuefeng washes the rice and dirt away, there is still something unwholesome left.

TEACHER: Yes, there is. That is why Dongshan pursued the question a little further.

STUDENT: That unwholesome entity—I won't talk about it.

TEACHER: You couldn't if you tried because whatever you would say wouldn't be it.

STUDENT: I won't talk about it anyway.

TEACHER: That's convenient.

STUDENT: Thank you for your answer.

TEACHER: May your life go well.

STUDENT: You are the spiritual cook of this monastery. Why do you cook?

TEACHER: I don't know. I have absolutely no idea. Chances are if I knew, I wouldn't be doing it. My teacher didn't understand; his teacher didn't know. Do you understand?

STUDENT: Thank you for your answer.
TEACHER: May your life go well.

STUDENT: Does the work of a chief cook hinge on cultivating the parental mind, the joyful mind, and the great mind?
TEACHER: Yes. Cultivating that kind of mind immediately implies a special kind of attitude towards everything—nothing is wasted. There is a story about a monk who was heading up a mountain to visit a monastery. As he was hiking up the trail, following a stream, halfway up he notices a cabbage leaf floating down the stream. Disappointed, he was about to turn back, not willing to join a community that allowed even this amount of waste, when he saw the chief cook running down the mountain after the cabbage leaf. We practice the same attitude during *oryoki*, our formal monastery meal. Oryoki means just the right amount. It doesn't mean that you starve yourself. We don't fast in Zen. We embody just the right amount. A big person eats more; a small person eats less. Nothing wasted; nothing left over. Even the waste water is consumed. It is respect and gratitude for the life we call "food."
STUDENT: That means doing everything wholeheartedly?
TEACHER: Yes.
STUDENT: Could something done wholeheartedly be at the same time done selfishly?
TEACHER: With the whole body and mind?
STUDENT: Yes.
TEACHER: Implicit in the statement "whole body and mind" is no self. In a sense, that's very, very selfish. There is nothing more selfish than an enlightened being. The whole universe is that being's realized self. She takes care of everything because it is herself. Every person, every rock, every plant, every animal, every planet, every star is nothing but the self. The great mind doesn't differentiate. It sees a pound in an ounce; it sees the universe in an atom.
STUDENT: Thank you for your answer.
TEACHER: May your life go well.

STUDENT: No rice, no water, no sand. Where is kind mind?
TEACHER: Kind mind is Dongshan's response. Xuefeng was taking away everything. And Dongshan stopped him, "How are you going to feed the monastics?" Immediately Xuefeng brought it all back. Bam! He threw the bowl upside

down. One of the scholars that translated this passage interpreted Xuefeng's gesture as covering the bowl. That misses it; it is a very different understanding of what happened. Xuefeng threw it upside down. No rice, no water, no sand is no eye, ear, nose, tongue, body, mind. If there is no eye, ear, nose, tongue, body, mind, how will you feed yourself, let alone the other monastics? How will you feed the starving people of the world? How will you stop the environmental destruction? How will you take care of the homeless people in the street? Dongshan presses the question of relevance—how will you manifest the life of compassion? Xuefeng simply turned the bowl upside down. Like this! In the world!

STUDENT: Thank you for your answer.

TEACHER: The expression on your face was worth it! Thank you.

STUDENT: I think I have a problem of trying too hard. Should I do things wholeheartedly?

TEACHER: You should climb to the top of Mount Tremper, right to the edge of a cliff, and leap off. Now could you do that?

STUDENT: Not without your help. I don't know what to do with my life. My effort is a way of hiding from that fact.

TEACHER: I don't have any answers for you. Even if I did, you shouldn't listen to them. I'm not going to solve your problems. I'm not going to give you a crutch. What will you do when I'm not around? How will I possibly impart any strength to you by giving you something? That belies the fact that you already have the strength; that you already are a manifestation of the sixteen-foot golden body of the Buddha. Anything I give you detracts from your perfection. Ask me another kind of question to get an answer. Do you understand what I'm saying?

STUDENT: Another kind of question?

TEACHER: You're asking me what to do with your life. I don't even know what I'm doing with my own. You simply have to be intimate with your life. When you're intimate, you don't need to classify, analyze, systematize, understand. You just do. When it rains you open an umbrella; if you don't have an umbrella, your head gets wet. That's the meaning of "with the whole body and mind." That's what it means to live wholeheartedly—to do what you're doing while you're doing it.

STUDENT: I'll do it anyhow.

TEACHER: Okay. Then don't do what you're doing while you're doing it! Will you do that? No place to hold on to, no place to stand. Isn't it wonderful?

STUDENT: It's scares the shit out of me.

TEACHER: When you pull back from it, it gets scary. Fear has always got to do with the next moment. What's the next thing that's going to happen? Right now, there is no fear. Fear is a thought about the next moment. No thoughts, and you are free and unhindered. So, stop thinking.

STUDENT: Thank you for your answer.

TEACHER: May your life go well.

The whole point of Zen practice is to knock out the wedges, pull out the nails, collapse the structure we are holding onto. Dogen's Dharma is not just the Dharma of isolating oneself on the mountain peak in a cloud of bliss. That's being stuck in the absolute. Much of half-baked spiritual teachings and practice end there. You make a big climb to the summit of the mountain, but you can't manifest this Dharma there. The world is not up there. You need to come down off the mountain and back into the marketplace before you can truly manifest the Dharma. The marketplace itself is not it. The peak of the mountain is not it. Then what is it? Where is the truth that is neither absolute nor relative? Where is the reality that is neither love nor hate, neither male nor female, neither heaven nor earth? That's the truth that is to be seen in this practice. Before we can actualize wisdom as compassion in the world, we need to realize that wisdom; we need to experience and personally verify that absolute basis of reality that is no eye, ear, nose, tongue, body, and mind. Once you see that, you throw it away and keep going, because wisdom must ultimately manifest itself as the ten thousand things in the world. And if we attach to those ten thousand things, that becomes a dead end. So, how do you manifest your life so that it neither attaches to absolute nor relative? "Instructions to the Chief Cook" is all about that: the practical day-to-day, moment-to-moment cooking of a meal, driving a car, practicing the Buddhadharma, saving the world, the cooking of a life.

9

MONASTIC RULE AND LAY LIFE

The theme for this dharma encounter is the Benedictine Rule and the emphasis it places on the vows of poverty, chastity, and obedience. These vows are also important in Zen training. Zen Mountain Monastery monastics have a practice of poverty, chastity—we don't call it that, but it is part of the third precept: honor the body, do not misuse sexuality—and obedience in the form of respect for our seniors and teachers. Though the underlying principles are the same in these two traditions, the rules themselves take very different shapes. In Zen, poverty does not mean living the life of a beggar. Even though Zen monastics are, in a way, mendicants who aspire to have only the robe and bowl as their possessions, when we use the word poverty, we are also talking about something much more profound.

The same is true of chastity. In the Third Grave Precept we speak of avoiding greed, of avoiding self-centered, manipulative sexuality. The Mahayana precepts relate not only to monastics but also to lay people, married and unmarried. What does the vow of chastity mean in terms of the Mahayana teachings and the precepts?

Last is the vow of obedience. Clearly, obedience is self-discipline. It does exist in Zen practice, but we also have statements like, "If you meet the Buddha, kill the Buddha," or, as Master Linji said, "Don't put any head on top of your own." How do these statements translate into actual practice?

I would like to discuss with you these vows of poverty, chastity, and obedience in terms of actual practice in the Zen tradition. What does it mean to practice poverty? What does it mean to practice chastity? What does it mean to practice obedience? Obedience to whom? Master Ruiyan said, "Master," and he answered, "Yes, Master." He said, "Do not be deceived by anyone, any time, any place." He answered, "Yes, Master." Clearly, the master of Ruiyan's house was Ruiyan, so whom did he obey? How do you understand poverty, chastity, and obedience in terms of the teaching of the Buddha? How do you actualize and manifest these vows in you life?

STUDENT: Making love with Daniel is really wonderful.
TEACHER: So much for chastity. How about poverty?
STUDENT: I don't know about that.
TEACHER: Mmmm.
STUDENT: I won't take out the garbage for my kids any more.
TEACHER: Don't ruin a good thing. You don't have to present anything else.
STUDENT: [Laughs.]
TEACHER: May your life go well.
STUDENT: Thank you for your answer.

STUDENT: All this talk about poverty, chastity, and obedience. You can't complete more than one action at a time. If I go straight ahead, I can't miss.
TEACHER: Straight ahead can also include the opposite of poverty, chastity, and obedience.
STUDENT: Definitely. [Leans forward.]
TEACHER: That doesn't help me with poverty. What is poverty?
STUDENT: I haven't found it yet.
TEACHER: Poverty is important in Zen. The real poverty is no eye, ear, nose, tongue, body, mind. Chastity is no eye, ear, nose, tongue, body, mind. Obedience is no eye, ear, nose, tongue, body, mind. What does that mean in life: every day, moment-to-moment ordinary life? That is the real question. Got it?
STUDENT: [Nods.]
TEACHER: So you're not going to fight today?
STUDENT: [Silence.]
TEACHER: May your life go well.
STUDENT: Thank you for your answer.

STUDENT: It seems to me that poverty, chastity, and obedience have to do with how I place myself with respect to the rest of the world; in poverty, not holding on to anything I think is myself; in chastity, not doing things for myself first; in obedience, not thinking about doing anything other than what has to be done.

TEACHER: In a sense, that is true. But it is a very intellectual presentation. The key is to be able to make it dynamic, to allow it to become the texture of your life. What does it mean to really be poor?

STUDENT: Do I have to let go of myself first?

TEACHER: When there is nothing left, when the self is completely forgotten, when the ego has fallen away, what remains? Everything. The whole universe. The only difference is that before you were separated from the whole universe. When the self is forgotten, the universe remains. What is gone is the idea of a separate self. This kind of poverty, in a sense, is boundlessly rich. That is why Caoshan challenged Qingrui when Qingrui said, "Help me. I'm destitute. I have nothing. Make me rich." Caoshan exclaimed, "Venerable Qingrui!" "Yes, Master." That calling and answering was the richness of manifesting the human life. Poverty is a form of plenty; it is a bursting and brimming over with everything.

STUDENT: Where do you suggest I look for it?

TEACHER: In your zazen. In your life.

STUDENT: I don't know how to look anymore.

TEACHER: Wholeness comes from letting go of all of your ideas. Attach to nothing. When you are holding on to nothing, including yourself, the ten thousand things return to the self, which is where they have always been, right from the beginning.

STUDENT: And if there is an idea about the ten thousand things, the ten thousand things wouldn't fit there.

TEACHER: The fact is that you and the ten thousand things are not separate from each other. But when we see ourselves, we see an idea. The self is an idea and it has boundaries—the skin. You are inside the skin and everything else is outside the skin. That is the central delusion that causes pain and suffering. That is the basic delusion that the precepts address. The basic fact is that you have no boundaries. The precepts come from that point of view.

STUDENT: Thank you for your answer.

TEACHER: May your life go well.

STUDENT: How is nothing experienced?

TEACHER: "Nothing" is an idea, a thought, a word. When there is no eye, ear, nose, tongue, body, mind; color, sound, smell, taste, touch, phenomena; no world of sight, no world of consciousness, how can you talk about nothing? How can you see it? How can it be contained? The moment the first thought arises, heaven and earth are separated, the ten thousand things spring into being, and there is you and there is the word "nothing," all separate and distinct. That is the activity of discriminating consciousness. To experience nothing, just become the word "nothing." Be nothing. No thing. Be it with your whole body and mind. No eye, ear, nose, tongue, body, mind; no color, sound, smell, taste, touch, phenomena; no world of sight, no world of consciousness. It is the same as being the koan Mu. Mu has absolutely, unequivocally no meaning whatsoever. But when you become it, the ten thousand things return to the self. That means that there is no way to measure it. The reference system is gone. There is no way to analyze it, characterize it, judge it, understand it. To be Mu is to be Mu—there is nothing else but Mu. It reaches everywhere. To be nothing is to be the oak tree in the garden. It is absolute poverty. The minute you say, "I've got it! This is it!," that's not it. That's an idea. When you say, "I have nothing," you have something. You have the something of "nothing!" That is what Master Zhaozhou was trying to get a monastic to see when he said let go of "nothing." Mu literally means "no." Be "no." Be "yes." I don't care what you be. But be it with the whole body and mind. Nothing held back. That is the first step. It is the absolute basis of reality. Everything else springs from that.

STUDENT: One more question. What should I obey?

TEACHER: What is your name?

STUDENT: Ray.

TEACHER: What does that mean to obey Ray? Is Ray separate and distinct from Daido? Different and distinct from the Buddha, Jesus, or Moses? Where do you place Ray? In that bag of skin? What does it mean to obey Ray, to be master of your life?

STUDENT: Thank you for your answer.

TEACHER: May your life go well.

STUDENT: The *zafu* is being used but no one is sitting.

TEACHER: That is a phrase that falls between the direct and an intellectual expression of the experience. It is a nice capping phrase, but it does not reach the heart of poverty. A capping phrase is a poetic summation of one's understanding that usually follows a direct presentation. How could you say what you started with, using live words?

STUDENT: I have no need for old baldheads!

TEACHER: Is that poverty? No. That is a capping phrase for obedience.

STUDENT: The abbot has his interviews.

TEACHER: Whom does he obey?

STUDENT: When I tell you, you will nod.

TEACHER: No. When you tell me, I will obey. The iron yoke of the abbot is the sangha. The puppet on a string is a teacher. The student is the one handling the strings. It is just like the dog-trainer and the dog. Who is being trained? The guy who holds up the pieces of meat and gives them to the dog when the animal stands on his hind legs, or the dog? Does the dog train the trainer or the trainer train the dog? It's the same with the dharma teaching. The teacher responds to questions like a puppet. Getting back to your first presentation, "The zafu is being used but no one is sitting." Can you go further?

STUDENT: [Groans.]

TEACHER: Much, much more personal; much, much more intimate than "sitting." Anything else?

STUDENT: No. Thank you for your answer.

TEACHER: May your life go well.

STUDENT: If mind-to-mind transmission occurs when the understanding of the student surpasses that of the teacher, are you more destitute than Shakyamuni Buddha?

TEACHER: More destitute; less destitute; Shakyamuni Buddha. Who are we talking about? I have no idea. Do you understand?

STUDENT: No.

TEACHER: That is the first sign that you can see. Do you understand that?

STUDENT: No.

TEACHER: Even better. When there is no knower and no thing that the knower knows, there is intimacy. It's the same thing. Get it?

STUDENT: [Stares blankly.]

TEACHER: Work on that "not knowing." It's very intimate, very intimate indeed. There's no reference system and nothing to compare it with. When you are the Buddha, there is no Buddha. No separation. Do you understand that?

STUDENT: No.

TEACHER: If only you really didn't understand, I would bow to you. Anything else?

STUDENT: No. Thank you for your answer.

TEACHER: May your life go well.

∞

STUDENT: Oowuggh!

TEACHER: What is that? Pain? Poverty? What about, "Ha! Ha! Ha! Ha!" What is that? Wealth? Are these two opposite sides?

STUDENT: Just pain.

TEACHER: When in pain, really be in pain, through and through. So much pain that there is no pain—that is poverty. But when you compare pain to non-pain, or choose to express poverty using pain instead of joy, then a bit of discrimination is working. Why not joy? Why not a nice big belly laugh? Isn't that poverty? When you don't separate from it, regardless of what "it" is—joy, pain, heaven, hell—that is always a manifestation of the absolute, because the self is forgotten. The problem is that this is very easy to say, but very hard to do; to really be the pain, through and through. That was the pain of Master Yunmen when his teacher slammed the door on his foot. He realized himself in it. Do you understand? Does it make sense? Do you see what I'm after? Easy to say but hard to do. That is the subtle difference between direct experience and the words that describe it.

STUDENT: Thank you for your answer.

TEACHER: May your life go well.

∞

STUDENT: At birth, there is poverty, chastity, and obedience. Is it possible to maintain that state until death?

TEACHER: Why do you say that at birth there is poverty, chastity, and obedience?

STUDENT: It seems to me that a newborn coming into the world is pure and unblemished by conditioning.

TEACHER: A monastic once asked Master Zhaozhou, "Does a newborn infant have the six senses?" Zhaozhou said, "It's like throwing a ball into the rapids."

STUDENT: When it is hungry, it cries.

TEACHER: Zhaozhou was referring to that moment-to-moment awareness that holds on to nothing. And you want to know if it's possible to grow up and maintain that kind of purity throughout one's life? Spiritual training doesn't commence until we become self-conscious and aware of our separation and suffering. We frequently think that our training is just about cessation of pain. That is a very self-centered way of looking at it. Training involves infinitely more. It is not just about taking care of yourself and realizing wisdom. Most importantly, it is about manifesting compassion. To stop at wisdom, isolating yourself from the world amidst your realization is the Hinayana teaching.

Mahayana teachings send you back into the world. You return back to what you have left and work for the benefit of all beings. Practice begins when you become aware of the world of pain and suffering, and when you decide to do something about it. The intelligence that is acquired through eye, ear, nose, tongue, body, and mind—the awareness of the world and your impact on the world—has to happen first, before the realization can be attained. Somehow, most of us never complete the cycle. We die before we fully come to know what it is to be human. To be human doesn't just mean to appreciate the First Noble Truth, but to thoroughly penetrate all four of the Noble Truths. Contained within the First Noble Truth, that life is suffering, is the cause of suffering and the cessation of suffering. That is all a part of being human.

STUDENT: Do you feel that a student who realizes their humanity in six months of training has brought that level of spiritual development from a past life?

TEACHER: Yes, but don't misunderstand what is meant by past life. Past life, from a Zen point of view, can be understood in terms of this very moment, in terms of the moment-to-moment awareness of our lives. A person who has been working on themselves, whose parents have been working on themselves, who is nourished by an environment conducive to self-exploration, has an established framework before they begin formal Zen practice. They will arrive at the Monastery with a degree of self-awareness or a spiritual drive. Or maybe they will have experienced an event which was a turning point in their life. All of this will definitely make a difference in how people will engage practice. But it is impossible to predict that ahead of time. It is very obvious though, when a student is grounded and has a deep spiritual drive. It is evident not in a sanctimonious posture and attitude but rather in the magic within them that is revealed in everything they do.

STUDENT: Why is it that certain people ...

TEACHER: We're back to those "why" questions. They appear very interesting but don't really tell you anything. Suppose I gave you the answer? You nod your head and go off. What good will that do you? Why is the sky blue?

STUDENT: Okay.

TEACHER: Rather than find out why, realize yourself! Do it in this life; not tomorrow or next year. Not even in this life, but in this moment. May your life go well.

STUDENT: Thank you for your answer.

STUDENT: It seems to me that the "whys?" are an important part of practice. They shed light on our experiences.

TEACHER: But what's on the other side of the "whys?"

STUDENT: My life.

TEACHER: That's an explanation. Beyond the "whys?", when you are really intimate with yourself, what is that?

STUDENT: [Silence.]

TEACHER: When you say, "Sarah, don't stay out late tonight," or "Hello, Zen Mountain Monastery," or "Maha Prajna Paramita Heart Sutra," or "You are hitting the bell too loud, Felicity!" this very life itself, from dawn to sunset, is the life of a buddha, whether it is realized or not. All of the little details. That is the crazy thing about this journey. Right from the very beginning, it is all there. Nothing is lacking. And yet, there is the "why?" The area of your doubt. That doubt is really important. You can't just brush it aside. To ignore it is anything-goes Zen, I-don't-know-I-don't-care-and-it-doesn't-matter-anyhow Zen. It is really important to resolve that great doubt and not just cast it aside. When somebody has got you by the throat and you are breathing your last breath, what will you do then? Will you be at peace with yourself? As Master Wumen says, "When your life comes to its end, you will be like a crab falling into a pot of boiling water, with eight arms and legs going. Don't say then that I didn't warn you." To really impart strength to yourself is to realize that your life is the life of a buddha.

STUDENT: Thank you for your answer.

TEACHER: May your life go well.

STUDENT: Not having been to the place of realization or even engaging in koan study, how can I hear and understand talks on koans or this dharma encounter?

TEACHER: If a person approaches spiritual training with a genuine drive to realize the ground of being, they will very likely be entering practice with a sense of trust, trust in themselves and trust of the process. Much of the process, at first, doesn't make any sense. I'm a lot more skilled in English than my teacher was, so I can explain the process better. My teacher's English was not so good and we, his students, had to accept the teachings on the basis of faith. In the early days of my practice I used to sit and listen to his dharma talks and I would think they were nonsense. He would present a koan and comment on it. Looking around the room, I saw people laugh and I would wonder what the joke was. Time continued and all of a sudden things started falling into place. I started to understand. After you have been listening to the Dharma with great faith, great doubt, and great determination—with the conviction that you can understand it—you will understand. Something turns and you begin to see. In a sense, this is no different from learning anything else, like math or science. There is a time when you struggle with it and all the problems seem very abstruse. You try to solve equations and they don't make any sense. Then suddenly everything falls into place. You can look at problems that were dark yesterday and immediately understand them. It's the same with koan practice. There are some seventeen hundred formal, recorded koans. We do seven hundred. You do those seven hundred and by the time you've sat with them, and chewed them up with your teacher, you can look at any koan and get an immediate appreciation of it. Once you connect with that way of perceiving reality, reality makes sense. The sutras make sense. The teachings of the Buddha make sense. At this point you are starting to learn that process.

STUDENT: When you are learning geometry, your homework is geometry. Here, in Zen training, the homework is what you do on the cushion, the homework is the koan. In the beginning phases of practice, that is sometimes very difficult to see and grasp clearly.

TEACHER: It is much more difficult to see that clearly at the later phases. It's impossible to see at the end of training. That is what Suzuki Roshi meant when he said, "Zen mind, beginner's mind." Beginner's mind is the most precious mind of practice. That's the mind that doesn't know everything clearly, that doesn't have the answers, that isn't categorizing, analyzing, or judging. It is innocent and full of wonder. The same innocence ultimately needs to reappear at the end of training. Coming down off the mountain back into the world, you are indistinguishable from the rest of the world, covered with dust, embracing all the imperfections.

STUDENT: When I hear a koan, I want to understand it. I have a goal. But my practice is my breath, and I end up struggling with all the ideas that the koan introduces and miss my breath.

TEACHER: Koans exhaust all the ideas.

STUDENT: But when you are not actively engaged in koan study...

TEACHER: According to what you are telling me, you are engaging them. You're doing it. And something is happening because you are doing it. A lot is happening, on the cushion and off the cushion, and a lot that you cannot even imagine, in relationship to koan study, in relationship to your understanding, in relationship to the way you will see it down the line. None of true practice is wasted. People get angry because they can't stay with their breath. Yesterday, they were with it all day long. Today they can't stay with it for a minute. Drifting off the breath is just as important as staying with it. It's learning. The mistakes teach you. And there are all kinds of mistakes to make, all kinds of delusions to explore and see through. There are a million ways for the mind to drift off. The more you experience it drifting off, the more you will understand about staying with it. If the failures don't happen now, they are going to happen later. The more you take care of it now, the better off you are. The same is true with the koans. They are pushing your buttons. You are very intellectual and the practice is specifically designed to frustrate the intellectual process. That is exactly what it is doing for you. It is happening now instead of later, when we work on the koans formally as part of the face-to-face teaching. And remember, there are all kinds of koans, not just the classical ones that are in the books. There are your own personal life koans. These are frequently far more important and powerful than those in books. And you work on them the same way. You can't figure them out intellectually. They frustrate you. And in practicing them you learn to approach problems differently—directly and intuitively. You learn to trust your intuition. That is what is going to get you through the difficulties of life—not logical sequential thought.

STUDENT: Thank you for your answer.

TEACHER: May your life go well.

STUDENT: Obedience: Riah does not wish to attend the University of Michigan. Her father says she must go. Who is right?

TEACHER: That situation is very conveniently abstract. In dealing with it, let me bring you back to what you are side-stepping. From the father's point of view, he is absolutely right. From Riah's point of view, she is absolutely right. Now let us get back to you. What does obedience mean to you? Who will you obey? What will you obey?

STUDENT: The moral decision.

TEACHER: How will you make that moral decision? What is the reference point for a "moral decision?"

STUDENT: No-self.

TEACHER: "No-self" is correct, but because it is intellectual, it is not yet it. When you express the truth from the intimate point of view of no-self, having experienced no-self, when no-self expresses no-self, then you will know what the moral basis is from your own experience. You won't need to check it out with anyone else.

STUDENT: Thank you for your answer.

TEACHER: May your life go well. And Riah's too.

STUDENT: Where have you been?

TEACHER: Where have you been looking?

STUDENT: My name is Martha.

TEACHER: My name is Daido. How do you do? What about poverty?

STUDENT: I don't even want to know poverty.

TEACHER: What do you know about it?

STUDENT: Do you see the forsythia all over the valley?

TEACHER: What about chastity?

STUDENT: I gave that up when I was a stripper.

TEACHER: What does that mean? That there is no chastity in Zen? What about obedience?

STUDENT: DAIDO!

TEACHER: Who is going to answer for him?

STUDENT: DAIDO!

TEACHER: I hear the calling. I don't hear the answering.

STUDENT: May your life go well.

TEACHER: That's something. Thank you for your answer.

STUDENT: Poverty is when you hold nothing and you have everything. Chastity is to keep from clinging to anything and it causes you to lose everything. Obedience is to follow that which allows us to keep everything.

TEACHER: The one flaw in all of this is that there is a self present. Express exactly the same thing, just as logically and intellectually, but without a self. That would be a lot closer to it.

STUDENT: If there was no self, then who would be here to talk?

TEACHER: I'm talking to myself. I've been doing that for years. All any of us can do is sit and nod to ourselves. There is nothing else. Do you understand?

STUDENT: Yes. Thank you for your answer.

TEACHER: May your life go well.

10 MYSTICAL REALISM

Mysticism is the realm of the mystery, and the mystic is one who studies and appreciates the mystery directly. Different religious traditions provide us with different perspectives and different ways of approaching the spiritual mysteries. In general, the mystical sphere is placed in opposition to the real. On one hand we have the ineffable and the mystical, on the other hand we have the tangible and the real. In Zen, those two polarities are seen as one reality. In Zen, mysticism is in fact realism in its most concrete manifestations. Mysticism is not other-worldly. It is the world itself.

In the "Mountains and Rivers Sutra," Master Dogen says, "To be in the mountains is a flower opening in the world." He says that the realization of Buddhism is the manifestation of the whole universe. In Zen practice, life is regarded not as an activity that takes place in the world, but rather as the activity of the world itself. Layman Pang said, "Isn't it mysterious, isn't it incredible—I chop wood and carry water." The mystical realism of work, the sacredness of work, is this very life. The truth that's been transmitted mind-to-mind, generation-to-generation, is the essence of everything we encounter in our everyday life.

Master Dogen, in his "Genjokoan," comments, "To carry the self forward and realize the ten thousand dharmas is delusion. That the ten thousand dharmas advance and realize the self is enlightenment." The ten thousand dharmas are the whole phenomenal universe—every thought, every action, every word, every thing, every particle, every star, every sound. To move toward the reality of the ten thousand dharmas is delusion—not knowing what's real. That the world advances and realizes the self is enlightenment. Dogen continues, "It is buddhas who enlighten delusion, and it is creatures who are deluded in enlightenment. Further, there are those who are enlightened above enlightenment and those who are deluded within delusion. When buddhas are truly buddhas, one need not be aware of being Buddha. However, one is the realized Buddha and further advances in realizing Buddha." There are those who are enlightened above enlightenment, and those who are deluded within delusion. Both are manifestations of the Way, of realization. "Deluded within delusion" is the life of the bodhisattva, a compassionate being. "Enlightened above enlightenment" is the life of the Buddha. It is buddhas who enlighten delusion. Within delusion itself, amidst the myriad things, the *samsara* of pain and suffering, is the enlightenment of all buddhas. Nirvana is samsara; samsara is nirvana. Delusion is enlightenment; enlightenment is delusion.

"It is creatures who are deluded in enlightenment" refers to the fact that each one of us is a buddha, perfect and complete, lacking nothing. In the midst of this enlightened perfection, we're deluded. Whether we realize it or not, enlightenment is here. Even though we consider ourselves deluded, lacking something and different from the buddhas, we are nonetheless buddhas. And ceaselessly, through practice we further realize buddhas. We realize the mystery of this life. All of reality is an opportunity to practice. All of reality is enlightenment itself.

STUDENT: When I was eight years old, I carried a broom into our garage to play cowgirls. Shanna was blinded by the end of the broom. My mother said, "Why didn't you know it was dangerous?" And I have mourned for thirty years. This is carrying the self forward.

TEACHER: You have that right. What you said is that you carried the broom into the garage to play cowgirls and Shanna was blinded by the end of the broom. This is to carry the self forward and realize the ten thousand dharmas. But you haven't told me what does it mean that the ten thousand dharmas advance and realize the self.

STUDENT: Who can know that?

TEACHER: I'll tell you! You blinded Shanna, not the end of the broom! Until you take full responsibility for that fact you can't let it go. You'll carry it for the next thirty years. The broom didn't do it. You did it. That the ten thousand dharmas advance and realize the self means to take responsibility for the whole universe; not just for what is immediately around us. Take responsibility for what is going on in Washington, in Tibet, for what happened a thousand years ago, and what will happen a thousand years hence. That is "all dharmas advancing and realizing the self." Please see that.

STUDENT: If I see it, will Shanna see it?

TEACHER: When you see it, Shanna will see it. When one sees it, the mountains and rivers and the great earth itself see it. All sentient beings see it, because there's no separation, except in the way we use our mind.

STUDENT: Thank you for you answer.

TEACHER: May your life go well.

STUDENT: Master Yunmen said that a good thing is not as good as nothing. Can you show me a thing that cannot be compared with nothing?

TEACHER: Yes. When Yunmen made that statement I would have turned over his meditation seat and beat him on the head with his zafu.

STUDENT: [Laughs.] Thank you.

TEACHER: May your life go well.

STUDENT: I don't feel very combative today. Thank you for your teaching on mystical realism.

TEACHER: Actually, I don't feel very combative today either.

STUDENT: You need a dharma nap. [Laughs.]

TEACHER: [Laughs.] Right. That's what I've been doing. Anything else?

STUDENT: That's all.

TEACHER: May your life go well.

STUDENT: The self moving forward, organizing, systematizing, putting this thing in order.

TEACHER: What thing are we talking about?

STUDENT: The self moving forward and realizing the ten thousand dharmas.

TEACHER: I know that. But when you say "putting this thing in order," what's the "thing" that you're referring to?

STUDENT: Oh, the thing. Me.

TEACHER: Oh, I see.

STUDENT: That real thing. When the ten thousand things move forward towards the self, it seems to me that that's like taking a walk through the woods and being surprised by a falling leaf.

TEACHER: Yeah, that's the problem, you know. That's the problem of really misunderstanding the teachings. We end up with misty landscapes and being startled by plum blossoms, which is all fine. But to carry the self forward and realize the ten thousand things, literally means to separate oneself from the world. That the ten thousand things advance and realize the self means to be intimate with the world. So, organizing board meetings, chopping wood—all of that is not something that happens to you. Nothing happens to you. What you do and what happens to you are the same thing. There's no separation between those two realities. In intimacy, the organizing organizes itself, the work creates itself. When you're separated, to carry the self forward and realize the ten thousand dharmas is "look at the pretty leaf." Master Jingqing asked, "What's that sound out there?" A monastic answered, "The sound of rain." And Jingqing said, "People these days are upside-down." That's not the sound of rain. What is it?

STUDENT: [Makes rushing noise like rain.]

TEACHER: What more can I say?

STUDENT: You could have said "shut up" at the very beginning.

TEACHER: May your life go well.

STUDENT: Thank you for your answer.

STUDENT: I want to ask you about the mystical teachings of the machete.

TEACHER: Indiscriminately wielding it. Cut, cut, cut.

STUDENT: [Whooshing noise.] It was my responsibility that those flowers be ready for the altars.

TEACHER: Clearly, the fault is mine. May your life go well.

STUDENT: Thank you for your answer.

STUDENT: A little while ago I took a shower in the bathhouse and it was very cold. I started to shiver and I'm still shivering. Is this delusion or enlightenment?

TEACHER: Was it that the water was cold, or was the heater in the building turned off?

STUDENT: The room was cold.

TEACHER: You should have turned the heater on. That's enlightenment. Shivering when there's a heater available is delusion.

STUDENT: The heater hasn't been started. I would have frozen to death trying to get it going.

TEACHER: It's an electric starter. All you have to do is push the button.

STUDENT: You would think so, but I tried it last year. It took a long time.

TEACHER: Maybe I should show you how to do it.

STUDENT: Maybe you should.

TEACHER: Okay. Anything else? Get warm.

STUDENT: I'll try. Thank you for your answer.

TEACHER: May your life go well.

STUDENT: I can barely take responsibility for my own spiritual practice. How can I take responsibility for everything?

TEACHER: Everything *is* your spiritual practice. So you're not taking responsibility for your own practice if you're leaving anything out. Do you understand?

STUDENT: I don't think I do.

TEACHER: The way you see it, what is your practice?

STUDENT: Getting up in the morning, doing zazen, trying to do work practice as well as I can, being centered.

TEACHER: Trying to do work practice as well as you can—where does that take place?

STUDENT: Out in the world?

TEACHER: Where does the world take place?

STUDENT: I think it's separate from myself.

TEACHER: Do you know why?

STUDENT: I can say why because someone's told me the answer, but I don't think I feel it.

TEACHER: Separate from myself. Myself, my self. The self. That's why. Get rid of self. What remains?

STUDENT: I don't know.

TEACHER: I don't know either. May your life go well.

STUDENT: I don't understand what use is it to come up here and have this encounter.

TEACHER: Neither do I. Guess what?

STUDENT: What?

TEACHER: You're on your own.

STUDENT: What a drag.

TEACHER: Bon voyage. May your life go well.

STUDENT: Am I supposed to thank you for that answer? [Laughs.] Thank you for your answer.

STUDENT: When you talk about the sacred teachings of work, I think about most people I know in the world. They're absolutely preoccupied with their work, tormented by their work. That's their life, night and day.

TEACHER: There's a difference between using the twenty-four hours of each day, and being used by the twenty-four hours of each day. Using the twenty-four hours days of each day is riding the ox backward into the Buddha Hall. Being used by the twenty-four hours of each day is having a ring stuck in your nose with a rope attached, and being led by it.

STUDENT: How am I letting work use me?

TEACHER: First of all, you're letting it torment you.

STUDENT: I've always done that.

TEACHER: Well, be nice to yourself.

STUDENT: But if I don't torment myself, it won't get done the right way. My father was told to retire from his job recently. Given how he depended on it, he's a dead man, you know. He'll either put a gun to his head, or he'll waste away.

TEACHER: Happens a lot.

STUDENT: Happens an incredible amount. It's something I think about a lot. My sister has worked herself to death. She has all kinds of physical problems. And look at me.

TEACHER: It's all in your hands. Only you can do something about it.

STUDENT: I guess it is.

TEACHER: Don't guess. It is. May your life go well.

STUDENT: Thank you.

STUDENT: I'm reading *The Cloud of Unknowing*. It's the quintessential Christian mystical text. I see great similarities in it with Zen. When the author speaks of love, however, it brings up something different in me than acceptance or openness, and when he talks of God, I wonder what is the corresponding reality in the Buddhist tradition. What is it that I'm open to? And I think, well, it's all said in words like "enlightenment," which feel very spacious, while I find the idea of God constricting. He's a man, and...

TEACHER: No it isn't. Who told you that?

STUDENT: Men are constricting.

TEACHER: First of all, she's black.

STUDENT: Not for that author, he's not. Not for the eleventh century when the book was written.

TEACHER: How about for this twentieth-century woman?

STUDENT: Yes, God is a man.

TEACHER: You should do something about that. Bring your tradition into it.

STUDENT: Oh, I see. If we speak of a goddess, I have a whole different set of images, values and attitudes. The goddess Hera was a great goddess.

TEACHER: So, your God is a woman?

STUDENT: Well, I think there's just a general problem with gods. That's the difference between the traditions, and if a Christian mystic doesn't go beyond his gods, then there's a big difference between us.

TEACHER: And how about your tradition? How do you see it?

STUDENT: I don't know enough of my tradition. As I read this Christian book, I wonder what is the corresponding text in our tradition?

TEACHER: The corresponding text in our tradition is your life. Anything else?

STUDENT: I'm speechless. There are no principles in my life to record.

TEACHER: Good. You're on the right track. Speechless and no principles. You can't go wrong. May your life go well.

STUDENT: I am still confused about taking responsibility for the ten thousand things. Would you please clarify that for me?

TEACHER: That kind of responsibility is based on realizing that cause and effect are actually one action. For every cause there's an effect. We usually see them as two different events. We think that cause initiates an effect, and then that effect becomes the cause of the next effect. The fact is that cause and effect are one. They are one like all dualities—good and bad, up and down, enlightenment and delusion. These are not two separate things. They are one reality. What that means is that what you do—cause, and what happens to you—effect, are the same thing. When you really see and realize this; that things don't happen to you, that you create them—whatever you experience—once you really understand that, you no longer separate cause and effect. We say, "He made me angry." He can't make you angry. Only *you* can make you angry. That's the huge difference between blaming and being a victim of your life, and taking full responsibility for the totality of your life. When you take responsibility, there's something you can do about it; about anger, about stress, about fear. But when we point outside of ourselves to the cause, there's nothing we can do about it, then we're just a victim of circumstances. It's very empowering to realize that cause and effect are one. It's very empowering to realize that I'm responsible for the ten thousand things. Whatever it is that exists, I create.

STUDENT: I get hints of that. Where the difficulties arise is when I move to see the problems of the whole world as my problems.

TEACHER: Sure.

STUDENT: Like the plane crash that just happened.

TEACHER: Sure. There's no intellectual justification for this way of seeing and being. This argument for taking responsibility for the whole world wouldn't stand up for five minutes against a good debater. The proof of it is in your own practice and life. When there's "no eye, ear, nose, tongue, body, mind," you see that all that exists, that all of existence including the self, is something that you create. You realize that it's the mind that's creating it all. So, the joy is my joy. The pain is my pain. That's why we say, be the barrier. Because when you become your obstacle, you return it to yourself, where it belongs. You realize that it's you.

STUDENT: I think I have a way to go.

TEACHER: Me too. We'll have a good trip together.

STUDENT: Thank you for your answer.

TEACHER: May your life go well.

STUDENT: I'm in the process of creating a home and whenever I come here I hear you talking about leaving home. How does one leave home without leaving home?

TEACHER: Leaving home is a monastic practice. The lay practice is to do exactly what you're doing, creating a home. And as far as I'm concerned, maintaining a household, having children, holding a job, are by far the most difficult practices. It's much easier, having let go of that, to deepen one's practice in a supportive community and to unify with the ten thousand things. But to unify with the ten thousand things in the midst of the ten thousand things is a lot more challenging. That's why I have unending respect for lay practitioners who are committed to that type of Zen practice. But the accent is on "committed." They are doing zazen and sesshin in addition to taking care of their children, spouse, home, and work. To really do it right, it means giving full attention to children, spouse, home, and work, and to express a deep gratitude to them for making it possible to practice. It's difficult, no question about it.

STUDENT: Thank you for your answer.

TEACHER: May your life go well.

STUDENT: You asked about the mystical realism of work. Where is this perfection of work? I would have to say, "Garbage along the highway. Dirty coffee cups left on the dining hall table."

TEACHER: I don't buy it. That's the anything-goes Zen syndrome; whatever-I-do-is-my-practice sickness. "Look, I'm a slob, but you know, I'm perfect as a slob." Not at this training center.

STUDENT: Whatever I do, that's my practice.

TEACHER: Horseshit. Anything else? May your life go well.

STUDENT: Thank you for your answer.

Those who regard the secular as a hindrance to practice only realize that in the secular nothing is sacred. What they haven't realized is that in sacredness nothing is secular. It's easy to say, whatever I do is my practice. But what does it mean to practice? Practice means doing, but all of life is doing. Is all of life practice? In a sense yes, and in a sense no. There's a very fine line here, and that fine line makes all the difference in the world between self-styled Zen and the genuine and authentic Zen of the ancestors. What does it really mean to practice one's life, to practice the breath, to practice a barrier, to practice the Buddha Way? Master Dogen says that practice and enlightenment are one. Practice is not a process that takes you to enlightenment. It's enlightenment itself. So what is it? It's very important to be clear on that. This reality is the same reality before enlightenment and after enlightenment. The only difference is how we perceive it. That's mystical realism. What changes with enlightenment is how we perceive ourselves and how we perceive the universe. That's something that can't be given, and it can't be received. The reason it can't be given and it can't be received is that it's already the life of each one of us—obscured, hidden—but here. And it's through the process of our zazen, of our practice, that we uncover and reveal it. So it is critical that we really take care of the question, "What is practice?"

11

MAKING VISIBLE THE INVISIBLE

In many centers and temples in the West, Zen liturgy has either been abandoned altogether or is done in a rote way. In general, Americans have a difficult time with liturgy. At this monastery liturgy is the area of training that generates the most questions and in which beginning practitioners encounter the most challenges. On the surface, Zen liturgy has the appearance of a Judeo-Christian worship service. There's an officiant; there's an altar; there's chanting and bowing. Most practitioners come to Zen from either a Jewish or a Christian background, traditions that have elaborate liturgy that has been institutionalized in significant ways. Many of them have left their original religions being disillusioned or dissatisfied with the empty forms they encountered. Zen seems very appealing to them. It's sparse, simple, and very direct. Buoyed by their expectations, people are sometimes shocked when they come to a Zen center and find liturgy punctuating all facets of the day. We have all the liturgy that exists in any other religion, and more—daily liturgy, sutras, liturgy for death, for marriage, for birth, liturgy for taking a meal, liturgy for work. But since Zen is non-theistic, it's hard to understand why Zen liturgy exists in the first place. What is it that we're doing in liturgy? What is it all about?

The English definition of liturgy is "a rite or body of rites prescribed for public worship," as well as "reverence to a divine being or supernatural power." Is that what's going on in Zen liturgy? My teacher Maezumi Roshi once said, "The invitation for the manifestation of the Three Treasures is included as part of our ceremonies." Each time he did the ceremony for receiving the precepts, or the ordination of a monastic, he used to begin the service by saying, "I ask all of the buddhas and bodhisattvas to be with us to verify and confirm our ceremonies."

What does that mean? Is it some sort of magic? Is Buddhism theistic after all and we just mouth that it's not?

A service dedicated to hungry ghosts begins with the supplication for raising the bodhi mind. Maezumi Roshi said, "We begin by offering the service to the hungry ghosts, which literally fill all space and time, both inwardly and outwardly." Hungry ghosts form part of one of the six realms of existence: heavenly creatures, human beings, jealous gods, hungry ghosts, animals, and demons. What do these realms represent? About hungry ghosts Maezumi Roshi said: "We have certain kinds of thirst and hunger. How do we really feel? Not the hunger we feel in the stomach, but the hunger and thirst we feel through our emotions and in the domain of our mind or spirit. However we call those insatiable frustrations and anxieties, how can we make ourselves really satisfied? That itself is the most fundamental koan. You already have the answer." In other words, he called these insatiable desires, appetites, frustrations, and anxieties the demons and hungry ghosts. Just within ourselves there's all kinds of maneuvering going on. These six worlds exist within ourselves. So having a service like this, who are we really serving and offering it to?

We offer our services to everything and everybody—all creatures and creations, beings animate and inanimate. This is the most basic principle of the Buddha's teaching. In one of the dedications of our Sunday service we intone, "When this devoted invocation is sent forth, it is perceived and subtly answered." Who is the perceiver? Who is the respondent?

Each morning we chant, "Vast is the robe of liberation, a formless field of benefaction. I wear the Tathagata's teachings, saving all sentient beings." What are the Tathagata's teachings? It's really important that we don't just repeat the words. That type of mindless mimicry makes religions dead. We really need to challenge everything that we hear and see. We need to keep our great doubt just as strong as our great faith and great determination.

We chant, "All Buddhas throughout space and time; All Bodhisattva Mahasattvas, Maha Prajna Paramita." Who are all the buddhas throughout space and time? What are all the mahasattvas and bodhisattvas? Are they all Buddhists? If we say that the buddha nature pervades everywhere, in trees, rocks, and rivers, then surely if a tree is a buddha, the image on the altar must also be a buddha since it's made from a tree. And the altar itself must be a buddha. Jesus must be one. Moses must be one.

So, how do you understand the liturgy that you perform every day here? How do you understand the liturgy that you perform in your secular life—the liturgy of brushing your teeth, taking a meal, the liturgy of a baseball game, the liturgy of opening a Senate hearing, of the cop standing in the middle of the street directing traffic? How do you identify with it? What does it mean to you? Liturgy is usually an expression of the common experience of a congregation, a group of people. What is the common experience of Zen practitioners? Let's restate it for ourselves.

STUDENT: Between heaven and earth, I am the only one.
TEACHER: That leaves nothing behind. There's no picking, no choosing; there's no life, no death; no buddhas. There are no creatures, no enlightenment, no delusion. Where does liturgy fit into that?
STUDENT: [Chants the Sho Sai Myo Kichijo Dharani.] *No mo san man da moto nan ...*
TEACHER: May your life go well.
STUDENT: Aren't you going to squeeze my head a bit more?
TEACHER: If you really understand what you've said, you'll know there is nothing to squeeze.
STUDENT: Thank you for your answer.

STUDENT: There is an incredible computer screen—all blank. On it I can type "buddhas," "demons," and "hungry ghosts." On it I type, *"Mountain Record. Fall Issue. Liturgy."*
TEACHER: Is that buddhas or is that demons?
STUDENT: Page two, dharma discourse. Daido Roshi, "Manifesting the Invisible."
TEACHER: How will you type buddhas?
STUDENT: Tap, tap, tap, tap...
TEACHER: And how will you type demons?
STUDENT: I don't know.
TEACHER: Are you a demon?
STUDENT: [Shouts.]
TEACHER: Are you a buddha?
STUDENT: I don't know.
TEACHER: Are you neither?
STUDENT: Tap, tap, tap, tap...
TEACHER: On one side we have the buddhas. On the other side we have the typewriter. You have the ability to create either of them. What is it that you're creating?
STUDENT: There's a great computer screen. On it I type *"Mountain Record. Fall Issue. Liturgy."*
TEACHER: Is it buddhas or demons?
STUDENT: It's *"Mountain Record. Fall Issue. Liturgy."*
TEACHER: May your life go well.
STUDENT: Thank you for your answer.

∞

STUDENT: I have an insatiable appetite. After our meals I take the hungry ghost offerings to the kitchen and eat them all, and I'm still hungry. What can I do?

TEACHER: Where does the hunger come from?

STUDENT: I just want more...

TEACHER: More what?

STUDENT: Food.

TEACHER: What kind of food?

STUDENT: Food I can really chew, eat, digest, and shit out.

TEACHER: Do you feel that food is something outside yourself being dispensed by someone?

STUDENT: No. It goes right through me and comes right out again.

TEACHER: Where will you get it? Who will give it to you?

STUDENT: Do you have any?

TEACHER: I have nothing.

STUDENT: Then I'll have to give it to myself.

TEACHER: "Give" also puts it outside yourself.

STUDENT: That's okay. I'll take it and eat that, too.

TEACHER: But you'll never satisfy yourself.

STUDENT: I know. It's a real problem.

TEACHER: So, what is the problem?

STUDENT: I'm hungry.

TEACHER: That means food is outside the skin bag along with everything else, and you're inside. What will you do about that skin bag?

STUDENT: I'll have to consume the whole thing.

TEACHER: The whole universe! Then there's no inside or outside.

STUDENT: Does it taste good?

TEACHER: Beats me.

STUDENT: Thank you for your answer.

TEACHER: May your life go well.

∞

STUDENT: I hate service. It makes me pass out; it makes me sick to my stomach, and so liturgy is trying not to pass out or just letting go of wanting to pass out, but that makes me feel like a dead horse. I get very numb.

TEACHER: Are you asking a question?

STUDENT: That's just a statement.

TEACHER: I feel sorry for you. It doesn't need to be like that, but maybe that's your liturgy.

STUDENT: Does letting go make you a dead horse?

TEACHER: Letting go of what?

STUDENT: Letting go of liking and hating, manipulating things around to make them fit. The answer is "no," but why does it feel like it does?

TEACHER: You'd better ask the feeler why it feels the way it does. Who is the feeler?

STUDENT: Me.

TEACHER: Who is the juggler?

STUDENT: Me.

TEACHER: Where does all that stuff take place?

STUDENT: In my head; in my body.

TEACHER: If you know that you're the creator of pain, you must also know that you're the creator of joy. If there is manipulation, there is also the possibility of no manipulation. The minute one is created, the other arises. If you have pain, you have the possibility of the cessation of pain, and the instant you have this possibility, it's clear how to do it. The Four Noble Truths arise from the existence of that first element, pain.

STUDENT: It seems like the only time I'm not in joy or pain, or manipulating, is when I'm asleep.

TEACHER: Why don't you throw away all of it—joy, pain, heaven, earth, good, bad? That's what it means to be the breath. The breath then consumes the entire universe. That's what it means to be the chant, the bow. When you bow, just bow. Anything else?

STUDENT: Thank you for your answer.

TEACHER: May your life go well.

STUDENT: Is bowing the same activity that trees do when they drop all their leaves in the fall? They just give it all back.

TEACHER: That's a nice, poetic way of looking at it, but what is bowing?

STUDENT: Letting everything go...

TEACHER: Without using words to describe it, what's the thing itself?

STUDENT: When bowing bows.

TEACHER: That's an explanation; a good one, but it's still an explanation. What's the truth?

STUDENT: I really don't know.

TEACHER: Sure you do.

STUDENT: Maybe that's my problem. It's always been a difficult part of practice to get down and then get back up, although I do it constantly anyway. You can't get up and down off a cushion without a certain amount of bowing. You can't pick up a handkerchief that you dropped without bowing.

TEACHER: Picking up a handkerchief is picking up a handkerchief. Bowing is bowing. Walking is walking. Sometimes bowing doesn't involve putting your head down and kneeling on the floor. Sometimes this is bowing [Demonstrates.] So, what's the truth of bowing?

STUDENT: [Silence.]

TEACHER: [Bows.] It's just that. May your life go well.

STUDENT: Thank you for your answer.

STUDENT: I pledge allegiance to the flag of the United States of America.

TEACHER: What is that?

STUDENT: I pledge allegiance to the flag of the United States of America.

TEACHER: Are you answering a question for me or just showing me secular liturgy?

STUDENT: I'm just showing secular liturgy.

TEACHER: Well, we already know that. Can you come up with something fresh?

STUDENT: Sure. [Yawns and stretches.]

TEACHER: What's going to happen to my Dharma?

STUDENT: You hid it too well.

TEACHER: Anything else?

STUDENT: No.

TEACHER: May your life go well.

STUDENT: Thank you for your answer.

STUDENT: If the water is free, why is it so damned hard to sell it?

TEACHER: It's not so hard to sell it. Look at all of us. We've just finished a meditation retreat with eighty people; there are five hundred students at this monastery alone, thousands throughout the country, all of us doing the same thing, buying water right alongside the river. A guy's got a fancy stand set up with a hose that runs right into the river and he's dispensing water.

STUDENT: Is that ever going to stop?

TEACHER: Yes. When you figure out what he's doing. Then you'll set up a stand next to him. That's what I did when I figured out what my teacher, Maezumi Roshi was doing.

STUDENT: What about just drinking the water from the river?

TEACHER: Nobody wants it.

STUDENT: Why not?

TEACHER: I don't know. People pass it up all the time. They are like fish in the middle of the ocean saying, "I'm thirsty, I'm thirsty."

STUDENT: What's going to happen to those people selling the water when people just go down to the river and drink it?

TEACHER: That would be wonderful. It would be the most wonderful thing that could happen, but chances are it won't. Why do *you* buy the water?

STUDENT: Well...

TEACHER: I know why I sell it. Why do you buy it?

STUDENT: Because I'm not sure enough that I could get the water without buying it...

TEACHER: Louise, Louise, Louise.

STUDENT: ...for another twenty years.

TEACHER: May your life go well.

STUDENT: Thank you for your answer.

STUDENT: Under the Buddha statue there are pictures of animals, trees, landscapes. Is this appropriate or not?

TEACHER: Which Buddha statue?

STUDENT: The one behind you.

TEACHER: In front of the Buddha statue there are people in robes on cushions, chanting and bowing. Is that appropriate? Behind the Buddha statue, on the outside wall of this building, is the resurrected Christ facing East, hands spread apart. Is that appropriate?

STUDENT: [Silence.]

TEACHER: What do you say?

STUDENT: Amen.

TEACHER: Amen. May your life go well.

STUDENT: Thank you for your answer.

STUDENT: I don't seem to have problems with liturgy. For me it is a chance to go into the zendo and yell my head off. I really like to do that but the problem is that while I yell so much I lose track of the words and don't appreciate them enough.

TEACHER: The key is to appreciate what's going on. What are we doing when we do liturgy? What's really happening? When we do the first service, we dedicate it to Shakyamuni Buddha. Why do we do that? He's dead. Then we chant, "All buddhas throughout space and time." What does that mean? What do the words of the *Heart Sutra* signify? Every one of those lines is a koan. What does, "Form is emptiness, emptiness is form" mean? What does, "no old age and death" mean? Are we denying what we see when we see old age and death? In the second service we chant the names of the ancestors, even though they're all deceased. Why are we chanting their names? The third service is dedicated to our family heritage, our personal ancestors. A lot of people hate their ancestors and wonder, "Why do I want to dedicate a service to my father or my mother?" The last service is a healing service. Who is healing? Who is receiving? Who is responding? What are the teachings of this service? There is nothing extra in Zen. It is all functioning very precisely and it is all pointing to the same place—everything we do, all eighty-four thousand gestures. So stop shouting and just *be* it.

STUDENT: Thank you for your answer.

TEACHER: May your life go well.

∞

STUDENT: [Blows his nose.]

TEACHER: What's that?

STUDENT: I have a cold. I guess it's my liturgy for today.

TEACHER: What's the point of that liturgy? If you take, for example, the liturgy of the Marines, "From the Halls of Montezuma to the shores of Tripoli, we will fight our country's battles on the land and on the sea," and go from that to, "O, Shariputra, form is no other than emptiness, emptiness no other than form" and then to, "I believe in God the Father, Creator of Heaven and Earth, and in Jesus Christ, his only Son, our Lord, born of the Virgin Mary," each of these says something very distinct. So, what's the point of blowing your nose? What is it expressing?

STUDENT: Blowing my nose seems to be some sort of an excuse. I have tremendous fear when liturgy comes up. I don't want to do it. But as soon as I begin the process, this fear changes.

TEACHER: Blowing your nose can be liturgy in the same way that [shouts] is liturgy when it consumes the whole body and mind. Isn't that what Zen liturgy is about? Isn't it pointing to the nature of the self? Blowing your nose can fill the whole universe the way raising a stick or blinking an eye fills the whole universe.

STUDENT: Thank you for your answer.

TEACHER: May your life go well.

∞

STUDENT: "Not knowing" is no body, mind, sight, phenomena. How does this "not knowing" function in the relative world?

TEACHER: I don't know.

STUDENT: That's my answer.

TEACHER: Do you understand?

STUDENT: No. That's why I'm asking.

TEACHER: And I'm telling you: I don't know. Do you understand that's how it functions?

STUDENT: Say that again. I have to think about it.

TEACHER: Don't think about it. Just don't know.

STUDENT: All right.

TEACHER: May your life go well.

STUDENT: Thank you for your answer.

STUDENT: Without breathing I will die; without breathing I will not die. "Reading words you should grasp the great reality." Chanting, I'm breathing.

TEACHER: Have you every tried to stop breathing? We had a fellow in residence once, a young boy who really didn't want to be here. He was seventeen years old and his parents sent him here because they thought Zen training would be good for him. He was hiding in his room one evening when it was time for zazen. I went up and talked to him. He said, "I'm afraid I'm going to stop breathing." I asked him, "Do you know what happens when you stop breathing?" He said, "Yes, I'll die." I said, "No, you'll pass out, and when you pass out you'll start breathing again." It's not something you choose to do.

STUDENT: How do I die and breathe?

TEACHER: What kind of dying are you talking about?

STUDENT: The Great Death.

TEACHER: Let go of breathing and not breathing.

STUDENT: And I shall die.

TEACHER: You shall die the Great Death—the death of the ego, the death of the self that separates you from the ten thousand things, the death of the self that creates breathing and not breathing, good and bad, enlightenment and delusion. Throw it all away.

STUDENT: Will you bury me when I'm dead?

TEACHER: Be happy to.

STUDENT: Thank you.

TEACHER: In fact, there will be nothing to bury. May your life go well.

STUDENT: There may be different forms of liturgy, but when I bow, there's a divine being with supernatural powers.

TEACHER: Only if it consumes the whole universe. There's nothing that's not a divine being with supernatural powers. Anything else?

STUDENT: No.

TEACHER: That's why I like you for my attendant. I need a divine being with supernatural powers. May your life go well.
STUDENT: Thank you for your answer.

∞

STUDENT: Our liturgy is boring. It has been the same for years and years. It's not just me. Everybody thinks so.
TEACHER: What would you do?
STUDENT: Couldn't we put a keyboard in the zendo and jazz it up a bit? Make it more fun.
TEACHER: It is jazzy.
STUDENT: Which part?
TEACHER: All of it.
STUDENT: Seems pretty boring to me
TEACHER: Don't separate yourself. Make liturgy go away by being it. The keyboard too. Make it go away.
STUDENT: Thank you for your answer.
TEACHER: May your life go well.

∞

STUDENT: When I started practicing, I hated services. Now I do liturgy and don't hate it, but I don't like it, either. I wonder what liturgy is doing for me.
TEACHER: When people don't like liturgy they either react violently to it, or they ignore it. From a teacher's perspective, give me the violent reaction any day. I can work with that. There is a possibility of provoking a response, of seeing something. On the other hand, the person who is numb to liturgy is dead to the possibility of learning. Before I got involved in Zen Buddhism, I was violently opposed to religion. My position was to burn down the churches, take the gold and give it to the poor. I felt very strongly about this and I was overtly active against organized religion. This went on for a long time. Everybody else could see the truth of how I felt except me. People used to call me Pope John, the Atheist. They saw that I was very religious in my own way. When a student doesn't respond or react, there's nothing I can do for them except a memorial service, because they're dead.
STUDENT: But when I react, nobody likes it. They tell me to do this, do that. I'm not up to your rules. Why those rules?
TEACHER: Those rules are the whip. There are different kinds of students. There are students who move at the shadow of a suggestion...

STUDENT: But you reach a point when you get used to that, and then it's not interesting any more.

TEACHER: The poking is meant to get you riled up. Anything else?

STUDENT: No.

TEACHER: May your life go well.

STUDENT: Thank you for your answer.

STUDENT: I get a lot out of liturgy, but the one place where I have difficulty is bowing in front of the altar when I am working as a server in the back of the zendo. I pass back and forth in front of the altar, maybe twenty-five times in the space of half an hour, and I just find it irritating to have to stop when getting from one side of the hallway to the other. If I'm carrying a bowl of rice and I'm intent on carrying it safely to the entrance of the zendo, why should I stop and bow to this wooden figure?

TEACHER: That's the problem—bowing to a wooden figure. Indeed, why should you bow to the wooden figure? I agree.

STUDENT: Right. So my bowing, in fact, would be in the carrying of the rice.

TEACHER: No, no. You can bow to the Buddha.

STUDENT: The Buddha is the rice.

TEACHER: Yes. You can bow to it.

STUDENT: Why stop bowing to one buddha in order to turn to this other buddha that doesn't concern me at that moment?

TEACHER: Why discriminate?

STUDENT: But you're discriminating by saying we should bow to the Buddha.

TEACHER: No, I actually didn't. My teacher, Maezumi Roshi, came visiting one day. As he walked through the hallway he turned and bowed towards the altar. He turned to look at me and said, "We should bow when we pass here." I said, "Fine," and from that day on, everybody bows when they pass the altar. I was just a good student. My teacher told me to do it, and I do it.

STUDENT: Would you mind if I didn't?

TEACHER: Would you mind if I stepped on your head? That's what you're doing if you don't bow—you step on my head.

STUDENT: How come?

TEACHER: By not bowing to the Buddha.

STUDENT: Fifteen times in the space of three minutes!

TEACHER: It irritates you.

STUDENT: What if I drop the rice?

TEACHER: But it irritates you. If it didn't irritate you, it would be different. When

Maezumi Roshi went to Europe, he spoke to a group of practicing Buddhists who were vocally non-theistic. In his talk Roshi kept emphasizing that there is a God, without a question, and that he believed in her wholeheartedly. His next talk was directed to an audience that was largely made up of Catholic priests and Jesuits. There he said, "There is no God. I don't believe in God." Which is the truth? At which of those extremes did Roshi really stand? Is it right to bow or not to bow? Is it important to be practical? Is it important to be aware? Is it important to be irritated or not irritated? For you it is important to recognize your irritation.

STUDENT: So, when I stop being irritated, I can give up bowing.

TEACHER: We'll find something else to push your buttons. Anything else?

STUDENT: There is a reverence, then.

TEACHER: Absolutely. But to whom?

STUDENT: What about the monastic who went up and sat on a Manjushri statue on the altar?

TEACHER: That was an incredibly profound reverence.

STUDENT: I guess I don't understand that.

TEACHER: I don't know. Do you?

STUDENT: No.

TEACHER: In reverence there is no self. That's the whole point of everything we do, to realize the fact of that no separation.

STUDENT: Am I being separate in my irritation?

TEACHER: Definitely. May your life go well.

STUDENT: Thank you for your answer.

STUDENT: When I first heard the Four Bodhisattva Vows they really tickled me because they seemed so impossible. I thought it was just amazing that every day we would vow to accomplish them as if it was a given. I still think it's funny, but now I see that the impossibility is pointing at something. I just don't know what.

TEACHER: When you first came here, your beginner's mind immediately saw the truth of the Bodhisattva Vows. Aren't they incredible? Sentient beings are numberless; I vow to save them. Impossible. Desires are inexhaustible; I vow to put an end to them. Impossible. The dharmas are boundless; I vow to master them. Impossible. The Buddha Way is unattainable; I vow to attain it. Impossible. That's the spirit, the heart of this practice—the impossibility of it all. If nothing else, most people develop incredible perseverance in this practice. Take dokusan, for example, where day after day students are rejected:

"No. Go deeper." There's no approval, even when you have insight. It takes an incredible amount of self-reliance. That trust in oneself is the whole point. It doesn't mean that we're not trying to fulfill those vows. We are wholeheartedly committed to them, even though it's deluded to try to save all sentient beings, and it's deluded to try to put an end to all desires. But what a wonderful delusion! May your life go well.

STUDENT: Thank you for your answer.

STUDENT: It's not about self-reliance. It's about much more than that. Self-reliance is a petty attitude.

TEACHER: Anything else?

STUDENT: Yeah!

TEACHER: You want a fight.

STUDENT: Yes, I want a fight.

TEACHER: Yell, scream, punch. Get it out. It's okay.

STUDENT: I can't learn anything here.

TEACHER: Anything else?

STUDENT: There's nothing to learn. That's just it. Another game.

TEACHER: [Laughs.] Every morning, first thing when you get up, sit on the edge of your bed and [Prolonged hearty laughter.] Then get on with the day. May your life go well.

STUDENT: Thank you for your answer.

STUDENT: I'm an ex-Catholic. I like the ritual here and it means a lot to me. We sit zazen and there's nothing. Then we all get up and we bow. Then we have a service. There's a lot going on. Once I was an usher and I had to take care of things fast, but at the same time it seemed like we were still sitting. Since I don't have a problem with liturgy, where is the edge of that practice for me?

TEACHER: Just practice it. Just do it with the whole body and mind. Ritual, service, liturgy—all of it is a form of dharma food. It has endless possibilities. Sometimes what we see is just the tip of the iceberg. Really look at it; look at the words that we chant; look at the different forms. We do some thirty different services here—renewal of vows, marriage ceremony, memorial service, birthing service, ordination, jukai, planting the garden, breaking the ground to erect a building. All of these services are rites of passage. In Zen, teaching is always taking place in each activity. Liturgy is not just prayer; it's not a petition. It is always a teaching. Try to see what that teaching is. Anything else?

STUDENT: No.

TEACHER: May your life go well.

STUDENT: Thank you for your answer.

∞

STUDENT: For deposit only. Zen Mountain Monastery, Inc. [Bangs floor.]

TEACHER: What is that liturgy directed to?

STUDENT: [Sings.] We're in the black...we're in the red...we're in the black ... we're in the red...

TEACHER: One of the joys of my life is watching you when you chant. I love the way you throw yourself into it. Is that throwing yourself into it?

STUDENT: Baby, I love making a deposit. I love it especially when it's big.

TEACHER: I do, too. Thank you for your practice, but don't be greedy.

STUDENT: Thank you for your practice.

TEACHER: May your life go well.

STUDENT: Thank you for your answer.

∞

When you do something with the whole body and mind, each moment is the first moment of your life. You see it in a way that's fresh and new. It can never be boring. Living this way, each weed that you pick is the first weed and the last weed of your life. And when you put it down you let it go completely, so that the next weed is again the first and the last weed of your life. That's what it means to really do liturgy. When you bow, just bow; when you eat, just eat; when you walk, just walk. Seen in this way, every moment is perfect and complete, lacking nothing. In fact, the incredible, the extraordinary truth of the matter is that, whether you realize it or not, each moment is perfect and complete, lacking nothing. Each one of us is a buddha, realized or not. It just makes this life a lot easier and a lot more beautiful when you realize it. Whether you do or not is ultimately up to you—it's your decision. You can take a blank piece of paper. If you draw a buddha on it, a buddha appears; if you draw a demon, a demon appears. Isn't that incredible?

12
CAUSE AND EFFECT ARE ONE

The functioning of cause and effect is a fundamental teaching of Buddhism, and the clarification of cause and effect in one's life is an integral aspect of Zen training. In general, when we talk about karma we tend to oversimplify it. We approach it from the perspective shaped by our scientific appreciation of causality, framed by the polarities of action and reaction. In an essay, "Wondrous Cause and Effect," Master Dogen says that "cause does not precede effect nor does effect follow cause." Cause and effect are one. They occur simultaneously. But we also speak of the seeds of karma. Every action produces the seeds of another action—a new cause. Indeed, one characteristic of cause and effect is the force to propagate itself.

Cause and effect, in and of themselves, are neither good nor bad. They are simply action and reaction. But when we evaluate them, we do so within a reference system. Not only is there individual karma, there is also group karma, family karma, national karma—karma that we inherit through our participation. Cause and/or effect may be the consequence of what you walk into. When you join an organization, your karma becomes part of the already existing karma of that organization.

In the koan, "Baizhang and the Fox" the question of causality and its relationship to karma is dealt with in a way that has been held in very high esteem by most Zen traditions. One of the pivotal teachings in the Buddhist sutras is that an enlightened being does not fall into cause and effect. The whole point of practice and enlightenment is to free oneself from the cycle of birth and death, from causality. Yet in this case which appears in all of the traditional koan collections, the teaching is much more subtle and profound. When the abbot of what later became Baizhang's monastery was once asked by a monastic, "Does an enlightened being fall into cause and effect?" and he responded, "He does not," according with the sutras, he was made to live five hundred years as a fox. In Chinese tradition the life of a fox is regarded as a horrible curse, so this is a way of saying that he suffered karmic consequences for his answer. After a long period of suffering as a fox, the abbot resurfaced on Baizhang Mountain. He told his story to Baizhang, begging him to say a turning word so that he could be free of the karma he created with his answer. Baizhang told him to ask his question, and the old man queried, "Does an enlightened being fall into causation or not?" Baizhang said, "He does not ignore it." Immediately, the old man was freed from his fox body; in other words, he was enlightened. He requested that Baizhang search for a dead fox in a cave on the other side of the mountain, and give it a burial as if for a deceased monastic. Baizhang took all his monastics around the mountainside, where they came upon a cave. He poked with a stick and pulled out a dead fox. They cremated the fox body in an elaborate funeral ceremony usually reserved for monastics.

After the funeral, Baizhang mounted the high seat and told his monastics the whole story of the old man's dilemma: how he used to come to the lectures and sit in the back of the room, how he finally asked his question, how he was freed of the fox body. The old man had finally understood the nature of cause and effect and its relationship to enlightenment. As Baizhang concluded his talk, Huangbo, the head monastic, got up and challenged Baizhang, "You say that the old man answered wrong when asked if an enlightened being falls into causality or not. What would he have become had he answered correctly?" Baizhang said, "Please come forward and I'll tell you." Huangbo approached Baizhang and, as he got close enough, he hit his master. Immediately Baizhang clapped his hands, burst out laughing, and exclaimed, "Isn't it wonderful? All along I thought you were a red-bearded barbarian and now I see you're a barbarian with a red beard."

In probing the topic of cause and effect, there are a number of questions begging to be addressed. What did Dogen mean when he said that cause and effect are one, that cause doesn't precede effect, effect doesn't follow cause? If that is the case, why do we speak of the seeds of karma? How is the old man's answer, "doesn't fall into causation" different from Baizhang's answer, "doesn't ignore karma?" Why was the old man made to live the life of a fox when he answered, "an enlightened being doesn't fall into causation?" Obviously, the old man fell into causation by his answer "does not fall into causation." How did Baizhang free him? Evidently his words enlightened the old man. When he was enlightened, was he free from causation? What would he have turned into had he answered correctly? Most important of all, what does cause and effect mean in terms of your life, practice, and actions?

STUDENT: Yesterday I lifted three boards. Today, "Oh, my shoulder!"

TEACHER: Is that cause and effect?

STUDENT: That's, "Yesterday I lifted three boards. Today, 'Oh, my shoulder!'"

TEACHER: Did one precede the other?

STUDENT: Yesterday I lifted three boards. Today, "Oh, my shoulder!"

TEACHER: I want to know what is the relationship of pain to lifting the boards.

STUDENT: Aghhh!

TEACHER: Does that follow or precede it?

STUDENT: Aghhh!

TEACHER: What is that "Aghh!?"

STUDENT: Aghhh!

TEACHER: May your life go well.

STUDENT: I don't understand. When the old man answered the monastic in a way that sounds correct, he was transformed into a fox and made to suffer. Why?

TEACHER: You have to look at what is right and wrong. You are almost there when you make that first statement, "I don't understand." Then you lose it. What is right? What is wrong? How do you determine right and wrong? That's where the whole truth resides. Recently, I was watching a Star Wars episode over my son's shoulder. One of the characters, Obi-wan Kenobi, was explaining that truth is always presented in terms of somebody's reference system, and that we should take that into account when considering the fairness of the situations we encounter. So what is the "right" answer and what is the "wrong" answer? Genuine Zen practice is beyond words and phrases, and exists outside of the scriptures. It is a direct pointing to the human mind and the attainment of Buddhahood. That is enlightenment. Explanations, judgments, and analyses are outside of it. The minute Obi-wan started explaining, he missed it. But isn't Baizhang's response to the old man an explanation? How did Baizhang's answer differ from the old man's answer? That is the key. The key is to be found in abandoning the reference system. The old man was stuck in a particular point of view. Baizhang freed him from it. And Baizhang should have been made to live five hundred years as a fox for his response. Do you understand?

STUDENT: Thank you for your answer.

TEACHER: May your life go well.

STUDENT: Why do I practice?

TEACHER: I don't even know why I practice. How could I know why you practice? Why do you?

STUDENT: I could give all kinds of answers.

TEACHER: There is only one. Master Yunmen once posed the same question to his assembly, "All you monastics, when the bell sounds why do you put on your priestly robes?" He was asking, "Why do you practice?" I ask you, why do you want to be a postulant? Before you can become a novice, you will have to pass through this koan. See if you can stop all the analysis and justifications, and directly and intimately look at your practice and answer the question of why you do it. Why are you really here? Why do you smile? Why is the sky blue?

STUDENT: Because it is.

TEACHER: That is just a little better than a twenty-page treatise on the topic, but not yet the heart of the matter. Why? The only way to answer these questions is the same way you answer Mu—be completely intimate with it. The answer is in the intimacy, in not separating yourself from anything. The answer to every single koan is intimacy. The precepts and all of Zen liturgy have to do with intimacy. Intimacy with what? With yourself. Really be intimate with yourself. That doesn't mean ego-tripping or self indulgence. Ego tripping is separation, not intimacy.

STUDENT: I'm afraid. What if I go in the wrong direction?

TEACHER: Why would you go in the wrong direction?

STUDENT: Because I have some goal in my mind.

TEACHER: Some goal outside of yourself? That's the same as Zhaozhou asking his teacher about the Buddha Way. When Nanquan replied, "Ordinary mind is the Way," Zhaozhou said, "Shall I direct myself towards it?" "The minute you direct yourself toward it, you're moving away from it," Nanquan corrected. Why? Because the Way is already where you are. This has to do with the subtle difference between aspiration and expectation. Really look at the question of "Why practice?" It's a central koan. The only way to see it is to be intimate with that question of "Why?" Then you will see it, and to see it clearly is to experience the enlightenment of the Buddha.

STUDENT: Thank you for your answer.

TEACHER: May your life go well.

STUDENT: The old man lived five hundred glorious years as a fox because of the "FOX!"

TEACHER: What is "fox?"

STUDENT: FOX!

TEACHER: I want you to show me the fox.

STUDENT: I can't.

TEACHER: You can show me Mu. You can show me the sixteen-foot golden Buddha. It always comes down to the same thing—no separation. Be intimate. Be intimate with yourself. That is what Dogen is talking about when he says, "Cause and effect are one." He did not say, "Cause was yesterday and the effect will be tomorrow." It is the same thing, simultaneous and immediate—fox. You're heading in the right direction but it's still intellectual. What is the thing itself? Anything else?

STUDENT: No. Thank you for your answer.

TEACHER: May your life go well.

STUDENT: You could just as easily say "effect and cause" as "cause and effect." Couldn't you?

TEACHER: No. Dogen clarifies this by saying that cause does not precede effect nor does effect follow cause. You could also go on to say that effect doesn't precede cause and cause doesn't follow effect.

STUDENT: Is it that I can't quite get that clear because I'm locked into a different sense of time?

TEACHER: It has to do with our language; how it relates to reality and how we use it. It is very difficult, if not impossible, to comprehend Zen through language. For example, look at the phrase, "form is emptiness," the central tenet of the Mahayana *Perfection of Wisdom* scriptures. Form is the phenomenal world, all of physical reality. Emptiness is "no eye, ear, nose, tongue, body, mind." Form is differentiation, a realm filled with activity and distinctions. Emptiness is devoid of any characteristics. They are two extremes. Nothing could be more opposite. Yet, in the *Heart Sutra* it says, "O, Shariputra, form is no other than emptiness; emptiness no other than form. Form is exactly emptiness, emptiness exactly form." This statement boggles the mind because it is a blatant contradiction. Dogen is saying something similar—cause and effect are one. When you try to place them in a sequence, within a linear progression, within language, you make them into something other than one. You make them into two separate entities. That misses the truth. One means exactly that—one. When you attribute your problem of understanding to your misconception of time, in a sense, that is true. Time is an illusion. Sometimes you sit in zazen and a thirty-five minute meditation period is five hundred lives of a fox. Another time, it's a flash. Once you abandon your reference system, time loses its meaning. The relationship of time and space to intimacy is very important. When you are totally intimate with something, beyond the attributes of thought and language, there is nothing else in the whole universe. When you are totally intimate with Mu, there is nothing in the universe but Mu. Mu becomes everything and there is no longer anything to compare it to. You can't measure, evaluate, analyze, or judge it. It's only when you come back out of the experience of Mu that you can look at it in terms of your reference system. Only then can you know something about it. In intimacy itself there is no knowing. In cause and effect itself, there is no knowing. There is just the thing itself—the direct, immediate, intimate experience of simultaneous cause and effect.

STUDENT: Thank you for your answer.

TEACHER: May your life go well.

STUDENT: If the teacher is wrong, the teacher is also right, and if the student is right, the student is also wrong.

TEACHER: You have to define right and wrong. So long as you're in the realm of right and wrong, you can call anything right and wrong.

STUDENT: So who is making the rules?

TEACHER: Anyone who says right and wrong has a set of rules.

STUDENT: If the rules are unclear, when do they become clear?

TEACHER: When the person understands them.

STUDENT: And what if the understanding changes?

TEACHER: Life constantly changes. People constantly change. The world and everything in it is in a constant state of flux. Rules change and you change with them. That's what a "true person of no rank" means—you are not fixed anywhere. In other words, when in Rome, do as the Romans do. It makes life a lot easier.

STUDENT: Thank you.

TEACHER: Also see that this has a lot to do with cause and effect. It has a lot to do with karma. When we say that what you do and what happens to you is the same thing, it means that you are in control of the consequences of your life. Your life doesn't happen to you. You create it. That's the basis of cause and effect; how it affects what we do, our work, our relationships; how it affects our well-being or our pain and suffering. Life always happens in a particular context and the context determines our experience. When I was in Israel, I once drove through the Hasidic section of Jerusalem on a Saturday. When in Israel, you don't drive through the Hasidic section on the Sabbath, unless you want to get your head cracked. And so I was stoned. Karma—action, reaction. Was I right? Was I wrong?

STUDENT: That's how wars start.

TEACHER: Peace and war are one; good and bad are one; heaven and earth are one and the same thing. All the dualities are two parts of the same reality. Heads and tails are two parts of the same coin. They are one thing and two things, simultaneously. You can't have one without the other. They are mutually arising, mutually co-existing, mutually interdependent. That's true not only for dualities but for multiplicities, because everything in the universe is connected. Each thing, every speck of dust, every person, every being, every cell, every planet, every thought, every color, *everything* is connected to every other thing in the universe, past, present, and future. And you cannot shake one part without shaking the whole of Indra's Net.

STUDENT: Thank you for your answer.

TEACHER: May your life go well.

STUDENT: It seems to me that falling or not falling into cause and effect implies someone to fall and somewhere to fall.

TEACHER: You're halfway there. The first thing you said is absolutely true. When we begin to talk about falling or not falling, we're talking about somebody doing it. And falling or not falling someplace immediately implies separation. That is why I said that Baizhang should also have received five hundred years as a fox for his reply. We might have some compassion for Baizhang though, because every teacher has to get into the mud in the process of teaching. At a certain point in my training, it was embarrassing to talk to my teacher, because he knew and I knew that no matter what I said, it missed it. But Baizhang, just like all good teachers, was muddying himself for the sake of the old man who was locked in the life of a fox. For the sake of that old man and his monastics, Baizhang was stinking up Zen.

STUDENT: He shouldn't have agreed.

TEACHER: He didn't agree. He gave a turning word. He helped the old man, pointing out where he was wrong. But in the process of doing it, he tied himself into a knot. He entered the weeds of delusion out of his great compassion. You understand the first half; you should also understand the second half. And, once you understand that, I have another question. Why didn't Baizhang get to live five hundred years as a fox?

STUDENT: Why didn't he?

TEACHER: Yeah. Put the old man, now enlightened, in charge of the monastery and turn Baizhang into a fox? It's an interesting question. Anything else?

STUDENT: I see how I create cause and effect in my everyday judgments. How does that relate to responsibility?

TEACHER: When you realize responsibility for causality, you make yourself free. Prior to that time, it will seem like anything could be causing an event or creating a situation. But when you realize that you are responsible for the situations and the conditions of your life, it empowers you to do something about them. If you think that somebody else made you angry, it's their fault and the way you solve the problem is to say, "Please stop making me angry," or, "You made me angry; do something about it or else." But, in reality, nobody can make you angry. It's you who makes you angry. Once you clearly realize that, you can do something about it.

STUDENT: So, we bring it upon ourselves.

TEACHER: Exactly. Dogen said, "If you're the effect, you must also be the cause."

STUDENT: Thank you for your answer.

TEACHER: May your life go well.

STUDENT: A man who had been angry for much of his life was angry again today. He had a heart attack and died. Were the anger and the death two or one?

TEACHER: Were his past, his present, and his future three?

STUDENT: Fruit is not picked until it's ripe.

TEACHER: But is the fruit any different from the seed?

STUDENT: No, the seed is produced by the fruit and then the seed produces the fruit.

TEACHER: Are they any different?

STUDENT: No.

TEACHER: Does that answer your question?

STUDENT: Yes.

TEACHER: Anything else?

STUDENT: No.

TEACHER: Yet, the anger may not have had anything to do with his death.

STUDENT: I believe that it did.

TEACHER: Yesterday I was fit to be tied when, on five different occasions, people came through my bedroom ceiling while they were fixing the parsonage roof. I was angry but I didn't have a heart attack. But I also have seen incredibly angry people get heart attacks. Ask a doctor what the cause of a person's death was and she might say "cholesterol." A psychologist might say "stress." A nutritionist might say "a lousy diet—too much meat and not enough carrots." Everybody sees the truth in a different way. So the truth, or the cause and effect of that death, is not so clear or simple or linear. Understanding cause and effect has to do with understanding intimacy, as well as our reference system, the flaws in it, and how it evolves and changes from day to day, hour to hour, moment to moment. The minute you let go of the reference system and become the thing itself—whatever that is—there is a whole different reality to be seen. Whether the thing itself is the person who suffered a heart attack, the koan Mu, the cypress tree in the garden, the refugees in Kosovo, or your President—whatever the barrier or difficulty—your ways of perceiving it and seeing what needs to be done are turned inside out if you don't separate yourself from it. Responsibility takes on a quality and a dimension that cannot even be imagined when there is separation.

STUDENT: So back to Baizhang. Once he opened his mouth, karma was created.

TEACHER: Absolutely. Even before he opened his mouth, karma was created because body, mouth, and thought all create karma.

STUDENT: It was not a chain of events. It simply was.

TEACHER: In that moment, cause and effect were one.

STUDENT: Thank you for your answer.

TEACHER: May your life go well.

STUDENT: What is moral and ethical about the Zen precepts?

TEACHER: By definition the adjectives "ethical and moral" imply that the precepts function within a reference system. They are specifically designed to deal with the relative world of differentiation, but are grounded in the reality of the absolute, and arise from the point of view of no-self. They are a definition of the enlightened life. If you live the precepts, you live your life as a buddha. What makes them ethical and moral is that they create no-self. No-self creates no karma—no action and no reaction. No-self is not fixed in any place. It is not separated from the rest of the universe. When you realize no-self, that is all there is in the whole universe. The person who falls and is in pain is no one but yourself. You take care of the universe and all sentient beings as you would take care of your own body, because they *are* your body, they are your mind, they are your life itself. Because the precepts are relative, they are constantly changing. They are always to be understood in terms of time, place, position, and degree—the shifting attributes of the circumstances we encounter. What is acceptable at one time is not acceptable at another time. Sometimes it's unequivocally necessary to lie. If you don't, you violate the precept, "Do not lie." Every precept needs to be understood in terms of compassion and reverence for life, and in terms of the absolute nature of reality. This allows them to be incredibly flexible and relevant, as well as ethical and moral. The precepts are not given until a person is ready to receive them. In order to begin understanding their scope and subtlety, commitment to practicing them is necessary. You hear differently when you make a commitment. You can't hear the spiritual teaching of Buddhism unless you have a commitment to Buddhist practice. When you commit you begin to hear. Before that, the door is closed. The precepts teachings that I offer are for people who are already Buddhists. They haven't completed the ceremony, but they have committed themselves to a moral and ethical life. They are practicing the precepts already, so they are ready to receive them.

STUDENT: Thank you for your answer.

TEACHER: May your life go well.

STUDENT: The Buddha Way is unsurpassable; I vow to attain it.

TEACHER: How will you attain it?

STUDENT: I get up, I do zazen. Later in the morning I prepare breakfast.

TEACHER: But it's said that even Shakyamuni hasn't attained it.

STUDENT: This mountain is covered with foxes.

TEACHER: Who is the fox?

STUDENT: [Makes motions like a fox.]

TEACHER: What a strange fox! The Dharma is not bad, but the biology is way off. Anything else?

STUDENT: Thank you for your teaching.

TEACHER: May your life go well.

I don't feel like you gave me an opportunity to really push you into new territory. This was dharma shadow-boxing, not all-out combat. Bringing your personal experience to these encounters makes them sparkle and reverberate. We learn a lot when the questions are real, pertaining to the immediacy of our lives. That is why Zen teachers traditionally create problems where none exist. If they didn't, and everything remained smooth and harmonious, with tranquil and misty landscapes and twittering birds, then nobody would learn anything. Everybody would be self-satisfied. When there are no challenges, Zen teachers go around poking, pulling rugs out from under students' feet, squeezing heads, and churning things up. That's what is meant by "creating waves where none exist." Every time I ask a question, I'm creating waves where none exist. We should all be turned into foxes. But that is the occupational hazard of Zen teachers. You can't do this without creating an all-pervading stink of Zen. For that I apologize.

Engage all of your life as you would zazen. Don't be cautious. Throw yourself into it. That's where you learn. Our tendency is to go with what is familiar and safe. Yet, the familiar and the safe have nothing to teach. It's only the challenges of a new territory that have something to reveal to you. But it means risking something, taking a chance. It means living and practicing the edge, not backing away from it. In doing that we engage the incredible Dharma that is now available to us.

13
ENLIGHTENMENT IS DELUSION

Our current understanding of the physical universe, from the cosmological to subatomic scale, is highly developed and intricate. Yet, as highly developed as our scientific theories and experimental confirmations are, we continuously fail to comprehend the fundamental aspects of human existence and the basic nature of the human mind. We do not appreciate the reality, or even the possibility, of our enlightenment. In the *Flower Garland Sutra*, the Buddha says this about his own enlightenment:

> At that time, the Tathagata, with his unobstructed pure eye of wisdom, universally beheld all sentient beings throughout the universe and said, "How amazing, how amazing! How can it be that these sentient beings are fully endowed with the wisdom of the Tathagata and yet being ignorant and confused, do not know it, do not see it? I must teach them the Noble Path enabling them to be forever free from deluded thinking and to achieve for themselves the seeing of the broad and vast wisdom of the Tathagata within themselves and so be no different from the buddhas."

During one of his retreats at the Monastery Buddhist scholar Peter Gregory said the following concerning the relationship between Buddha's enlightenment and practice on a Buddhist path:

> Although the Buddha's enlightenment is the paradigm for sentient beings' experience of enlightenment, it must also be pointed out that what is meant by "sudden enlightenment" in Zen differs significantly from the enlightenment experienced by the Buddha, which all Buddhist traditions have characterized as

supreme perfect enlightenment: annutara-samyaksambodhi. Sudden enlightenment followed by gradual cultivation refers to initial awakening—only the first
stage in a process of spiritual cultivation. The Buddha's enlightenment, on the
other hand, would correspond to the final culmination of enlightenment.

In terms of training at Zen Mountain Monastery, the process leading to enlightenment can be understood in terms of the Ten Stages. In the third stage, we see the
nature of the self. Although that initial seeing is, in fact, realization, it is only a glimpse.
You know you saw something but its features are not fully distinguishable. By the
fourth stage the nature of the self is seen more clearly. It can be taken hold of. And it's
that taking hold of the self that is the basis of the *dharmakaya*, the absolute ground of
being. This view still needs to be refined, however, and this clarification process takes
place from the fifth to the eighth stage of training. In the eighth stage there is the
experience of *shunyata*—falling away of body and mind; not for a moment, not for a
day, not for a week, but a permanent falling away of a distinct self. What in the third
and fourth stage of training was only a glimpse now becomes the pure dharmakaya.
The ninth stage is the *sambhogakaya*—the body of bliss or the reward body. Then,
having finally attained the realization of the Tathagata—annutara-samyaksambodhi—
you return to the world in the tenth stage of *nirmanakaya*. Realization is now manifested as one's life, but no trace of enlightenment remains. The realized being looks
like any other person in the world. Her enlightenment carries no stink about it.
There's no smell of holiness. She is manifesting holy buddhahood in everything, yet
it cannot be detected. She is indistinguishable from all sentient beings.

By the Buddha's own realization, all sentient beings are perfect and complete
right from the beginning. Still, in the *Flower Garland Sutra* Buddha reiterates:

> Thus, although the experience of enlightenment is sudden, one must still engage
> in a long process of cultivation in order to remove the deeply-rooted seeds of the
> false view of the substantial self that has become ingrained over a period of innu-
> merable kalpas. Even though one suddenly realizes that the dharmakaya, the true
> mind, is identical with Buddha, still, since for innumerable kalpas one has delud-
> edly clung to the four elements as constituting oneself so that this view has
> become second nature and is difficult to do away with all at once, so, one must cul-
> tivate oneself on the basis of this experience of enlightenment. When one has
> reduced it and further reduced it until there is nothing left to reduce, then it is
> called the attaining of Buddhahood.

So, the question we need to address is what is the role of enlightenment in our
practice, its relationship to our lives. How do you understand enlightenment?

STUDENT: This enlightenment is really tired and fuzzy-headed. I don't know about this enlightenment. Is this what the Buddha meant?

TEACHER: What do you think?

STUDENT: Ah, the Buddha. The Buddha thinks so.

TEACHER: Fuzzy-headedness, clarity, pain, joy are all part of the realization of the Buddha. Someone asked me recently, since after realization there is still pain and suffering what is the point of practice and enlightenment? Parents who were having problems with their kids would still be having difficulties. The nuclear threat would still exist. The environment would still be polluted. If before enlightenment this is so and after enlightenment it is still so, what is the point of going through all this practice? That's a good question. We should all look at it very closely. Sometimes we feel so miserable that we think there is, after all, something to be said for "a short and happy life." How would you answer this question?

STUDENT: What's the purpose of practice? Is that the question?

TEACHER: Let me take the questioner's place. Here I am, in terrible pain. I'm working on my first koan, going to sesshins and pushing myself, hoping to become enlightened. Yet, from what I've read and heard, I understand that after I'm enlightened the pain is still going to be there. Enlightened people feel pain and die. Enlightened people have all of the human experiences unenlightened people have. In fact, there is no difference between the two and, furthermore, all of the world's problems are still there. The world doesn't change. So, what's the payoff of practice?

STUDENT: The payoff is in the doing of it. It's like fundraising—having to deal with people's reactions when you ask them for money, having to deal with the issue of money itself, and what it means to solicit others for it. The point, of course, is to raise money, but it's also the actual process of doing it; just doing it; being told "no" and still continuing.

TEACHER: But why?

STUDENT: There's no reason. You have to do it. If you don't have to do it, you don't have to do it.

TEACHER: That's a reasonable way of looking at it. But there's more to be said about it. Maybe other people can elaborate. Thank you for your answer.

STUDENT: Thank you for your teaching.

STUDENT: I read that we shouldn't try to get rid of evil thoughts because they're also part of enlightenment. At the same time, I thought that having evil thoughts could produce bad effects.

TEACHER: Where does it say you shouldn't try to get rid of evil thoughts?

STUDENT: Well, it doesn't say exactly not to get rid of them, but that evil thoughts are all part of enlightenment.

TEACHER: What does it mean to practice the breath? You sit in zazen and you start counting the breath. The intent is to stay with the breath; to let body and mind fall away. A thought pops up and you get wrapped up in the ensuing story line. In the meantime, while you're doing that, you've lost the breath. You're no longer in contact with your physical body and the breath. You're now caught up with a chain of thoughts. You notice that, acknowledge the thought, release it, and come back to the breath, beginning at "one." Each time you do that, you empower yourself. You know from your own experience that at first you can't get past "one," or you get past "one" and end up at "two hundred," realizing that you haven't stopped at "ten," when you were supposed to return to "one." But, after a while, you're able to get to "two" and then to "three," "four," "five," and eventually to "ten." Eventually, with practice, body and mind do fall away. You practice the precepts in the same way. There is "Realize self and other as one. Do not elevate the self and blame others." Yet, I find myself saying, "That asshole doesn't know how to hit the bell like I can hit it." There, you have done it! You broke the precepts! Practicing the precepts, first you acknowledge that. You acknowledge the fact that in breaking the precepts, you separate yourself from them. In breaking the precepts, you intensify the illusion that you and the person you just belittled are two separate entities. But after a while you take note of the fact that, actually, when they don't hit the bell right, *you* don't hit it right. You acknowledge this and come back to the precepts again. You return to the life of the Buddha. Five seconds later you're off again. Yet, when you practice those precepts, when you practice the breath, you practice the wisdom and compassion of the life of a buddha. That's the way you progress. That's the way you arrive. When the evil thoughts pop up, you acknowledge them. You know that they create karma, so you deal with it. You acknowledge it and let it go. Each time you do that, it is an expression of the enlightened life. The process is the goal.

STUDENT: Thank you for your answer.

TEACHER: May your life go well.

STUDENT: Is there something other than just doing what needs to be done?

TEACHER: It depends on how you see what needs to be done. If you're deluded, then what needs to be done is always seen in terms of the individual self and is self-centered. If you're not deluded, then what needs to be done has to do with everyone and the whole universe. These two views generate very different results. Both Gandhi and Hitler were doing what they thought needed to be done. Yet, their actions affected countless numbers of people in dramatically different ways. So there's more to it than just doing what needs to be done.

STUDENT: How can you be clear enough to do your best?

TEACHER: That's a different question than your first one. To do your best means to exert meticulous effort, to manifest oryoki—just the right amount. Just the right amount varies from person to person, from circumstance to circumstance. If you're not holding back, you're at that edge. That's different than just doing what needs to be done.

STUDENT: But how can you be clear on what to do, how to do it, and when?

TEACHER: It's always helpful to be tuned into your feelings, to cultivate the intuitive aspect of your consciousness. Some of us are more comfortable operating intellectually, using logic and rational analysis to understand and solve problems. Others function more in terms of their feelings or intuition. In general, our intuition tends to be more precise and immediate in getting a direct appreciation of the situation, although it, like the domain of our ideas, can also be deluded. As a person practices zazen and develops clarity, the intuitive aspect of their consciousness becomes more accessible and available. It appears along with the clear understanding of the nature of the self. Intuition enables you to function in the world spontaneously and out of that understanding. That's what I mean by clarity, as in "being clear on what you have to do."

STUDENT: Thank you for your answer.

TEACHER: May your life go well.

STUDENT: The purpose of enlightenment is to be selfless and devoted to the service of all of humanity. That's a very distant goal for me. I give to my family but to no one else.

TEACHER: Maybe you can appreciate it in terms of your family. When you make yourself empty you allow yourself to express compassion. When you express compassion, you're experiencing the pain of the other person as your own. I used to hate face-to-face teaching. I loved to sit zazen and could really get lost in my sitting. Sesshins were wonderful, but during sesshin I was expected to go in to do interview with the teacher. I knew that my head would get squeezed. I really hated that interruption even though I always learned something from the exchanges. I remember the anguish of working with the koan Mu—the desperation of wanting to see it, the endless rejections. Then finally seeing it, and after that having to do more koans. I used to live for the day when all that crap would be over; I'd be enlightened and I'd never have to do another koan again. What happened instead is that now I go through the same agony with every student that works on Mu. I want them to see it more than I ever wanted it for myself. I want them to see it so badly that I would feed it to them if I could. I would do anything for them. It's that painful. Every time a person comes to dokusan I think to myself, "Are they going to see it this time?" Then, when they don't, I feel worse than they feel. And that's only the first koan. And there are several hundred students! It's a hopeless continuum of precisely what I wanted to get rid of. I'm still experiencing pain, whether it's somebody else's pain or my own. Pain is still pain. So why do it? Why practice?

STUDENT: You get to a point when you don't evade the discomfort. You actually create it or at least you receive it naturally.

TEACHER: Yes. That's what it boils down to. There are no choices, anymore than you can choose to take your next breath.

STUDENT: I've noticed that pain is almost constant. It's always here or just around the corner. If I accept it and make friends with it, it's easier to handle.

TEACHER: Pain always occurs in reference to no pain. When you stand back from it, you will always have something to compare it to, but when you are the pain itself there is no longer a reference system. When you are the barrier itself, the barrier is no longer there. When you are the koan, you've seen it. To see it means to forget the self. In a sense, when you're totally in pain, there's no pain.

STUDENT: When I notice that I've improved in this or that, there's the "Hurrah!" and that's usually a problem.

TEACHER: That's the illusion of the goal. But you also have to be careful of not withdrawing and settling into numbness. To make yourself numb is another way of not feeling pain. There are a lot of numb people in this world, walking the streets with vacant, lifeless eyes. They're not living their lives anymore. They're just barely existing. That's not the same as not attaching to a goal.

STUDENT: Thank you for your answer.

TEACHER: May your life go well.

STUDENT: Is the difference between someone realized and someone deluded that the realized person is always in the moment, with no hindrances in their life?

TEACHER: How can you be any place other than where you are? Show me "not being in the moment."

STUDENT: [Silence.]

TEACHER: You can't do it. That's why the slogan, "Be here now" is so utterly ridiculous. How can you be anywhere else? No, the difference must be something else. Or maybe there is no difference. Do you remember the Tenth Grave Precept—"Experience the intimacy of things; do not defile the Three Treasures?" Do you know what that means?

STUDENT: Do not speak ill of the Three Treasures.

TEACHER: Do you know how to do that?

STUDENT: To say you are the Three Treasures?

TEACHER: To say that is to proclaim the truth. To defile the Three Treasures means to give rise to the thought that there is a difference between buddhas and ordinary beings. Just to give rise to that thought violates that precept. The fact is that there is no difference between the two.

STUDENT: Then why do we strive?

TEACHER: Do you know the story about the Ugly Duckling? The Ugly Duckling was perfect and complete, but he felt miserable. There was nothing he needed to do but he was looking for something. He was looking for perfection, not knowing that he was already perfect. When he realized that he was a swan all along and that there was nothing wrong with his color, beak, honk, or anything else—that he was indeed perfect—all the pain disappeared. If you are an observer looking at the Ugly Duckling after his realization, you see everything happening just as it did before his enlightenment, but the Ugly Duckling is living in a very different way.

STUDENT: In a different reference system?

TEACHER: No reference system. The self is the reference system. That is the illusion. Get rid of the self and what do you have? The whole universe. Forget the self. Every atom, every color, everything past, present, and future. But there's no longer a bag of skin separating you from it. Actually, there's no bag of skin right now, even though you think there is. Anything else?

STUDENT: Thank you for your answer.

TEACHER: May your life go well.

STUDENT: The measurement of enlightenment—how fast or slow we get there— is not a good use of the mind. It's just rambling ideas.

TEACHER: What is a good use of the mind?

STUDENT: To take a line from Dogen and meditate on it; to allow it to touch you deeply.

TEACHER: Isn't that just ideas rambling around?

STUDENT: It's the level of involvement that makes the difference between real understanding or empty repetition.

TEACHER: That's more ideas about levels, about deep and shallow. We were talking about the challenge of realizing ourselves within a universe where there is pain and suffering. You were born into this catastrophe. Your birthright includes nuclear threat, pollution of the atmosphere, millions of starving people, imminent wars, ethnic cleansing, as well as the satisfaction of intimate relationships, the joy of good health, and accomplishments at work. All of that is part of your existence. The question is, how do you deal with all of that? What's your responsibility? How can you take care of this life and how can you help other people?

STUDENT: We must approach everything with love and understanding.

TEACHER: But the Third Ancestor of Zen says in the *Faith Mind Sutra* that love is just another delusion. He stresses, "When love and hate are *both* absent, then the Way is clear and undisguised." The minute you create love, you create hate.

STUDENT: You're using a particular definition of love. I don't mean it that way.

TEACHER: This applies to any kind of love. Love is always opposed to hate.

STUDENT: No, it's not. Not when it accepts all things.

TEACHER: The minute you have "acceptance" and "all things," you have separation.

STUDENT: What do you mean by "separation?"

TEACHER: You have a self. You need a self in order to accept something.

STUDENT: I'm using language to describe, just as you are.

TEACHER: Language is always used to describe. And language is always dualistic. The moment you say "enlightenment," that's dualistic, because on the other side of enlightenment is delusion. The moment you say "buddhas," there are "ordinary beings." The moment you say "up," there's "down." There's no way to avoid it. And it doesn't mean those realities don't exist. But are you and I the same or are we different?

STUDENT: [Silence.]

TEACHER: You and I are exactly the same thing, and yet I'm not you and you're not me. Both of these statements are true. If you only see that you and I are the same thing and cannot see that I'm not you and you're not me, you've got a problem. Or if you can only see that you and I are not the same and cannot see that we are exactly the same, you've got a problem. Zen practice is the integration of both of these polarities. So, when love and hate are both absent, when both extremes are let go of, the way is clear and undisguised. Yet, there is love and there is hate, and the minute you create love, you create hate.

STUDENT: It's possible to step out of the dichotomy of thought.

TEACHER: How?

STUDENT: I don't judge who is evil; I don't judge who is good.

TEACHER: Isn't judging in the realm of dichotomies?

STUDENT: It's a way to use language! And there is a difference between an

Einstein and someone struggling with "one plus one equals two." You're not ready to accept that difference and so our discussion goes on like this.

TEACHER: I am willing to accept the difference. That's why we have academic study.

STUDENT: I don't want to read someone who is having trouble with "one plus one equals two." I want to read Einstein.

TEACHER: Who are you reading that has trouble like that?

STUDENT: The people who are commenting on how we get enlightened, creating all these artificial complications.

TEACHER: I see. You don't approve of Peter Gregory? How about the *Flower Garland Sutra* itself?

STUDENT: I haven't gotten to that yet. I probably wouldn't like it.

TEACHER: I think you will find it a lot more complicated than Peter Gregory's commentary on it. And that sutra is supposedly the Buddha's own words.

STUDENT: If all he can do is decide whether enlightenment is fast or slow, and take twenty pages to write badly about it?

TEACHER: He's not deciding. He's simply commenting on the different schools of Buddhism. There are people who are interested in that.

STUDENT: I think if he was really interested, he would have done it differently.

TEACHER: You should do it then.

STUDENT: No, I don't think that's a good use of the mind.

TEACHER: Getting back to your original statement then, show me a good use of the mind.

STUDENT: [Silence.]

TEACHER: Silence doesn't reach it. That's another dead end. How do you do it without silence and without speech?

STUDENT: Without silence and without speech?

TEACHER: Right. It's neither speech nor silence, neither enlightenment nor delusion, neither love nor hate. When you see it you can express it. You see annutara-samyak-sambodhi. That's what the Buddha is talking about in the *Flower Garland Sutra*. Zen is the middle way. The minute you say, "This is right and this is wrong," you have problems. And when you say, "This is right and this is right," or "This is wrong and this is wrong," there are problems.

STUDENT: Understanding is not to be stupid. It is to differentiate but not to judge. It is to see but not to injure. It is to distinguish but not to cast aside.

TEACHER: These are wonderful words, but I want you to show me. That's what this boils down to: neither speech nor silence. It's not words, not concepts. Show me the living reality itself. When you show it, you show the life of a buddha.

STUDENT: I'm afraid the way I live is far from it.

TEACHER: Keep in mind that you always show the life of a buddha. Anything else?

STUDENT: Thank you for your answer.

TEACHER: May your life go well.

STUDENT: Ever since we began doing the pledge drive, I've been wondering why I practice. When I found out that I was going to be on the phone asking people for money, I died inside. What I encountered over these past couple of weeks though, is that even with all of the rejections, it's becoming a little bit more okay. In the beginning I wasn't really into it that much. Now I actually prefer the rejections to the donations because then I get the chance to stay with that person a bit longer, to get to know them, practicing patience throughout the conversation.

TEACHER: I know what you're saying. When I first saw pictures of monastics in Japan doing begging for alms, I thought to myself, "It is stupid to put on your robe and a silly hat to run around begging with a bowl. So they get a little bit of rice. They don't need the rice. That's not supporting the monastery. Why are they doing it?" It's easy to comment on something you're not doing yourself. I should have put the hat on and gone out with the rice bowl, then criticized the practice. You said you died inside when you found out you were going to be doing the fundraising. If you had really died—not just inside but completely— then there could be no rejection. When the self no longer exists, then there can't be any successes or failures. There is only the other person. When giver and receiver merge, there is no giving and there is no receiving. That's the essence and function of compassion. That's why real giving is *dana paramita*, perfection of giving, the wisdom of the other shore.

STUDENT: They're giving to us but . . .

TEACHER: That's the flaw in your way of understanding it. You're giving and they're giving. You're receiving and they're receiving. That's what's happening. I'm teaching; you're learning. You're teaching; I'm learning. If that's not happening, the process is one-sided and it isn't really working. If I were doing that in my teaching, if I were just giving you something, I would be ripping you off. You can't truly give without receiving and you can't receive without giving.

STUDENT: Getting back to why I practice and the issue of payoff, all I know now is that doing what I dreaded like crazy, when I threw myself into it, I felt more alive.

TEACHER: Thank you.

STUDENT: I have a problem with intellectualizing everything. I'm even afraid of reading now, because I don't want to add more fuel to an already out-of-control fire.

TEACHER: What happens when you don't read?

STUDENT: I just practice.

TEACHER: What does that mean? What kind of practice? Does it include liturgy, meditation, academic study?

STUDENT: Practice in ways that I can. Sometimes just reading, or just thinking. For me it's hard to just think.

TEACHER: Do you know how just not to think?

STUDENT: Not right now.

TEACHER: The problem is we're always thinking. Whether we're studying or not studying, we're constantly thinking. When people start looking at their thoughts, they are usually shocked. What they encounter is white noise—pure gibberish and little clips of nonsense. The unmitigated stream of consciousness. The mind hops from one thing to another, on and on and on. That's what we do all the time. Even when Master Dogen says, "Think non-thinking," isn't that a thought? Isn't working with your breath in zazen a thought? Master Keizan said, "Sweep as you may, you'll never empty the mind!" What is he telling us?

STUDENT: I'm going to have to do it.

TEACHER: Why?

STUDENT: [Laughs.]

TEACHER: Because I said so?

STUDENT: [Silence.]

TEACHER: Look at that. Anything else?

STUDENT: Thank you for your answer.

TEACHER: May your life go well.

∞

STUDENT: My question relates to work. Please help me see how working hard to get approval is to miss my buddha nature. I feel compelled to work hard. Is there a way of working hard towards perfection that recognizes that we are perfect?

TEACHER: It depends on who the approval is coming from, whether or not you're separating yourself from your buddha nature. If you're looking for the approval outside of yourself, that in itself separates. If you recognize that you are totally responsible and that the approval comes from you, then you are verifying your buddha nature. How can you work so that you're really doing a good job and at the same time not being caught up in the goals? Thich Nhat Han says that there are two ways to wash the dishes. One way to wash the dishes is to have clean dishes. The other way to wash the dishes is simply to wash the dishes. Essentially that means, do what you're doing while you're doing it. The activity itself, moment-to-moment, is the complete perfection. The moment you get ahead of yourself, or behind yourself, you're missing it. When you look outside of yourself, outside of the moment, you miss it.

STUDENT: Outside of the moment, outside of the situation or whatever is in front of me?

TEACHER: When you pull back from a situation, separate yourself from it, recognize that it is nothing but the self. You practice work the way you practice any barrier. Be the barrier, be the koan, be the breath, be your work.

STUDENT: Thank you for your answer.

TEACHER: May your life go well.

STUDENT: Why practice? That's a good question. I sure don't know.

TEACHER: How do you practice "Desires are inexhaustible"?

STUDENT: God, would I like a cigarette!

TEACHER: How do you put an end to "Desires are inexhaustible?"

STUDENT: [Holds her breath.]

TEACHER: And how do you practice "The dharmas are boundless; I vow to master them?"

STUDENT: I get up in the morning, walk my dog…

TEACHER: How about "The Buddha Way is unsurpassable; I vow to attain it?"

STUDENT: [Loudly.] I really want a cigarette.

TEACHER: [Laughs.] Thank you for your answer.

Zen is a lifetime practice. To realize oneself is the beginning. Actually, the very beginning is to raise the bodhi mind, to take that first step and say, "I want to experience the truth of my life," or to ask the questions, "Who am I?" "What is life?" "What is death?" That step contains all the stages of a spiritual journey, from the beginning to the realization of annutara-samyaksambodhi. It contains all the fifty-three stages of the bodhisattva. It's like pregnancy. You're either pregnant or you're not. The moment you're pregnant, implicit in that pregnancy is the totality of a human life and the lives that will follow that life, and all of the phases of growth and development from embryo to full adulthood and death. Raising the bodhi mind works in the same way. It contains the totality. So you don't wait until you've experienced annutara-samyaksambodhi to help people. You do it even though you stumble through it. You don't wait until you've realized yourself to put an end to desires. You immediately start working on putting an end to them. You immediately practice the precepts. You don't wait until you've received them formally to start practicing them. That very first awareness is the totality of anuttara-samyaksambodhi. In a sense, the way of looking at gradual or sudden, realized or unrealized, sentient beings or rocks, doesn't make any difference. Annutara-samyaksambodhi, supreme enlightenment, is the enlightenment of this very mountain, of the people who live on it, of deer, trees, and rivers. All of it is the mind of the Buddha. All of it is constantly teaching, constantly speaking the Dharma, whether we realize it or not. That's our life. When we realize it, then our life manifests the life of a buddha. But whether we realize it or don't realize it, our life manifests the life of a buddha. If it doesn't make any difference—if before you're enlightened and after you're enlightened the same things are going on in the world—why practice? The person that asks that question hasn't really taken that first step. When you've taken that first step, you realize that there is no choice, no choice whatsoever.

When you realize the nature of the self, you realize the nature of the universe. Your whole way of perceiving yourself and the universe is completely transformed. This allows you to realize your own strength, and it allows you to impart strength to others, and there is no choice in the doing of that. To realize yourself immediately reveals the fact that there was never a distinction between yourself and all sentient beings. That's what the Buddha realized: all sentient beings are enlightened. He realized that he was all sentient beings, the whole catastrophe, all of it. It excludes nothing—not a single molecule, not a most distant galaxy. And he realized that when you affect one speck of dust in this universe, you affect the entire universe— past, present, and future. That's the *Flower Garland Sutra*. That's what we need to transmit into the twenty-first century if we, all species and this planet, are to survive.

14
JUST AVOID PICKING AND CHOOSING

A monastic once visited Master Zhaozhou. He quoted the opening lines from the *Faith Mind Sutra* of the Third Patriarch, "The Great Way is not difficult; only avoid picking and choosing," and then asked, "What is it that is not picking and choosing?" Zhaozhou said, "Between heaven and earth I alone am the World-Honored One." The monastic challenged, "That's picking and choosing." Zhaozhou responded, "Asshole! Where is the picking and choosing?"

Picking and choosing are the workings of the discriminating mind. They have to do with gain and loss, aversion and attachment, as well as the separation of self and other. According to the *Faith Mind Sutra*, the Buddha Way is not difficult if you avoid picking and choosing, gain and loss—all of the dualities. The monastic wanted to know what in the universe didn't fall into the realm of discrimination; how dualities could be avoided. He was asking for instruction from Zhaozhou but he was also testing the teacher. Zhaozhou, very kindly, answered the monastic, "Between heaven and earth, I alone am the World-Honored One." The monastic didn't accept that answer, saying that it also was a dimension of picking and choosing. Zhaozhou's reply to that was very strong: "Asshole! Where is the picking and choosing?" The monastic fell silent.

In our everyday life there is a constant stream of apparent picking and choosing. How can we get from one side of the street to the other without discrimination? Isn't zendo discipline picking and choosing? How can we avoid it? Who is it that is not picking and choosing? Zhaozhou said, "Between heaven and earth I alone am the World-Honored One." He answered the question. From where he stands picking and choosing cannot happen. How is that? What was Zhaozhou talking about? In your practice, how do you avoid picking and choosing? In your life, when do you pick and choose, and when do you not? What is the difference?

STUDENT: A leaf floats down a stream. When there's no self there's no picking or choosing.
TEACHER: That's a nice philosophy. What does it mean? I don't understand.
STUDENT: [Kisses the teacher.]
TEACHER: Thank you, that was nice. Is that picking and choosing or not picking and choosing?
STUDENT: That depends on how you look at it.
TEACHER: How do you look at it?
STUDENT: [Silence.]
TEACHER: It's a simple question. You kissed me on the cheek. Was that picking and choosing or not?
STUDENT: No.
TEACHER: And if you were picking and choosing how would it be?
STUDENT: [Silence.]
TEACHER: You need to see that side. May your life go well.

STUDENT: I apologize for my outburst in the zendo this morning, and for disturbing the harmony of the Sangha.
TEACHER: Thank you. I appreciate that. I appreciate you.
STUDENT: When I lose my temper like this, is this picking or choosing or not?
TEACHER: You tell me.
STUDENT: SHUT UP!
TEACHER: Thank you for your answer.

STUDENT: "Jori, do you think I want to be sitting here arguing with you about your homework? I would much rather be sitting zazen."
TEACHER: Zhaozhou said, "I alone am the World-Honored One." What did he mean?
STUDENT: I don't know what he meant since I alone am the World-Honored One.
TEACHER: May your life go well.

∞

STUDENT: I want to do what I want to do and you can't keep me from doing it.

TEACHER: What is that?

STUDENT: That's what I feel like saying, and that's definitely picking and choosing.

TEACHER: It most definitely is. Can you see why?

STUDENT: I'm setting up a barrier between my likes and dislikes.

TEACHER: In a sense, Zhaozhou is doing that, too. Whatever Zhaozhou did would have been picking and choosing. So, how come we say it was not picking and choosing? Carole says kissing me on the cheek is not picking and choosing, but kissing me on the cheek *is* picking and choosing. What's the difference? When is an activity picking and choosing and when is it not? When are you discriminating and when aren't you?

STUDENT: I don't know.

TEACHER: This is critically important. Zhaozhou was coming from the absolute point of view. The monastic was coming from a relative point of view. If you're standing in the relative domain, everything that you see is in terms of the relative. Picking and choosing are functioning. But from the absolute point of view, there can't be any picking and choosing. In order for picking and choosing to manifest, there needs to be something separate from you. When the monastic asked his question, "What's not picking and choosing," Zhaozhou pointed to the absolute. He told him, "I alone am the Honored One." That may sound like an ego-trip but it's exactly the opposite. Zhaozhou was verifying the enlightenment statement of Shakyamuni Buddha, "Between heaven and earth, I alone am the World-Honored One." There is nothing outside of Zhaozhou. He contains the totality of the universe. Every star, every sound, every color, is nothing but himself. How could there be picking and choosing? How could there be gain and loss? How could there be a beginning and an end, birth and death? The monastic didn't get it and continued, "That's picking and choosing." At this point Zhaozhou became more direct.

STUDENT: But what do I need to do to get to that point of not picking and choosing?

TEACHER: You can forget the self. But what does "forget the self" mean?

STUDENT: [Silence.]

TEACHER: To study the Buddha Way is to study the self. To study the self is to forget the self. To forget the self is zazen. May your life go well.

STUDENT: Thank you for your answer.

STUDENT: At this moment, is there anything to pick and choose?
TEACHER: It depends on what "this moment" means to you. It's easy to say, "this moment." It's quite another thing to be totally immersed in this moment. We can make ourselves numb in order to avoid really experiencing ourselves and our lives. It is possible to be here and not even know that you're here and alive. "Being in the moment" is a very nice and reassuring idea, but what does it mean?
STUDENT: That's it?
TEACHER: That's it.
STUDENT: Thank you for your answer.
TEACHER: May your life go well.

STUDENT: There is deciding and not deciding, yet you once said that they are the same. What's the same?
TEACHER: Deciding and not deciding.
STUDENT: Who says that?
TEACHER: Daido. Not only are deciding and not deciding the same; heaven and earth are the same. Good and bad are the same. You and I are the same.
STUDENT: That's being stuck in enlightenment.
TEACHER: If I stick in enlightenment that's being stuck. When Zhaozhou said, "I alone am the World-Honored One," we could say that he was stuck in enlightenment. But he wasn't stuck anywhere. The monastic just needed to probe a bit to find that out.
STUDENT: How?
TEACHER: ASSHOLE! THAT'S A STUPID QUESTION. Do you see the difference? "Between heaven and earth, I alone am the World-Honored One" means there's nothing outside of me. When there's nothing outside of me, left and right are the same thing, up and down are the same thing. What's to be found outside of me? When I strike out and shout as Zhaozhou did, "Asshole!" I separate and the relative is manifested. You and I are the same thing. You say I'm stuck in enlightenment. I'm not you and you're not me. You say I'm stuck in the relative. Being stuck is when you don't move, when you can't move. But when you're free to move, there's no sticking. In fact, because there's no picking and choosing, I pick and I choose. Do you understand?
STUDENT: Thank you for your answer.
TEACHER: May your life go well.

STUDENT: I call it David.

TEACHER: What do you call David?

STUDENT: Between heaven and earth I alone am the World-Honored One.

TEACHER: It's sufficient to just say, "I alone am the World-Honored One." Why are you calling it David?

STUDENT: Because you told me to.

TEACHER: That's picking and choosing. What is it when it's not picking and choosing?

STUDENT: DAVID!

TEACHER: That's only half. What's the other half?

STUDENT: You don't know what you're talking about.

TEACHER: Better, but there's still a little bit to go.

STUDENT: Very enervating.

TEACHER: The other half of David is, "Where's the picking and choosing?" That's picking and choosing.

STUDENT: Thank you for your answer.

TEACHER: May your life go well.

15 NEITHER GOOD NOR EVIL

The reality of Zen is not to be found in either of the realms of absolute or relative. We come into Zen practice caught up in the phenomenal world and in differentiation. Through the practice of zazen, little by little, the mind gets quiet, and at some point, we see and experience for ourselves the absolute basis of reality—the experience of shunyata, the falling away of body and mind. But our practice doesn't end with shunyata. Emptiness is "no eye, ear, nose, tongue, body, mind." Somebody with "no eye, ear, nose, tongue, body, mind" can't function; they can't differentiate, so if they cross the street, they might get hit by a car. Obviously practice must go further. We call the phase of training after realization of the absolute "descending the mountain" training. We come back into the world, manifesting that which has been realized in our lives. And yet, when we really look at it—phenomena and differentiation are not it; the absolute basis of reality is not it. The truth can't be found in either of these extremes. So, the basic question remains, what is it? What is it that transcends the dualities of good and evil, up and down, absolute and relative?

There's a koan that deals with this question. The Sixth Ancestor was once being pursued by Monastic Myo. The Ancestor, seeing Myo coming, laid the robe and bowl on a stone and said, "This robe symbolizes faith. How can it be fought for by force? I'll leave it to you to take it." Myo tried to take up the robe, but it was as unmovable as a mountain. Myo was terrified and hesitated. He said, "I've come for the Dharma, not for the robe. I beg you, please teach me, lay brother." The Sixth Ancestor said, "Think neither good nor evil. At such a moment, what is the true self of Monastic Myo?" At this, Myo was at once enlightened. His whole body dripped with sweat. With tears, he made a bow and asked, "Beside these secret words and meanings, is there any further significance or not?" The Ancestor said, "What I have just told you is not a secret. If you will realize your true self, what is secret is in you yourself." Myo said, "Although at Obai I followed the other monastics in training, I did not awaken to my true self. Thanks to your instruction, which is to the point, I am like one who has drunk water and actually experienced himself whether it is cold or warm. You are really my teacher, lay brother." The Ancestor said, "If you are so awakened, both you and I have Obai as our teacher. Live up to your attainment with care."

Wumen, on making up a poem about this koan, said:

> You may describe it, but in vain,
> Picture it, but to no avail.
> You can never praise it fully.
> Stop all your groping and maneuvering.
> There is nowhere to hide the true self.
> When the world collapses, it is indestructible.

So, how do you think neither good nor evil? How do you transcend dualistic opposition? What is the truth that's not absolute and not relative? Indeed, what is truth itself? What is reality? What is God? Who are you? How will you know?

STUDENT: In the evening, this Monastic Myo is really fat. She eats up everything. She's so fat that when you crawl around on her you can't find her edges. But in the morning she wakes up hungry. Day after day: fat, hungry, fat, hungry. There's no end to it.

TEACHER: There's an end to it. This Monastic Myo hasn't found it. The Monastic Myo from the koan found it. What is the end of it? Night and morning— where do they come together?

STUDENT: Gobble, gobble, gobble, gobble, gobble.

TEACHER: Anything else?

STUDENT: Are you satisfied?

TEACHER: Are *you* satisfied?

STUDENT: Gobble, gobble, gobble, gobble, gobble, gobble.

TEACHER: What happened to "hungry in the morning"?

STUDENT: [Remains silent.]

TEACHER: Silence is stinky.

STUDENT: Uhm.

TEACHER: May your life go well.
STUDENT: Thank you for your answer.

STUDENT: You've pretty much completed your Zen training and have been transmitted to. I was wondering, do you know more or less than you did at the beginning of this journey?
TEACHER: First of all, I haven't completed my training, so let's put that to rest. Zen training never ends. Practice continues endlessly. The teacher may disappear at some point, but when that happens the whole phenomenal universe becomes a teacher. All of my students become teachers. What was the second part of the question? I have a very short memory.
STUDENT: Do you know more or less now than you did in the beginning?
TEACHER: During my formal training my teacher put a lot of time and effort in helping me be stupid. When I went to him with my koan presentations and would rattle off everything I read, he would say, "Daido, please try to be stupid."
STUDENT: Are you stupid?
TEACHER: I hope so.
STUDENT: But you're not sure.
TEACHER: I'm not sure.
STUDENT: When will you be sure?
TEACHER: I don't know.
STUDENT: You said that you're doing this dharma encounter as a practice for your upcoming ceremony, but I presume your practice is at the Fifth Rank of Master Dongshan. There's no practice at that rank. What are you doing then?
TEACHER: Fifth Rank of Master Dongshan doesn't exclude the other four ranks. Each rank contains all five. The first rank is nothing other than all five ranks, the second rank is all five ranks.
STUDENT: But what are you practicing for?
TEACHER: I don't know.
STUDENT: This is your practice, to—
TEACHER: If you say so.
STUDENT: You said so.
TEACHER: Oh, okay. [Both laugh.] So I'm practicing.
STUDENT: What are you practicing?
TEACHER: I'm practicing to be a good monastic for all of you when I do this ceremony.
STUDENT: So you're not a good monastic yet?
TEACHER: I don't think so, but I don't know.

STUDENT: What would make you a good monastic?
TEACHER: Beats me.
STUDENT: You got a lot of work to do.
TEACHER: Right. You too.

STUDENT: Zen is a teaching outside the scriptures, with no reliance on words
and letters. It's a direct pointing to the human mind. What would a Zen
Training Introductory Workshop be like if it were to truly exemplify this?
TEACHER: There were no Zen Training Workshops in Japan or China. Lay practitioners did not get involved very much in Zen training, and the training of the
monastics depended heavily on direct pointing. When a prospective monastic
arrived at a monastery, nothing was explained. In fact, they didn't even let the
monastic in. They made it difficult for him to enter training. Once he was in,
he took his position with all the other monastics and began the routine of
monastic life. Because everything he encountered was new, he made a lot of
mistakes. He didn't know how to wear a *kesa*, how to use his bowls, how to
chant. Everybody who got there even an hour before him was senior to him
and in a position to correct him. He would continuously hear, "You don't wash
the windows that way, you wash the windows *this* way." Constantly making
mistakes, constantly being corrected, in a very short period of time he became
an expert on maintaining awareness. Since nobody was explaining anything,
the only way he learned was to notice what everybody else was doing, and to
catch all the subtleties. His awareness developed and deepened. That's how he
learned, and he started working with a teacher in that context.
STUDENT: That's the essential and the fun aspect of Zen practice. When I started,
I was in residence for three months before I did a Zen Training Workshop.
Experience first, and then reflect on your experience.
TEACHER: I don't think many people in the West are ready for an introduction to
Zen that relies exclusively on experiential teaching. In order to enter training
that way a clear commitment to realizing oneself has to be in place. A lot of
people are looking into Zen practice for other reasons. In this culture, there is
a prevalent "quick-fix" mentality about spiritual practice. Americans are not
satisfied with pure experience. They want explanations. They want explanations even when they hear that the words and ideas that describe reality, miss
the reality itself. People persist in holding onto the paradigm of intellectual
understanding. So, there's actually a subtle danger in presenting Zen through
explanations. But these workshops also provide an entry into practice for
many people who would otherwise never taste Zen practice.

STUDENT: Couldn't it be the other way around: experience first and then?

TEACHER: We try to combine experience and explanations. Participants not only hear lectures, but they sit zazen, do work practice, chant and bow in liturgy. And even with all the explanations, there are still reactions to these experiences. We're a culture that has no Buddhist traditions and context. In beginning our practice, we have to sink a foundation.

STUDENT: Thank you for your answer.

TEACHER: May your life go well.

∞

STUDENT: I'm still hating the Catholic Church for handing me, at the age of seven, a booklet with one hundred and twenty questions and answers as to what I was all about.

TEACHER: I got the same book around that age, and I got into a lot of trouble because of it. And yet, I'm really grateful for that little book, because it precipitated my spiritual search. The first question in it was, "Who made the world?" The answer was, "God made the world." The second question was "Who made God?" "God always was, is, and will be, world without end. Amen." Or something like that. When I got to question number two, I asked the nun who was teaching the class, "How do you know?" I wasn't seven actually, but eleven. It was just before my confirmation and all hell broke loose. She answered, "You just know." And I persisted, "But how? I mean, have you ever seen God?" She said, "You're being insolent, Mr. Loori." I said, "Well, I need to know." In exasperation, she said, "Go see Father Santora," and chased me out of the room. Father Santora was outside playing softball with other kids. As I approached, he looked up and said, "Loori, are you here again? You've got a week to go before you get your confirmation. Why don't you just shut your mouth, sit in there and learn from Sister Assunta?" I went back but I was pissed. I knew I had to do confirmation—my mother and father wanted me to do it—but I was dissatisfied and decided to become an atheist right then and there. At the same time, I also started the process of asking and investigating these fundamental questions.

STUDENT: You didn't shut your mouth, though.

TEACHER: No, I never have. That's been my problem. It took some time to get a handle on it. But you seem to have learned not to shut yours, too.

STUDENT: I go through periods when I shut up for a while.

TEACHER: The great doubt, the questioning, is really the heart of our practice. Always keep asking. Keep doubting.

STUDENT: Thank you for your answer.

TEACHER: May your life go well.

STUDENT: There's a phrase that's been coming up for me a lot lately. It goes something like this, "Most people think that in the mundane there's nothing sacred."

TEACHER: Isn't that what Daido said?

STUDENT: That's what I'm saying. Okay, let me start again. Daido may have said that, but I'm saying this now: "Most people think that in the mundane there's nothing sacred, but what they don't know is that in the sacred there's nothing mundane."

TEACHER: The saying is actually a paraphrasing from Master Dogen: "There are those who understand that in the mundane there is nothing sacred. What they have not yet understood is that in sacredness there is nothing mundane."

STUDENT: The first part says that the way we discuss the Dharma and our common understanding are the realm of the mundane. The second part, "In the sacredness there is nothing mundane," says that looking at the clock it's getting late, and I have so many things to do today that I really can't tell you about this.

TEACHER: The way you're presenting it is rather indirect, a little wishy-washy, but it's okay. How could you say it straight out?

STUDENT: Thank you for your answer.

TEACHER: May your life go well.

STUDENT: Today I'm practicing Buddhism; tomorrow I practice Judaism. As a Buddhist, I don't feel conflict. As a Jew, I feel conflict and guilt. Which is the truth?

TEACHER: You're practicing Buddhism and you're practicing Judaism. Right there is the problem. You've got them separated. When you stop practicing Buddhism and Judaism, you'll find the truth.

STUDENT: Thank you for you answer.

TEACHER: May your life go well.

∞

STUDENT: I have a great deal of difficulty with words. They seem to cause a lot of separation. Frequently I don't know what to do with them.

TEACHER: What do you think you need the words for?

STUDENT: That's part of the problem. Ultimately, I don't see that the words are of any use.

TEACHER: That's understandable. Since you're a visual artist, your inclination would be toward communicating in other ways than words. But there are a lot of writers and poets in this room that would disagree. So what's the truth: your way of doing it or their way of doing it? What's the right way?

STUDENT: I can only give you my way; I can't give you the other one.

TEACHER: May your life go well.

STUDENT: Thank you for your answer.

STUDENT: I'm curious about the witness and where it fits in relation to my concept of myself, and in relation to the absolute and relative. How do I get rid of it?

TEACHER: The witness is the cardinal problem. The witness is what's constantly analyzing, categorizing, evaluating, and judging. People come into the dokusan room and say, "I've experienced the falling away of body and mind." I ask, "How do you know?" And I get all sorts of descriptions—the witness is still there watching the experience of falling away of body and mind. That's not it. So long as you're reflecting on it, it's not falling away of body and mind. The witness is nothing but those reflective thoughts. And when you let go of these thoughts, nobody's watching anymore. For most people, that's kind of scary. It requires trust. You have to trust yourself to let go. When the breath breathes itself, there's no witness. When you're doing something with the whole body and mind, there's no witness. The witness is the internal dialogue.

STUDENT: Thank you for your answer.

TEACHER: May your life go well.

STUDENT: Yesterday was a special day for insects. Summer was gone, autumn was coming. I saw some beautiful caterpillars. They were furry, brown in the center and black on the ends. I enjoyed seeing them as I walked to the monastery. When I walked back, I noticed one on the road. It wasn't moving. It was dead. I picked it up and put it to the side so it would wither with the leaves and the gravel, and I went on my way.

TEACHER: Any questions?

STUDENT: You asked about life and death.

TEACHER: Where is that caterpillar now?

STUDENT: The body is not alive.

TEACHER: Yes, but where is the caterpillar itself? Where will you be when your body withers and falls apart? What are you?

STUDENT: My life is not my body. My life is not Barbara.

TEACHER: An ancient master said, "When the world is destroyed, the true self is not destroyed." If it's not your body, then what is it?

STUDENT: [Pause.] It's life.

TEACHER: That's an explanation. What's the truth? Show me the true self.

STUDENT: [Pause.] I was going to show you the flower, but the flower is form.

TEACHER: You've shown it to me, but you don't know you've shown it to me. Thank you for your answer.

STUDENT: Thank you.

STUDENT: [Crying.] I feel more trapped than liberated by faith and doubt.

TEACHER: Faith and doubt are not yet liberation; they are going to bring you to liberation. Faith, doubt, and determination cut through all the stuff that you're struggling with. To realize yourself is to "break the rhinoceros horn of doubt." To make yourself completely free is to eradicate all doubt, to kill buddhas and ancestors and topple mountains and temples.

STUDENT: But I feel so unsure.

TEACHER: Everybody does. That's one of the motivations for spiritual practice. What happens when you practice? When you sit zazen, each time you let go of a thought and come back to the moment you empower yourself; you generate *joriki*, the power of concentration. It manifests as mental clarity, physical prowess, psychological stability, and emotional sensitivity. And you get all that from nobody else but yourself. Eventually, the joriki becomes strong enough to allow us to smash that great doubt, to penetrate all the questions to their bottom. But it's important to have the questions to begin with. The questions provide the cutting edge of the search and practice. Ultimately though, you throw it all away.

STUDENT: But sometimes I just don't know what is more real. Part of me feels wholeheartedly that this practice is for me, that you're my teacher and I want to be here now. Another part of me says maybe I'm not a Zen person; maybe I'm not?

TEACHER: And when you're absolutely sure that you're on the right path and I'm your teacher, I'll do everything in my power to convince you that you're not. This practice has to come forth from your own intention and power, not some idealized, romantic notion of it. I have nothing to give. I can't give you anything because you already have it.

STUDENT: How do I know whether what I have is real?

TEACHER: That's what you will have to discover for yourself. And first of all, you will need to understand what "real" means. What's real? Is this real? Are your ideas real? What is reality? Is your reality any different than my reality? Those are the questions that will bring you to the place called "peace of mind." So keep questioning, keep doubting. It doesn't need to be a struggle. Trust yourself. There's nothing else, no outside. There's only you.

STUDENT: Sometimes I hate you.

TEACHER: I know. Just doing my job. May your life go well.

STUDENT: This practice never ceases to amaze me; how everything seems to fit so well. After you talked about the need to trust yourself, I now seem to suffer from an inordinate amount of faith in myself. I think that I can do everything really well, including failing.

TEACHER: You're right.

STUDENT: Hmm.

TEACHER: Don't confuse faith and arrogance. There's a big difference between the two. Faith doesn't mean that everything's going to come out like you expected. When you have faith in somebody, it doesn't mean they're going to perform according to your expectations. Faith has nothing to do with expectation. Faith has to do with allowing things to be as they are, in giving yourself permission to succeed or to fail. It's no big deal. Either way is okay. Success doesn't blow off the top of your head; failure doesn't depress you. That's faith, that's trusting yourself. Arrogance, on the other hand, has to do with lack of confidence and fear. It's usually people who are frightened who are arrogant.

STUDENT: Thanks.

TEACHER: You're welcome. May your life go well.

STUDENT: When I first started practicing Zen, I had a lot of painful questions. Now, I don't have the answers, but the painful questions aren't there anymore. It seems that any time a question comes up, if I even ask you the question, then in some way I've missed it. It seems that what I have to do is just to let go of the questions somehow.

TEACHER: No, the questions need to be resolved. You need to understand that the answer comes from the same place that the question comes from. That doesn't mean throwing the questions away. That turns you into a mindless zombie.

STUDENT: I'm puzzled then about why, although I don't have any answers, the terrible pain that I used to have disappeared.

TEACHER: Maybe, if things are that comfortable, I have to squeeze your head more.

STUDENT: No. It's not like things are wonderful, but it seems that, most of the time, I can handle what comes up. I was crying on the phone yesterday, because a lot of people with whom I have been involved are dying. And I wasn't sure if it was okay to cry, because I interpreted from what you said that to be effective when you're working with people, you have to let go of the emotions.

TEACHER: What do you mean when you say let go? How do you let go of anger?

STUDENT: First I get really angry. But what I find is that, if I'm really aware, I can see the anger before it comes up.

TEACHER: When you're really angry, where's the anger?

STUDENT: [Shouts.] Fuck you!

TEACHER: Letting go doesn't mean suppressing. It means being it with the whole body and mind. Be the anger with the whole body and mind. Be the fear with the whole body and mind. When you cry, just cry with the whole body and mind. There's nothing wrong with crying. Since when has there ever been anything wrong with crying? And what makes you think that an Italian teacher would tell you that there is something wrong with crying? *Mama mia!* May your life go well.

STUDENT: Thank you for your answer.

STUDENT: Last night someone asked me what your teaching style is, and I said, "Sometimes meeooooww, sometimes ggrrrowwwll." What would you have said?

TEACHER: I don't know. My answer is very different from your answer, because I'm very different from you. I'm tall, you're short. I'm a tall buddha, you're a short buddha. If someone asked me about your teaching style, I would say, "Sometimes grrruummmbllle, sometimes hahahahahahaha." What would you have said?

STUDENT: I don't know.

TEACHER: May your life go well.

STUDENT: Thank you for your answer.

STUDENT: Sometimes I want to be a mystic and devote my life to cultivating sublime experiences. Other times I want to be a gambler because it's exciting and a bit dangerous. Sometimes I want to be an itinerant farm worker because the adversities of that kind of life seem like worthy barriers to cross. Sometimes I want to be a bum on skid row. Frankly, I don't care which one of these things I do as long as, when I'm doing one of them, I don't want to be doing something else. How does one accomplish that? How does one do something without wanting to do something else, without thinking that they should be doing something else?

TEACHER: Thinking about it is one thing; doing it is another thing. You're a seaman; how come? Despite all of the "sometimes this, sometimes that," that's what you did. How did you know what to do? What's the right way? Ultimately, it comes down to trusting yourself, with all of it. How do you pick a mate, try out all of the possibilities in the world? No. You trust yourself. You tune into yourself and you trust your instincts. They may turn out wrong, or they may turn out right, but either way, you trust yourself. It's the only way you can do it, anyway.

STUDENT: Okay.

TEACHER: Anything else?

STUDENT: Yeah, there is one other thing. I understand what you mean when you say that arrogance is lack of trust in oneself, but I don't understand when, in a particular field, people who are the best in that field are still arrogant assholes. If you're the best in the field and you know you're the best, and everyone else does too, how can you still lack confidence in yourself?

TEACHER: People are like that. Maybe they know something we don't know.

STUDENT: Thank you for your answer.

TEACHER: May your life go well.

∞

STUDENT: If we're not to distinguish between good and evil, how can there be right action?

TEACHER: Right action has to do with taking a precise hold of that question. For example, the precepts are what we call right action, and the precepts say, "Cease from evil. Do good. Do good for others." Those are the Three Pure Precepts. Then the Ten Grave Precepts tell you how to do that. Yet, those very precepts arise from a tradition that says, "Think neither good nor evil. At that moment, what's your true self?" That "think neither good nor evil. What's your true self at such a time?" is about the realization of the absolute basis of reality, the experience of "no eye, ear, nose, tongue, body, mind." That's one side of reality. There's another side, and that is where there *is* a body and mind. How do we resolve these apparent opposites? The precepts are that experience of no-self functioning in the world. Basically, right action is compassionate action. But what's compassion? It is the activity of wisdom.

Wisdom is the realization of no-self. Compassion is the action of no-self. Compassion happens the way you grow your hair. It doesn't require any effort. It's not necessarily a matter of doing good. Sometimes compassion may seem like an evil act. Kicking the crutches out from under someone and letting them walk under their own power can be a very compassionate act. It's not always doing good, and it has nothing to do with doing. Compassion is a very natural, effortless act. It comes out of no separation. The golden rule: "Do unto others as you would have them do unto you," when seen from the point of view of wisdom and compassion translates as, "What you do to others, you do to yourself." The act of compassion is really an act of self-centeredness, but that self now consumes the whole universe. It's the universe caring for itself, the same way the hand scratches the face when there's an itch. That's right action. But doing good misses it. And doing evil misses it.

STUDENT: Thank you for your answer.

TEACHER: May your life go well.

STUDENT: I'm hungry in the morning, and I'm hungry at night when I go to bed. I am hungry all the time. What should I do?

TEACHER: You should eat. What's keeping you from eating?

STUDENT: I eat and I'm still hungry.

TEACHER: Maybe you don't eat enough. You have to eat just the right amount.

STUDENT: I feel like there's food all around me. I take it in, and I still want more. I just crave knowing more.

TEACHER: Maybe what you want is not outside. The more you take in from the outside, the more you realize that it's not filling you. The more you look to me for your answers, the more disappointed you're going to be. Only you have the answers, not me, not the Buddha, not the ancestors. The teachings repeatedly warn you: don't put another head on top of the one you already have.

STUDENT: I often feel content with what I understand, and I have more than enough to do to work on my practice, and it's still not enough.

TEACHER: What are you looking for?

STUDENT: A spark. I feel too passive.

TEACHER: How long have you been practicing?

STUDENT: Four months.

TEACHER: Be patient. I'm going to give you more sparks than you can handle, when the time comes. Right now you really have to create a solid foundation. Be patient. Try not to be so greedy. You'll see it.

STUDENT: I feel like I'm running out of time.

TEACHER: Think you're going to die?

STUDENT: Well, someday.

TEACHER: Before you realize it?

STUDENT: I think that gets in the way.

TEACHER: The most important thing that you can realize is that what you're looking for is not out there. Chew on that for a while. If it's not out there, then what is it? Not *where* is it; *what* is it? Don't tell me. Show me. Show me the "it" that is not destroyed when the world collapses. [Pause.] Anything to say?

STUDENT: No. The words get in the way.

TEACHER: Don't give me words. Show me.

STUDENT: This, this.

TEACHER: This? Be specific. Point to it.

STUDENT: [Big gesture.]

TEACHER: That's dualistic. Point to it!

STUDENT: I'm all there is!

TEACHER: If you say so.

STUDENT: I say so.

TEACHER: May your life go well.

∞

STUDENT: When this body becomes all mind, does anyone polish the mind?

TEACHER: Body and mind are one reality to begin with. They're not two separate things.

STUDENT: So there's no one to polish the mind anymore.

TEACHER: What is it that you're polishing? Bring the mind to me. Let me see it. What is it? Where is it?

STUDENT: Next week I will complete my three months of residential training. Who is descending the mountain?

TEACHER: What do you say?

STUDENT: Who is going back to the city?

TEACHER: What do you say?

STUDENT: Thank you for your teaching.

TEACHER: May your life go well. [Pause.] This is a tough practice. No matter where you turn, it always comes back to you. When you realize that what you do and what happens to you are the same thing, you can't push off the responsibility on anybody else anymore. You have to take responsibility for your life. When you do that, you realize that you, and no one else, is the master of your life. That's why we say there are no Zen teachers, nor is there anything to teach.

STUDENT: Maybe that's why I'm so depressed lately. I'm really realizing that I'm responsible for my life, and there's really nobody else that's going to do it for me.

TEACHER: So instead of creating "depressed," why don't you create "happy?"

STUDENT: [Laughs.] That's a good question. How can I get to the bottom of why I tend to create "depressed" so much?

TEACHER: When depressed, really be depressed. Not only do you get to the bottom of it, you get to the place where it fills the whole universe, and there's no longer a reference system.

STUDENT: What about letting go, though, letting go of the thought of "I'm depressed?"

TEACHER: Really be depressed. That's the same as letting go. Who's going to let go of what? Is depression something other than you? Is it something that happens to you, or is it a manifestation of your own body and mind? Is your joy anything other than a manifestation of your own body and mind? You have the capacity to be either depression or joy. Empower yourself. Take charge. Life is not happening to you. It's what you do.

STUDENT: Thank you for your answer.

TEACHER: May your life go well.

STUDENT: I find that when the confusion of right and wrong comes up, I don't want to struggle, but would rather go to the answer that will make me comfortable. Also, I had a thought about the koan: perhaps the reason that Monastic Myo could not pick up the robe and bowls was that time was sewn into the lining of that robe.

TEACHER: What made the robe so heavy was his own doubt. But, concerning your first point, you say that you're looking for comfort and you want to get away from discomfort, and almost always, you have to get through discomfort to get to comfort. You struggle with ego in your zazen and the whole point of it is to realize the self, to free oneself from pain and suffering. That's definitely not easy. That freeing oneself of pain and suffering is basically the comfort that you're talking about. Sometimes there's no way to avoid the struggle along the way. Very few people that I know of in the history of mysticism, East or West, have realized it without some kind of a struggle. Unfortunately, struggle seems to be part of the process. Anything else?

STUDENT: No.

TEACHER: May your life go well.
STUDENT: Thank you for your answer.

STUDENT: Yesterday we contrasted Christian and Zen truths. We asked which is better; are they the same? Well, Zen truth is the truth. The only thing is that at night I can't find it, but in the morning [sings] "Bringing in the sheaves, bringing in the sheaves."
TEACHER: Yeah, I feel the same way about chocolate ice cream versus vanilla ice cream. There are a lot of people who think vanilla ice cream is the best, but there's no question about it: the best ice cream is chocolate. May your life go well.
STUDENT: Thank you for your answer.

Often we find ourselves looking for easy answers to complicated questions of life and death, good and evil, responsibility. In addressing these questions, we don't want to put our heads on the block, our asses on the line. Consequently, we resort to bowing to authority. We turn into a bunch of sheep. We don't want to struggle, we don't want to probe ourselves, we don't want to take the responsibility of finding out. We want to ask somebody and have them tell us. We want the irrevocable truth from high above. Zen practice is definitely not like that. It may appear like there is authority—the discipline, teachers, monasteries, ancestors—but when you really look at it, you will begin to see that it always turns you back to yourself. How do you know which is the right way? Trust. If you don't trust yourself, you can't trust anybody and anything. It starts with you. Again and again, throughout our lives we have to make decisions, and sometimes those decisions are contrary to what everybody else is doing. It may mean banging your head against the wall. But life is about taking risks, and being able to take risks is about trusting yourself. It's a precious gift to be born human. Most of us don't appreciate it. We're involved so deeply in our own personal drama that we don't see the beauty of our lives. Human life is an incredible gift. It's a shame to waste it. It doesn't need to be a struggle. To really put the matter of life and death to rest means to really go deep into yourself. Zazen is a practice that has to do with liberation, not with easy certainties. There is no rule book to go by. You have to delve deep into yourself to find the foundations of it, and then learn to live your life out of that which has been realized; not what you've been told, or what you believe or what you understand, but from your own direct experience. That's what "Give life to the Buddha" means.

16
THE MOUNTAINS AND RIVERS SUTRA

In the "Mountains and Rivers Sutra," Master Dogen uses the images of the mountains and rivers as a way of presenting the Dharma. For Dogen, the mountains and rivers themselves are a sutra. Sutras are the collected teachings of the Buddha, so in this chapter of the *Shobogenzo,* Dogen is saying that these mountains and rivers are the Buddha's teachings. We should see and receive them this way.

In this dharma encounter I would like to focus on a couple of key passages: "We should understand that the mountains are not within the human realm, nor within the realm of heaven." Dogen places the mountains in a very unique position. He doesn't want us to get confused by seeing them only as the mountains and rivers of everyday life. Then he says,

> From time immemorial the mountains have been the dwelling place of the great sages. Wise ones and sages have all made the mountains their own chambers, their own body and mind. And through these wise ones and sages, the mountains have been actualized. However many great sages and wise ones we suppose have assembled in the mountains, ever since they entered the mountains, no one has ever met a single one of them. There is only the actualization of the life of the mountains. Not a single trace of their having entered remains…
>
> …As for mountains, there are mountains hidden in jewels. There are mountains hidden in marshes. Mountains hidden in the sky. There are mountains hidden in mountains. There is the study of mountains hidden in hiddenness. An ancient buddha has said, "mountains are mountains, and rivers are rivers." The meaning of these words is not that mountains are mountains, but that mountains are

mountains. Therefore we should thoroughly study these mountains. When we thoroughly study the mountains, this is the mountain training. Such mountains and rivers themselves spontaneously become wise ones and sages.

What does it mean that mountains are hidden in jewels, hidden in marshes, hidden in the sky, hidden in mountains? What does it mean to thoroughly study these mountains? What is the mountain training?

In his writings, Dogen uses certain words both to refer to a particular object, and as a metaphor for something else. So a mountain is a mountain the way we usually understand it, and it is also a metaphor for the relative. Sometimes he uses different metaphors in the same paragraph, making the text very poetic and subtle.

In this sutra he generally uses mountains as a symbol for phenomena, existence, form. Water is a symbol for emptiness, formlessness. But because in Zen form and emptiness are completely interpenetrated, because there is the identity of the relative and the absolute, the mountains and rivers present both form and emptiness. When we speak of form, it contains emptiness. When we speak of emptiness it contains form. When we speak of mountains they contain rivers. When we speak of rivers they contain mountains.

Although much of Dogen's teachings sound confusing, he is not making anything up. He's describing the reality of our lives. He is describing the nature of the universe. Throughout the sutra he shifts his perspective, from existence in emptiness, to emptiness in existence, to the fundamental unity of both. He examines the relativity between subject and object. He is interested in obliterating the notions that things are just as one views them, that emptiness is nothingness, that permanence is constant, that impermanence is annihilation.

The phrase "mountains are mountains" can be traced back to various sources. Master Wumen used to say, "Monastics, do not have deluded notions. Heaven is heaven, earth is earth, mountains are mountains and rivers are rivers, monastics are monastics, and lay practitioners are lay practitioners." Another master said, "Thirty years ago, before I had studied Zen, I saw mountains as mountains and rivers as rivers. Later, when I had more intimate knowledge I came to see mountains not as mountains, and rivers not as rivers. But now that I have attained the substance, I again see mountains just as mountains, and rivers just as rivers." When Dogen says "mountains are mountains" he is not referring to them in the ordinary way. He is talking about mountains as being the nature of all dharmas, and he is talking about water as the water of the Buddhadharma. And for Dogen, mountain training means a sense of devotion to the study and practice of the Way.

What does it mean to you? What does it mean to you to thoroughly study these mountains?

STUDENT: In your introduction, you clarified that the rivers represent the absolute and the mountains the relative aspects of reality. Yet, as I read the sutra, everything gets very intertwined. It feels like a koan. These teachings don't readily jump out at me. It seems that to really study Dogen you have to do concentrated zazen with his writings.

TEACHER: That's true. It's true of all sutras, for that matter. Take the lines that we chant daily in our liturgy: "Form is emptiness. Emptiness is form." "Absolute and relative are like the foot before and the foot behind in walking." "Darkness within light, light within darkness." What does that mean? These teachings are koans. They can be comprehended intellectually, and many scholars have offered interpretations of them, but they can also be seen as a direct pointing of the Dharma. That's the way Dogen intended them to be received. Indeed, the "Mountains and Rivers Sutra" is a koan. So, how do you take up the koan of the mountain training?

STUDENT: What is your name?

TEACHER: Can you do better than that?

STUDENT: I'm hungry. I didn't have any breakfast.

TEACHER: Is your complaining about hunger the way you do the mountain training? Say it so that everybody can understand it. Don't hide in Zen jargon.

STUDENT: Okay, okay. Today at two-thirty I'm going to drive back home to Greenfield and get ready for work tomorrow. It's what I have to do.

TEACHER: Be aware of how you do it. May your life go well.

STUDENT: Thank you for your answer.

STUDENT: How can I save all sentient beings in the mountains and rivers?

TEACHER: I mentioned right at the beginning that mountains are form, the world in which you live. To be in the mountains is a flower opening in the world, and whether you realize it or not, you're that flower. Do you understand? The "mountains" are another expression for the world. A flower opening in the world is realization in the world, and to realize oneself in the world is to save all sentient beings. In order to save all sentient beings you need to be saved by all sentient beings. That is, you and all sentient beings become one reality. It doesn't mean that you busily run around doing good. It means that you identify totally with all sentient beings, and then what needs to happen happens. May your life go well.

STUDENT: Thank you for your answer.

STUDENT: If my job is mountains, and my car and my apartment are mountains, is my attachment to these mountains here, literally and physically, an attachment I have to get over?

TEACHER: All attachments are attachments you have to get over. Who is attaching to what? Do you see the basic stupidity in attaching? If you and the ten thousand things are one reality, who will attach to what? When you attach to something you create an illusion of separation. That's simply not true.

STUDENT: Then, why do I feel more satisfied coming to an Apple Blossom Sesshin than an Orange Rind Sesshin?

TEACHER: You're attached.

STUDENT: Thank you for your answer.

TEACHER: May your life go well.

STUDENT: I've read this sutra about thirty times, in six different translations, and I haven't the faintest idea what Dogen is talking about. There are parts, though, that really strike me. They're mysterious and they really draw me into Dogen's reality, making me want to find out what he's talking about. You mentioned one of these lines in your introduction: "Although mountains belong to the nation, they belong to the people who love them," or something like that. What is Dogen talking about there?

TEACHER: He said, "Mountains don't belong to the country; they belong to those who love them."

STUDENT: What mountains?

TEACHER: Any mountains.

STUDENT: I don't see what he's saying.

TEACHER: What does it mean to love something?

STUDENT: When you and I are one.

TEACHER: Is that your understanding of love?

STUDENT: That's a characteristic of love.

TEACHER: Okay, I'll buy that. So, the mountains don't belong to the countryside. They belong to those who love them.

STUDENT: What's to belong?

TEACHER: Let's look at that. What's the definition of belong?

STUDENT: Possess, own, have.

TEACHER: Being part of.

STUDENT: So mountains love their masters?

TEACHER: No. That's another section. Let's get this section out of the way first. That's the problem. If you keep skipping all over the place, without going deep enough into any one section, you'll never get any of it. So, the mountains belong to those who love them.

STUDENT: It makes sense, but I don't see it.

TEACHER: Would you mind explaining that one to me; it makes sense, but you don't see it?

STUDENT: I understand what you're saying. I can explain it back to you just fine, but I don't see it that way when I look at it. It doesn't hit me.

TEACHER: Well, it probably doesn't hit you because your definition of love in relationship to the mountains hasn't happened yet. Right? So, I would advise you to make love to the mountains. In fact, start with this one. It needs it. May your life go well.

STUDENT: Thank you for your answer.

TEACHER: You need it too.

STUDENT: I started reading this sutra several times, and I never made it through the whole thing once. I have a hard enough time with my koan, so I don't have much time for other questions. But when I hear you elaborate on it, it all sounds wonderful, poetic, and edifying. It's beautiful. I want to understand it, but I don't know what Dogen is talking about, and I don't know how to begin working with it.

TEACHER: Working with your koan is an essential part of understanding what Dogen is presenting. He's talking about intimacy with these mountains and rivers. Intimacy gets a lot of lip service in our culture, but it's actually a very rare occurrence. Usually, we use the word in the context of sexual intimacy. For Dogen intimacy is seeing form with the whole body and mind; hearing sound with the whole body and mind. In other words, it's not something that takes place outside of you. A car is not something that's passing by on the street. The apple blossoms are not something that's flowering on the tree. Whole body and mind seeing involves you intimately. That kind of understanding is another way of saying enlightenment or realization. So, working on your koan, what you have to practice is intimacy. It's the only way you'll see the koan. You have to be intimate with it.

STUDENT: I have to be intimate with the mountains and rivers, and then the sutra makes sense?

TEACHER: Definitely. The fact is that, from the beginning, you're not separated from them. This is not a new thing. What you're going to discover is that you've always been intimate with them, but you just haven't realized it. That little shift changes your way of perceiving yourself and the universe. You can't treat these mountains and rivers, or their inhabitants poorly, when you see clearly that you and they are the same thing. Not similar. The same thing—identical.

STUDENT: I want to see that way more than anything.

TEACHER: You will. May your life go well.

STUDENT: Thank you for your teaching.

STUDENT: [Crying.] To be in the mountains—does that mean that if I want to help children, I have to vow to help the children, and then do something about it even if I can't help them all?

TEACHER: First of all, to be in the mountains means to really be yourself. Before you help anybody, you need to realize yourself; realize yourself as the mountains, the rivers, the great earth. And then, how to help, when to help, how much to help, what to do, becomes clear to you.

STUDENT: I'm trying and I think I see that.

TEACHER: That's still being separated. There is no helping. The only way to do it is through intimacy. It starts with being intimate with yourself. To really be yourself makes you intimate with the ten thousand things. Then your way of responding to circumstances is not from the perspective of the helper, but as the thing or person in need of help. You don't raise yourself up to help those below you. Do you understand?

STUDENT: Yes. I see.

TEACHER: In that way, when you work you're not debilitated. The work doesn't wear you out. It's hard to do what you want to do if you're not intimate. So, be intimate with it. Don't separate yourself. May your life go well.

STUDENT: Thank you for your answer.

STUDENT: As a grade school teacher, while I teach I feel like I'm being myself more than I have ever been. I feel I connect with the kids and help them, although I'm not sure exactly how I'm doing that. At the same time, I feel like I've been a wreck all of this semester. I've had diarrhea for the last three months, and no sleep.

TEACHER: Do the kids scare you?

STUDENT: They don't scare me.

TEACHER: Well, what's the barrier? Have you identified what the diarrhea is about?

STUDENT: Wanting to do what I do well.

TEACHER: So, you're attached to your results. When I encourage you to really be yourself I mean to give yourself permission to be yourself; I mean to trust yourself. If you trust yourself your heart is right. I don't think you're teaching because of the big salary. You're not doing it because you're power hungry. You're doing it out of your love for the kids and love for teaching. If your heart is right and you trust yourself, you can't go wrong.

STUDENT: So why do I have diarrhea?

TEACHER: Because you don't trust yourself. Do you?

STUDENT: I guess not.

TEACHER: You already said so much before. You're afraid that it won't go right. That's not trusting yourself. Empower yourself and give those kids a break. May your life go well.

STUDENT: Thank you for your answer.

STUDENT: I've always been in love with the ocean, but recently I seem to be pulled much more by the mountains. I don't know why, but I want to hike and climb. Just last week I picked up Neville Shuman's book *Zen and Climbing Mountains*. Do you know that book?

TEACHER: Yes.

STUDENT: Do you think it's a pop book?

TEACHER: I don't think it's either about Zen or mountain climbing.

STUDENT: Oh. Well, I was mesmerized by it. It's a story about the author climbing Mont Blanc. I guess I was captivated by the narrative because he was drawing analogies between his adventure and the process of Zen practice. In getting to the top of that mountain he had to fight many obstacles. He had to trust himself. He had to let go. He had to have determination. Without these qualities, he wouldn't have succeeded. When he reached the summit, because of his struggles, that moment was much more significant. After he got there and saw it, he turned around and made it back. On the way down he had to maintain the same amount of focus. He couldn't relax because his life was still on the line.

TEACHER: You mentioned some of the flaws of this book, and pop Zen books in general. Usually they're written by people who found a little bit of information about Zen. It sounds good to them and they assimilate it into their writing.

When you carefully look at what is being presented though, it is off. You said that he really had to fight to get to the top. Fighting obstacles is not the way to practice. Also, most importantly, practice is not about getting to the top. Practice is always right here, right now. It is not about a goal. We focus on the goal all the time. This whole culture is goal oriented. And in that obsession with getting somewhere, we miss the process. We miss this moment. We miss our lives. Practice is about unity with your life and the whole universe. It is not a struggle.

STUDENT: I thought Shuman was involved with the process.

TEACHER: It may be. But if he was fighting obstacles, as you said, that way of living is not the way of practice. In practice, don't fight your barriers. Be the barrier. Don't try to get to the top; don't try to be victorious. Just be victorious moment to moment. Remember that the process and the goal are the same thing. Your life takes place right here, right now—not tomorrow on top of the world, when all the goals have been reached.

STUDENT: Thank you for your answer.

TEACHER: May your life go well.

In closing, I want to reiterate that the "Mountains and Rivers Sutra" may be one of the most profound teachings of the Buddhadharma available to us. It is very relevant to what we're doing in our practice, individually and collectively, as Buddhism becomes Westernized. If you want to understand the Dharma, your life, and your practice, then study and appreciate the teachings of mountains and rivers.

17 MIND-TO-MIND TRANSMISSION

The principle and reality of the mind-to-mind transmission that has continued for two thousand five hundred years, beginning with Shakyamuni Buddha, and which is present right here and now on this mountain, lies at the heart of Zen training. But what is the direct truth of the mind-to-mind transmission? Master Dogen said:

The right transmission of all the buddhas and ancestors, from the time of the seven buddhas to the present, is the samadhi of practice and enlightenment, namely, following the right master and studying the teachings. When we follow the right master we sometimes see half our face and body, but then at other times we see all of our face and body. Sometimes we see half of ourselves and half of others. Sometimes the master reveals himself with the face of a god covered with hair [represents enlightenment], sometimes as a devil with horns [represents practice]. Different types of behavior confront us and personalities change unexpectedly. Searching for the Dharma is carried on throughout kalpas. This is the real function of study under a master—we meet our real selves and true form. Shakyamuni blinked, Kashyapa smiled, Eka received the marrow of Bodhidharma, Eno his bowls.

When we study the Way, we study our own skin, flesh, bones, and marrow. When we cast off our own skin, flesh, bones, and marrow, we realize that the mutual study and seeking of the Way between master and disciple is the spiritual and physical entwinement of buddhas and ancestors. This forms the life of the buddhas and ancestors. Their skin, flesh, bones, and marrow are the smile of Kashyapa. Generally, sages study in order to cut off the root of spiritual entanglement but do not use their entanglements to cut off entanglements. Do they know

205

how to use entanglements to transmit entanglements? It's rare to find anyone who knows that entanglements cannot be separated from the transmission of the Dharma. Few have experienced it or even heard it. How can it be possible for many people to experience it?

On Mount Gridhrakuta, Shakyamuni Buddha gave a talk. Two thousand people were in the assembly. Buddha blinked and held up a flower. At this all remained silent. The venerable Kashyapa alone broke into a smile. The World-Honored One said, "I have the all-pervading true Dharma, incomparable nirvana, exquisite teaching of formless form. It doesn't rely on letters and is transmitted outside of scriptures. I now hand it to Mahakashyapa."

Wumen's commentary on Shakyamuni's transmission to Mahakashyapa says:

> If at that time, when Shakyamuni blinked and held up the flower, everyone in the assembly had smiled, to whom would the true Dharma have been handed? Or again, if Kashyapa had not smiled, would the true Dharma have been transmitted? If you say that the true Dharma can be transmitted, then the yellow-faced old man with the loud voice was deceiving simple villagers. If you say the Dharma cannot be transmitted, then why was Kashyapa singled out from those two thousand people and given the transmission?

The twenty-eighth ancestor, Bodhidharma, said to his disciples, "The time has come for you to tell me what you have attained." The disciple Dofu said, "This is my viewpoint: neither be attached nor not attached to words or letters. Utilize that condition freely." Bodhidharma said, "You possess my skin." The nun Soji said, "This is my present understanding: after Ananda saw the Buddha land of Ashoka once, he never looked at it again." Bodhidharma said, "You possess my flesh." The third disciple, Doiku, said, "The four elements are empty and the five skandhas are nonexistent. In my view there is not one thing to be gained." The ancestor said, "You possess my bones." Finally, Eka made three prostrations without speaking and returned to his seat. Bodhidharma said, "You possess my marrow." Then Bodhidharma transmitted his dharma robe to Eka, designating him as the twenty-ninth ancestor of Zen.

Why did Bodhidharma say that among his four disciples, one possessed his skin, another his flesh, the third his bones, and the fourth his marrow, and transmitted the Dharma mind-to-mind only to Eka?

On this, Dogen wrote:

> We must study these words of Bodhidharma: "You possess my skin, flesh, bones, and marrow." These are the words of an ancestor. Each of the disciples had an

understanding and possessed some good points. Each of those points are the skin, flesh, bones, and marrow of the liberated body and mind—that is, the skin, flesh, bones, and marrow of the body and mind that has dropped off. We should not listen to or study any ancestor's words with superficial understanding or discrimination. The ancestor's words are not this nor that trying to describe the whole. Nevertheless, those who lack the right transmission think there is a difference between the levels of understanding of these four disciples and that there is a distinction in the ancestor's skin, flesh, bones, and marrow. They think that the First Ancestor's skin and flesh is further away than his bones and marrow. Also, they believe that the Second Ancestor was given the marrow because his understanding was the best. If we say such things, we have not studied the buddhas and ancestors nor received the right transmission. If we are able to open the eye of study and receive the seal of "You possess my skin," we will have found the correct way to possess Bodhidharma. It is his entire skin, flesh, bones, marrow, body, and mind that is transmitted. This mutual study and seeking of the Way between a master and disciple is called *kato*, the spiritual and physical entwinement of buddhas and ancestors. This forms the life of the buddhas and ancestors. It forms their skin, flesh, bones, and marrow. It forms the smile of Kashyapa, the blinking of the Buddha, the bowl of Eno.

Why then was the transmission only given to Eka and not to the monastic Dofu, nun Soji, or Doiku? Why did Shakyamuni only transmit to Kashyapa and not to Ananda, who was standing right next to him during the discourse, or to the two thousand people in the assembly? What if everyone had smiled? Who would have received it? What if no one had smiled? What would have happened to the Dharma? Is there anything to impart or not? Shakyamuni said that all sentient beings are endowed with the buddha nature. What then is there to impart? What was going on with, "You have my marrow" or "I transmit to you the marvelous mind of nirvana and the teaching of formless form?" If there is something to impart, then why only to certain people in each generation? If there is nothing to impart, then what is the deceit that is going on? What is using illusion to cut off illusion, using entanglements to cut off entanglements? What is the physical and spiritual entanglement of buddhas and ancestors that is transmitted from generation to generation? What does this all mean to you?

STUDENT: In regard to what is received... [Bangs on the floor several times with her fist.]
TEACHER: Where is that coming from?

STUDENT: [Bangs on the floor again.]

TEACHER: Received from whom, from what?

STUDENT: [Bangs on the floor again.]

TEACHER: Then what are all the sutras, the oceanic storehouse of the teachings, the marvelous mind of nirvana and all the other teachings that the Buddhist masters have been passing on for two thousand five hundred years?

STUDENT: Just appreciation of this condition.

TEACHER: What condition?

STUDENT: [Wails loudly.]

TEACHER: That condition closes out the whole universe. What about the world and the ten thousand things?

STUDENT: Gratitude is gratitude. Telling my son to use shampoo when he takes a shower; telling my daughter not to hit the cat.

TEACHER: What is the relationship between that and this [knocks on the floor] that you presented?

STUDENT: Don't hit the cat!

TEACHER: May your life go well.

∞

STUDENT: Let's say my right hand is entangled with my left but I don't see it that way. How do you see it? [Student entwines her arm.]

TEACHER: I see your arms wrapped around each other.

STUDENT: You do?

TEACHER: Yes, and I'm afraid that if you don't, you're going to have a hard time going through life like this.

STUDENT: Which arm is wrapped in which?

TEACHER: Beats me. What does spiritual and physical entanglement mean?

STUDENT: [Entwines her arms.]

TEACHER: Doesn't reach it.

STUDENT: [Crosses her eyes.]

TEACHER: Doesn't reach it. Anything else?

STUDENT: No.

TEACHER: Find out how it doesn't reach it. May your life go well.

STUDENT: Thank you for your answer.

∞

STUDENT: Yesterday I heard a talk about Zen Buddhism, but I didn't see it. When you shouted I saw it, but I lost it the instant I saw it.

TEACHER: Do you think that Zen Buddhism is a shout?

STUDENT: No. Seeing it and letting it go. You become attached but you have to let go, and that's hard.

TEACHER: How could you get attached?

STUDENT: By wanting it.

TEACHER: But who is attached to what?

STUDENT: I guess I am.

TEACHER: What is the "I?"

STUDENT: I don't know. That's what I'm searching for.

TEACHER: That is the self that needs to be studied, and that is the self that ultimately needs to be forgotten. May your life go well.

STUDENT: Thank you for your answer.

STUDENT: Why do you bow in front of a buddha statue?

TEACHER: What would you like to do?

STUDENT: Smile.

TEACHER: Okay. You smile and I'll bow.

STUDENT: Why do you bow in front of him?

TEACHER: I don't bow "in front of him." Don't you see? Bowing in front of him would make that image something other than me. That's not what that image is. That image is nothing but me. You are nothing but me. This whole universe is nothing but me. And it is to that that I bow. Bowing is no separation. It is like nodding to yourself because there is nothing else.

STUDENT: Thank you for your answer.

TEACHER: May your life go well.

STUDENT: Why did Bodhidharma sit in that cave in the first place?

TEACHER: I don't know. What do you say?

STUDENT: Shhhh!

TEACHER: Don't separate yourself. Don't be the watchman keeping things quiet for Bodhidharma. Be Bodhidharma!

STUDENT: That's crazy!

TEACHER: Look at that. What does it mean to be the broken-toothed old barbarian who sat nine years facing the wall? When you see that, the question of why he was sitting there becomes very clear. A scholar would tell you that he was waiting for his successor. Is that why he was sitting there?

STUDENT: He was sitting there waiting for the four successors.

TEACHER: That's adequate for Buddhism 101, but it doesn't work in face-to-face teaching. Whether you realize it or not, what you are basically asking is, "What is the truth of the rightly transmitted Dharma?" Why was Bodhidharma sitting there? Why did he come from the West? Why did he transmit only to Eka? What is the truth of Zen? Those are all the same questions.

STUDENT: Thank you for your answer.

TEACHER: May your life go well.

STUDENT: Master Dogen once said that if you agree with everything your teacher says, he is probably not a very good teacher. I just want to thank you for helping me know that I have the right teacher. It's because you have so little to say and give that every Sunday I come in here for your discourse.

TEACHER: I have nothing to give. I have a lot to say but nothing to give. And I'm sorry I have nothing to give you.

STUDENT: I am, too.

TEACHER: You should be happy! May your life go well.

STUDENT: Thank you for your answer.

STUDENT: Using entanglements to cut off entanglements. How is that?

TEACHER: What do you think? Do you understand?

STUDENT: At the clinic where I work someone who comes in regularly is an incest victim.

TEACHER: That's the fact. What's the entanglement?

STUDENT: Living in that hell, even though it's not happening anymore.

TEACHER: Who is living in it?

STUDENT: The person who comes in.

TEACHER: How about you?

STUDENT: I live with it part of the time.

TEACHER: Are you talking about that person or are you talking about yourself? You can't cut somebody else's entanglements. You can only cut your own. What is your entanglement with respect to that?

STUDENT: [Silence.]

TEACHER: Are you holding on to something? What are you feeling? How will you deal with those feelings? How will you deal with your fear, anxiety, anger, love, and hate? When they become entangled, what will you do with them?

STUDENT: [Silence.]

TEACHER: Study that. Until you take care of your entanglements, there's no way that any kind of a healing relationship can form with someone else suffering from these entanglements. Your confusion and resistance simply compound the difficulty. Do you understand what I am saying?

STUDENT: Yes.

TEACHER: When we say, "Be the barrier," what is the barrier? And when you become the barrier, what's the consequence of that? Isn't that the transmission of entanglements? Isn't it using entanglements to cut entanglements?

STUDENT: [Silence.]

TEACHER: May your life go well.

STUDENT: Thank you for your answer.

STUDENT: Daidoshi! Daidoshi! Daidoshi! Daidoshi! Daidoshi!

TEACHER: [Silence.] Now what will you do? There's calling but no answering.

STUDENT: There's calling but there's never been any answering.

TEACHER: You can do something about that. You have half a face and half a body. Where will you get the other half?

STUDENT: "Kelly?"

TEACHER: Master Ruiyan used to call out every morning: "Master?" "Yes, Master!" "Never be deceived by anyone, any time, any place." "Yes, Master!"

STUDENT: It's no different than: "Daidoshi! Daidoshi!" "Yes, Kelly!"

TEACHER: Maybe. Maybe not.

STUDENT: It's hopeless...

TEACHER: Now there is the entanglement—hopelessness. What will you do about hopelessness?

STUDENT: We're never going to get the next issue of the journal out on time!

TEACHER: Be more direct! What will you do about hopelessness?

STUDENT: I can't do it!

TEACHER: Be hopeless. And then go on.

STUDENT: Thank you for your answer.

TEACHER: May your life go well.

STUDENT: Over the years of practice there have been quite a few moments when something incredible was transmitted. The aftermath of those moments is always the same: first there is the surprise, then tears, and then attachment. Are the surprise and tears attachment?

TEACHER: Attachment means separation. When you cry with the whole body and mind, the whole universe cries with you. When you dance with the whole body and mind, the whole universe dances with you. That is non-attachment. Anything else?
STUDENT: No. Thank you for your answer.
TEACHER: May your life go well.

∞

STUDENT: The more I accept how far away I am from realizing myself, the more hope I have.
TEACHER: You make that statement sitting in the Buddha's seat, wearing Buddha's clothes, and eating Buddha's food. That's how far away you are from realizing yourself. That's why there is no hope.
STUDENT: Thank you for your answer.
TEACHER: May your life go well.

∞

STUDENT: I've built a really good box. What do I do with it?
TEACHER: What are your alternatives?
STUDENT: Sitting inside of it, I could bounce off the walls; or I could lift the lid and look carefully inside.
TEACHER: There are couple of things you can do. You can lift the lid and stuff the whole universe into the box until there is nothing but that box. Or, you can take the box and manifest it as the whole universe. Either way the result is the same—no separation.
STUDENT: How do I do it right now?
TEACHER: You have the box, don't you?
STUDENT: Thank you for your answer.
TEACHER: May your life go well.

∞

STUDENT: About entanglements. I have to go to the bathroom, but I also have a question about Shakyamuni Buddha and what happened on Mount Gridhrakuta.
TEACHER: What's your question?
STUDENT: Should I go to the bathroom or ask my question?
TEACHER: What's your question?

STUDENT: If everyone smiled Mahakashyapa's smile would everyone have been enlightened?

TEACHER: Don't go to the bathroom on the floor here!

STUDENT: Has the entanglement been cut or am I still entangled?

TEACHER: What are you entangled with?

STUDENT: I was thinking that if I asked the question while my bladder was screaming for my attention, I wouldn't really be completely with my question. I would be thinking about going to the bathroom. But then I just asked the question.

TEACHER: You need to take care of both of these things by yourself. No one can go to the bathroom for you and no one can realize it for you. The answer comes from the same place that the questions come from.

STUDENT: Thank you for your answer.

TEACHER: May your life go well.

STUDENT: I'm tired of feeling this way. When this ceases to be you can feed my bones to the wolves.

TEACHER: When this ceases to be there'll be no bones to feed the wolves. And it will cease to be only when you let it in with the whole body and mind. Don't be "tired of feeling this way"—just feel this way! Then there are no longer any bones, marrow, skin, flesh, buddhas, or creatures. There is no life and no death. As long as you stand back from it, separating yourself from it, hating or loving it, naming, identifying, analyzing, categorizing it, it looms bigger and bigger until it becomes overpowering and it's impossible for you to do anything. So *be* it; it is nothing but yourself. There's no way that you can run from it or separate yourself from it. Let those feelings be. Feel them! Fill yourself with them! Be them until there is nothing else. That's the blinking of the eye, the smile of Mahakashyapa, the marrow of Bodhidharma. No separation. Do you understand?

STUDENT: That's the problem, I guess.

TEACHER: What's the problem?

STUDENT: That I understand.

TEACHER: You've got eighty percent of it. Now finish it. Do your best.

STUDENT: Thank you for your answer.

TEACHER: May your life go well.

STUDENT: How do you transmit "Nothing to transmit?"

TEACHER: Ask Brian.

STUDENT: That's a funny way to transmit it!

TEACHER: Where else could it come from?

STUDENT: How was it for you to receive "nothing to transmit?"

TEACHER: My teacher warned me right from the beginning that he had nothing to give me. Periodically he would apologize to me for having nothing to give, and I would say, "But you give me so much!" and he would walk away. Six months later, he would say, "I'm sorry I have nothing to give you." On his birthday, when I would give him a gift, he would say, "I'm sorry I have nothing to give you." I'd say, "Oh, but you give me so much," and again he would walk away.

STUDENT: Thank you.

TEACHER: I hope you don't think I gave you anything. May your life go well.

There is nothing more personal and intimate than the teacher-student spiritual training relationship. It starts with separation, but as it develops and matures, the gap between the teacher and student closes. In the beginning the teacher is a dot, a single point surrounded by a circle—the student. As time goes on, the circle shrinks, getting smaller and smaller until the student is also a perfect dot. That point is the life of the Buddha. To become that dot is to give life to the Buddha. Ultimately, it all boils down to intimacy, to really being intimate with yourself. When you are really intimate with the self, the whole universe returns to the self, where it has always been. When you finally put all your questions to rest, you make yourself free, in life and in death.

18

ACTUALIZING WISDOM

The Buddhist precepts have to do with relationships between self and other, yet they come from the realization of no-self. The precepts are based on no-self. They are the activity of the realized Buddha in the world of phenomena. When you really understand the precepts, they provide an extraordinary example of what realization in everyday life really means. They give the practitioner who has not yet come to full realization and actualization of the Way concrete guidelines on how to practice their life. The precepts become a guide not only for moral and ethical conduct, but for all action. They define our relationship with the environment, with each other, with our nation, indeed, with the universe itself. At the same time, they contain within them an incredible flexibility that allows for changing conditions, for the variables of time, place, position, and degree. The precepts are very practical as well as very profound.

In bringing up your questions about the precepts, make them real and practical. Let them come from the heart. Let them be connected to your life. When a question arises that way, the answer is more reachable. When the question comes from the heart, the answer penetrates the heart.

STUDENT: In the city, when I meet a street person who's asking for money, it's my responsibility that he's there. It's his responsibility that he's there. If I give him money, he may get drunk. If I don't give him money, he may starve.
TEACHER: Do you have a question?
STUDENT: Every time they ask, I say, "Here."

TEACHER: That's similar to what Mother Teresa used to say. Deal with the moment and not the possible consequences of your action.

STUDENT: When I see him take that dollar and go into the liquor store, I say, "Really enjoy it!"

TEACHER: Many years back, when I lived in the city, I encountered similar situations. One time I asked the guy who was panhandling what he wanted the money for and he said he was hungry. I said, "Okay, let's go get something to eat." He got really angry, as if I didn't trust him.

STUDENT: Was that doing good for others?

TEACHER: No, in that case, it wasn't. It was creating a lot of problems. But that's a key question. Are we truly helping? When we give money away, is it more than just an easy way out of an uncomfortable encounter? Are we really taking responsibility?

STUDENT: But in a sense, not giving money can also be coming from a self-centered point of view.

TEACHER: The answer may be somewhere else than those two extremes. What other action is possible? We get locked into extreme positions very frequently, not noticing or dismissing the endless spectrum of possibilities. Take the drug problem. Drug use is definitely a major issue in our society. Everybody agrees. We wage wars on drugs. We use military interventions to cut off the flow of drugs from abroad. We may decrease the influx by half but that causes the street prices to double with parallel increase in related crimes. With a scarcer commodity, we see more burglaries, more murders, more gangs. If we swing to the other extreme and legalize and make street drugs available to everyone, we end up supporting the habit of some people who can't handle these substances. How do we take care of the problem, not in a self-centered, self-righteous way, but creatively and effectively? In case of the beggars, I don't think the answer lies in either one of the two extremes. You have more than two alternatives, and as you genuinely engage the question, they will become apparent.

STUDENT: Thank you for your answer.

TEACHER: May your life go well.

STUDENT: The bell rings and I start to come up for service. Then our cat screeches and I run down to see what's wrong. I can't find her so I walk into the woods searching for her. The birds are singing and I do my liturgy with them. I listen carefully and hear the teachings from the frogs by the pond. Before I know it, it's sunset and I return back to the Monastery. People are really upset.

They say, "Where have you been?" And I say, "I've always been here. What's the problem?" What do you have to say about that?

TEACHER: There are consequences to your actions. If you've made a commitment to this place and vowed to take full responsibility for observing the monastic rules, then what I say is [yells at the top of his lungs], "Dammit! Be in here on time!"

STUDENT: But listen to the birds.

TEACHER: Birds are fine. Frogs are fine. But...

STUDENT: I'm always here on time. I'm on time when I'm out there.

TEACHER: Just by what you're saying and the way you're expressing it, it's not so. "I'm on time when I'm out there." What out there?

STUDENT: I take that away.

TEACHER: You can't take that away.

STUDENT: I can't bring it out either.

TEACHER: That's the truth. Anything else?

STUDENT: No. Thank you for your answer.

STUDENT: My job selling ads for the *Mountain Record* journal is getting me down. The job is actually okay, but I don't particularly love it. I'd rather do something else.

TEACHER: How'd you do this week?

STUDENT: Terrible.

TEACHER: How come?

STUDENT: Because I can't squeeze any more people. There aren't any more people to squeeze.

TEACHER: How about squeezing yourself?

STUDENT: I'm broke, I don't have any money...

TEACHER: No no no. I didn't mean squeeze yourself that way. Are you filled with exuberance for what you're selling?

STUDENT: I don't have anything inside me.

TEACHER: That's why you're not selling. Somebody who's empty can't cross the street, can't wipe their nose, and definitely can't help anybody else. So don't be empty. Get rid of emptiness.

STUDENT: Somebody who's empty can also cross the street, wipe their nose, and help other people.

TEACHER: No. It's only when you've come down off the mountain that you can manifest your wisdom.

STUDENT: But I have to go up a lot of mountains to sell ads.

TEACHER: No, you don't. You have to get back into the world, into the market-place to sell ads. That's where the people are—in the world. There is nobody on top of the mountain. There's no communication whatsoever on the peak.

STUDENT: So what's wrong with that?

TEACHER: It doesn't sell adds. It doesn't help people. It doesn't take care of the problems.

STUDENT: What if I'm not sure if I can really help anybody?

TEACHER: Then take care of that. It's up to you. You don't have to do it, you see. You don't have to practice. You don't have to sell ads. It's up to you.

STUDENT: Thank you for your answer.

TEACHER: May your life go well.

STUDENT: I don't understand how to use the precepts. I hear, "Cease from evil; practice good, actualize good for others," and I conjure up an idea that I should be that way—whatever that means. I try to do that and feel stuck trying to fulfill this ideal.

TEACHER: The Three Pure Precepts are the definition of the essential reality of the universe. The Ten Grave Precepts tell us how to do that—how to cease from evil, how to practice good, how to do good for others. The Three Pure Precepts function as the Ten Grave Precepts. You practice the Ten Grave Precepts the same way you practice your breath. You sit down and you vow to concentrate on your breath. "One...two...three...four...oh, the bird has stopped singing. That was a catbird. They are amazing at this time of year, stealing from other birds. I think they're part of the crow family...Oh, I forgot the breath." Then you let go of the catbird and come back to the breath. Each time you let go of the thought and return to the breath, you empower yourself. You build the power of concentration. You confirm and reinforce your intent through the practice of letting go and returning to the breath. You work the same way with the precepts. First of all you need to be aware of the precepts. To practice the breath you must be aware of the breath. To practice the pre-cepts you must be aware of the precepts. Once you're aware of the precepts, when you go off the precept, you notice that; you acknowledge that you went off it; you take responsibility for having gone off, and you return to the precept. That's practicing the precepts.

STUDENT: What does it mean that the Three Pure Precepts are the basis of reality?

TEACHER: It's a reality where everyone ceases from evil, does good, and does good for others. When you have a world like that, you don't have religious wars, eth-nic cleansing, terrorism; you don't have people fouling the air with pollution, chemical companies dumping waste into the rivers; you don't have ministers ripping off the congregation, elected officials taking bribes, because they ceased from evil. They do good and they do good for others. And if everybody's doing that for each other, we've got two hands washing each other. That's what makes it work, but as a civilization we're a long way from that. Even to create a microcosm of this reality in a place like a monastery is extremely difficult, because every time someone new comes in from the outside, they come in with all of their conditioning and they resist. They want to fight others; they want to fight the system. They try to reorganize the Monastery. They rarely think first of adapting to the circumstance. The immediate thought is how can I rearrange this to suit myself. As a result, we needed to set up rules and guidelines of sane behavior based on the precepts. It takes a lot of effort to maintain this harmony. When we first started the Monastery, it was impossible. It's possible now because we forged a tradition and there are senior practitioners setting an example. It's taken a long time and a lot of effort to bring it about, using the precepts, the teachings, the history, and the Dharma itself.

STUDENT: Thank you for your answer.

TEACHER: May your life go well.

STUDENT: I'm struggling with the question of trust in relation to the image of the bodhisattva's effort to fill the well with snow. I have a hard time with not thinking and worrying about why am I putting the snow in there. What's the purpose of this crazy endeavor? How long is it going to take? I always expected to have a goal to attain in order for my life to make sense.

TEACHER: Practicing the bodhisattva's vows doesn't mean that there shouldn't be goals. Goals are very important. You need them to know where you're going. Otherwise the journey becomes a "go with the flow" drift where nobody knows what they're doing or where they're going. You need to know where you're going. You need to know what you're going to accomplish and then you need to get rid of those expectations. Know them clearly and don't attach to them. Realize that each step of the process is the goal.

STUDENT: And that realization is not a thought?

TEACHER: Of course it's a thought. There's nothing wrong with thinking.

STUDENT: How do you deal with it on a daily basis when you're—

TEACHER: When you're thinking? Really think. And when it's time to not think, really not think. You should be able to do both freely.

STUDENT: How do you know when you're thinking too much?

TEACHER: When it starts getting in the way of your life. When you're doing it during zazen. Take a rifle, for example. It's important to be able to look down the barrel of a rifle to see if the bore is clear. It's also important to be able to shoot the rifle. If you try to look down the bore while you're shooting it, it doesn't work so well. That doesn't mean that looking down the bore is wrong or shooting it is wrong. It means that trying to do both at the same time creates a problem.

STUDENT: And that knowing when to think and how much comes from trusting the way things are?

TEACHER: It comes from trusting that you know. When you're overwhelmed with thoughts, when they become cyclic and getting nowhere, when you're no longer thinking but worrying; that's the time to be able to let go of the thoughts, to center yourself and make yourself empty. A person who can do that is a very powerful person. Goals are important. Not being attached to them is also important. Most of the time when we create and pursue goals, we don't have the information necessary to even know if that's the goal we really want to pursue. Halfway along in the process, we realize that's not really what we want. We have to let go of the old goal and shift. We need to be able to reassess what we are doing.

STUDENT: It means being patient with exactly what we're doing and things being just as they are?

TEACHER: It's important to be able to know when to back off. Basically, we're talking about common sense.

STUDENT: So you just know.

TEACHER: You trust yourself and you allow yourself the room to fail. There's nothing wrong with failing. But it's important to get up. That's what "seven times knocked down, eight times get up" means.

STUDENT: But when you fail you may catch hell.

TEACHER: That's fine. When someone asks, "What happens during zazen in the zendo if I really need to move?" I answer, "If you really need to move, move." Yes, the monitors are going to shout. You moved. If you move too many times, they'll throw you out of the zendo. If you keep doing that each time you come, they'll ask you not to sit in the zendo anymore. You'll have to sit in a room by yourself. There are consequences to everything that you do. If you're going to break the law, be prepared to get arrested. If it's important enough to you to break the law to draw attention to something, that's okay, but then know that you might get arrested. As Clarence Darrow said, "You want to fly? Fly. But the clouds are going to stink of gasoline and the birds are going to lose some of their mystery. But you can fly if you want." Every action has a consequence. You need to be able to know what it is that you need to do, and then proceed, along with the mistakes. I've watched many people make mistakes. I watch my children make mistakes these days. In sixty-five years of life you gain some experience. I can see the dynamics of a particular situation. I can see a relationship about to break up. But people in the midst of their drama can't possibly see it. That's why it is drama. It takes time for them to see it clearly. There's no way to intercede, to prevent learning from experience. I watch my children. I watch my students. I watch my friends. It's much easier to see the intricacies and implications when you're standing outside of a situation. It doesn't take any profound wisdom to be able to do that. But you have to allow the thing to happen. You practice patience. If you're watching water boil, patience helps. Being impatient doesn't make it boil any faster. But sometimes, if you're involved in a specific job, a little bit of impatience may get it done a little faster. There you can intercede. So be patient while you're waiting for the water to boil. Be patient as the fly ball crosses the sky and you wait for it to come down. There's no way you can rush that. It's going to have to take its own time, and gravity and the ball will determine when it's going to come to you. There's a time for patience and there's a time for impatience.

STUDENT: And trust is just accepting?

TEACHER: Trust is ninety-nine point nine percent trusting yourself. It's really got to do with nothing other than yourself. Once you trust yourself, the whole universe comes home. In a way, you become invulnerable. That's the key— trusting yourself, having faith in yourself. Anything else?

STUDENT: Thanks for being here.

TEACHER: Thank you. May your life go well.

STUDENT: At least once a month, especially during Zen training weekends, I sit in the zendo and hear monitors say, "It's not what you do with your knees in zazen, it's what you do with your mind." Every morning someone tells me and Shariputra, "form is emptiness." Then, during sesshin, when I can't sit in proper form, I find out that it's critical what my knees are doing, more important it seems at times than what my mind is doing.

TEACHER: If your mind is empty, it doesn't matter what your knees are doing. But when your mind becomes agitated, your knees hurt and you have to sit in a chair.

STUDENT: How much can my mind be emptied out as a beginning student?

TEACHER: Empty enough so that you can cut your arm off just like Eka did before Bodhidharma. Completely empty. You can go very deep into the stillness. Not everybody reaches it. Not everybody reaches it for long periods of time. But that's basically what the statement in the *Heart Sutra* means—there's no eye, ear, nose, tongue, body, or mind—your self disappears. That's what Avalokiteshvara is saying to Shariputra. When that happens, from your perspective no one is sitting. Anything else?

STUDENT: No. Thank you for your answer.
TEACHER: May your life go well.

STUDENT: My question comes up as an image. Think of a vessel and a field on a hot day. Someone very thirsty comes up and starts drinking out of that container. It's sweet water to them until it starts to taste bad because they've drunk too much. They throw the ladle back with a clang. In my relationships, I feel that I am that vessel and what I turn out to be depends on the point of view of people who relate with me. Should I use my humanity to let them drink freely or...
TEACHER: First of all, blast that vessel—gone! No more containers. Make yourself utterly empty. That's what it means to exhaustively study the self. That's zazen. To study the self is to forget the self. BOOM! No more self. No eye, ear, nose, tongue, body, mind; no color, sound, smell, taste, touch, phenomena.
STUDENT: Then, once you do that...
TEACHER: Then there's only then.
STUDENT: Being empty, how do you then re-enter the marketplace and not be egotistical?
TEACHER: There's no one to be egotistical and no one to enter the marketplace. You have to get rid of "once you are empty." That's yet another idea.
STUDENT: Thank you for your answer.
TEACHER: May your life go well.

STUDENT: What is the meaning of taking refuge in the Buddha, the Dharma, and the Sangha?
TEACHER: It is acknowledging the oneness of yourself and the Buddha, the Dharma, and the Sangha. We identify with the Three Treasures. We chant, "Being one with Buddha, Dharma, and Sangha." Buddha is not only the historical Buddha, but all individuals—yourself. Dharma is the teachings of the Buddha and at the same time it is the whole phenomenal universe. The ten thousand things are the dharmas. Sangha is the community of practitioners that practices the Buddhadharma and it's all sentient beings. In a sense, Buddha, Dharma, and Sangha is another way of saying self, which is none other than the whole universe itself. You're essentially identifying with that.
STUDENT: The word "refuge" seems to imply that there's something else that you're taking refuge from.

TEACHER: That's an unfortunate twist in the translation.
STUDENT: Thank you.
TEACHER: May your life go well.

∞

STUDENT: I don't take good care of you. I'm so sorry.
TEACHER: How can you take better care of me?
STUDENT: Don't forget to take your umbrella when you go back to the parsonage.
TEACHER: There's a much better way of taking good care of me.
STUDENT: Want a cup of coffee?
TEACHER: Much, much better... What's a better way?
STUDENT: [Silence.]
TEACHER: Open your own umbrella. Have a cup of coffee. Have a drink, and I'll get drunk. That's the only way. Otherwise, I'll go to my grave without any descendants. I've accepted that possibility. I may have to die without a successor. Zhaozhou did it, so I can do it. But, please, don't let me have to do that. Cover your head with the umbrella. Have a cup of coffee. May your life go well.
STUDENT: Thank you for your answer.

∞

STUDENT: Sean told me last week that I had morality up my ass. I think I know what he means. I take the precepts very seriously. And I don't know whether I should wait a long time, letting my practice become really strong before I do jukai or should I do it as soon as I'm eligible.
TEACHER: The time to do it is after you've taken an enema. Do you know what I mean?
STUDENT: No. I've never taken one.
TEACHER: I think the precepts have got you constipated and you've got to get rid of them.
STUDENT: What do you mean?
TEACHER: Get rid of the precepts. If you carry the precepts around like baggage, they are just going to get in the way.
STUDENT: Morality has always been baggage for me. If I took the precepts, I would probably love to wear a rakusu and say, yes, I'm a Buddhist.
TEACHER: A Dharma brother of mine who was a professor of Physics at the University of California was a student of Maezumi Roshi for about seventeen years. He almost completed koan study when he decided to become a monastic.

It was a big step for him. The evening before his ordination he went over to Roshi's house and knocked on the door. Roshi came out and said, "Hi. What's the matter?" "Well, tomorrow morning you're going to ordain me as a monastic. Do you have any last words that you'd like to say to me?" And Roshi said, "Yes. No big deal." And, boom, slammed the door. Roshi took away what he was holding on to. On the other hand, for someone who may be taking things very lightly, the message may be, "Get serious! This is one of the most important things you can ever do in your life." If the student points to the absolute, the teacher points to the relative. If the student points to the relative, the teacher is pointing to the absolute. And when a student points to neither the absolute nor relative, that's when the teacher manifests the sixteen-foot golden body of the Buddha in a pile of shit and rubbish. *That's* where the truth of this practice is. Not in any extremes.

STUDENT: Thank you for your answer.

TEACHER: When you're ready to take the precepts, let me know. You're the only one who will know when you're ready. May your life go well.

STUDENT: When I lose confidence or trust in myself, I hide in the right and wrong as if that could shield me. Then when I return to the practice of the moment, there are two karmas to deal with, not just one. Sometimes it seems hopeless.

TEACHER: What do you mean by "there are two karmas to deal with?"

STUDENT: That hiding itself, in addition to whatever it was that I created by heading for the extremes.

TEACHER: In a sense, what you're saying is true. You lose confidence when all of the extra gets thrown into action. The defense systems come up and you've got to make the other person wrong and yourself right. Good and bad spring up, rules, and all the other complications. When you're filled with trust, you're basically invulnerable even though you may be knocked down and trampled over. You get up and brush yourself off and get on with it.

STUDENT: It's true. But I still do both.

TEACHER: Well, do them well. May your life go well.

STUDENT: Thank you for your answer.

STUDENT: The only way I can figure out how to really practice the precepts is like this, "Hi, Don. How ya doin'?"

TEACHER: Well, maybe. But try that with somebody who has a knife at your throat and is threatening your life. How do you practice the precepts then?

STUDENT: I'm out of here. See ya later.

TEACHER: Identifying with the other person isn't always the solution. The precepts aren't static. When necessary, speak of the faults of others. "Officer, that guy just stole something from the store. I saw him do it." That's upholding the precepts.

STUDENT: You could also say that it's identifying with the person so deeply that it's what is appropriate for that person.

TEACHER: In a sense.

STUDENT: Identifying with my son doesn't mean that I see what he wants and I just let him do it.

TEACHER: It's a good point. Speaking of identifying, I caught hell from my son yesterday. He's not speaking to me because I wouldn't let him drive your car. But it's for his own benefit. He can't understand it. I've been watching him drive and he's definitely skillful; he knows how to pull it into a tight parking space and spin it around. But he doesn't have the appreciation that he's driving two tons of steel, that it's a deadly weapon. I said, "Not only can't you drive that car, but I'm not going to agree for you to get a learner's permit until you get your head straightened out about what driving a four-thousand-pound vehicle really means." So he hates me now. But, ultimately, it's...

STUDENT: ...Identification.

TEACHER: May your life go well.

STUDENT: Thank you for your answer.

These precepts are a major contribution that Zen Buddhism can make to Western society. They have become one of the most powerful guiding forces in my life. I always had difficulty with church rules, laws, and commandments because they are categorical and disempowering. The precepts work in a very different way. Instead of abdicating your responsibility by giving it over to the church, the minister, Jesus, or God, you realize that you are ultimately responsible for the whole universe. And that is freeing. One of the beautiful aspects of the precepts is that they provide guidelines and at the same time contain enough flexibility that ultimately the responsibility still comes back to you. You have to make the decision, but the precepts provide a moral and ethical matrix within which you can operate. Depending upon the circumstance, the guidelines may shift. You need to be completely awake, aware of details of the situations you encounter and navigate through. So "do not steal" can vary according to time, place, position, and degree. Acknowledging our interdependence and lack of an ultimate reference system, the practice of the precepts returns responsibility to us. That's a powerful addition to the moral and ethical framework that we need here in the West if we're ever to survive in the twenty-first century. Right now the precepts are in the hands of a small group of Buddhists and unknown to the general public. But as the years go on, and as practice in the West grows, the precepts will be increasingly manifested in the world. That's ultimately where it counts. Sooner or later they will affect our society and our ways of making decisions and living our lives.

19
BEYOND FORM AND EMPTINESS

As Buddhists of the next century, we are obliged to address the moral and ethical issues of that century, a century that will present us with many more, and more complicated, moral and ethical questions than we are confronting today. How do you see the causes of and the solutions to the problems and questions that face us? How do you understand the place of commitment to a spiritual practice in this very complex age we live in?

In regard to the issue of practice and moral and ethical life, Master Dogen says:

> Water is neither strong nor weak, neither wet nor dry, neither moving nor still, neither cold nor hot, neither being nor non-being, neither delusion nor enlightenment. Solidified, it is harder than diamond; who could break it? Melted, it is softer than milk; who could break it? So it is impossible to doubt all of the virtues realized by water. We should then study that time when the water of the ten directions is seen in the ten directions. And this is not the study only of how humans and devas see water. There is also the study of water seeing water. Because water practices and is enlightened by water, there is the study of water expounding water. We must bring to realization the path on which the self meets the self. We must move back and forth along and spring off from the vital path on which the other penetrates the other.

In general, when Dogen speaks of mountains and rivers, he is referring to mountains as form and to rivers as emptiness. But, of course, we all need to understand that form is none other than emptiness and that emptiness is none other than form. When we are speaking of form we are also speaking of emptiness, and when we are speaking of emptiness, we are also speaking of form. There is a constant interpenetration of form and emptiness. What can be said of form and emptiness can also be said of the ten thousand things, of all the dualities. They can be seen as separate and distinct or they can be seen as one and the same entity. The reality of existence can be found in neither of these extremes, but rather in the total inter-penetration and non-hindrance of all things.

"The water of the ten directions is seen in the ten directions." Because it is empty, the water, like the ten thousand things, is free, boundless, and unhindered. To see it in the ten directions is to realize that boundlessness that reaches every-where. "Because water practices and is enlightened by water, there is the study of water expounding water. We must bring to realization the path on which the self meets the self." Bringing to realization the path on which the self meets the self is water seeing water.

In "Genjokoan," Dogen says, "To study the Buddha Way is to study the self." Isn't this water seeing water? Isn't this emptiness seeing emptiness? "To study the self is to forget the self, and to forget the self is to be enlightened by the ten thou-sand things." Isn't this the water of the ten directions seen in the ten directions? Isn't this the self of the ten directions seen in the ten directions? "To be enlight-ened by the ten thousand things is to cast off body and mind of self and other. No trace of enlightenment remains and this traceless enlightenment continues end-lessly." What is the path on which the self encounters the self? We call it the Buddha Way, but what does it mean to be on the path of the Buddha Way? We've often said that practicing the precepts is like practicing the breath. It is like any kind of practice. When we violate the precepts, just as when a thought interferes with the breath, we see it, acknowledge it, and become at one with it. We atone. After taking responsibility, we then let it go. We release it and come back to the precept.

When we break a precept we create karma, a force to perpetuate the breaking of the precepts. When we maintain the precept, the same force to continue is present but now as the force to stay with the precept. The precepts are based on water seeing water. They are based on the self studying the self, forgetting the self, and being enlightened by the ten thousand things.

The precepts are based on no-self. Self-centeredness and deluded actions have to do with the little bag of skin that contains our bones and our history, and from which we have excluded the totality of the universe. From the perspective of self-centeredness, our actions take no account of the whole picture. The precepts provide us with a way to let go of the limited vision of an isolated individual, and bring us back onto the path upon which the self encounters the self.

"We must move back and forth along, and spring off from, the vital path on which the other penetrates the other." To penetrate the other is to be totally integrated with the ten thousand things. Ten thousand is just an arbitrary number to describe the whole universe. That boundless unity is the reality of our life. That's why Dogen teaches that practice and enlightenment are one. Practice doesn't lead you to enlightenment. Practice is enlightenment. To study the self is enlightenment. To walk the path on which the self meets the self, before even meeting the self, is enlightenment. And enlightenment is an absolute necessity for morality, real morality which does not exclude anything. And just as there can be no morality without enlightenment, there can be no enlightenment without morality. They are mutually dependent. They mutually arise and coexist, like practice and enlightenment.

When we take the precepts of the Buddha Way and begin practicing them, how do they inform the moral questions that we face today—questions of euthanasia, surrogate motherhood, cloning, the questions that we face in our legal and political system, the question of war, the questions of ecology? As Buddhists, we have a particular view based on those precepts available to us. That perspective is very different from the Judeo-Christian view. In a sense, the "person" in Buddhism is the totality of the universe. And it responds to the whole universe and takes care of it as if it was taking care of its own body. But how does that resolve itself into day by day morality and decision making? Decisions about what path to take, how to act, when to act? What criteria do you use to determine alternative modes of action within the matrix of the moral and ethical teachings of the Buddha?

If we don't look at the nitty-gritty situations in terms of the day-to-day morality of our practice, we'll never engage the precepts. And they're too valuable to be taken during a precept ceremony and then tucked away. They are meant to be actively engaged. When you actively engage them you manifest the life of the Buddha, a life of wisdom and compassion. How do you do that?

STUDENT: I should introduce myself. Between heaven and earth, I alone am the World-Honored One.
TEACHER: What will you do about the polluted streams, a dishonest president, religious wars, the homeless?
STUDENT: I'd like to inform my congressional advisors that I knew nothing about what was going on with the Contras.
TEACHER: The Buddha Way should have a little bit more to offer. What do you have to offer?
STUDENT: I can't find anything, but when the bell rings, I get up.
TEACHER: That doesn't reach the moral and ethical teachings of the Buddha. It retreats from them. The precepts are an active edge, functioning in the world. They're manifesting in the ten directions, in a multiplicity of forms, in the

various ways that different beings see. What considerations would you make?

STUDENT: When the bell rings, I get up. When the river is dirty, I roll up my jeans and get a shovel. I write letters and change policy, and I don't turn back.

TEACHER: Why will you do all that when the river is dirty?

STUDENT: When the river is dirty I roll up my jeans and I get a shovel.

TEACHER: What concern of yours is the river?

STUDENT: Between heaven and earth, I alone am the Honored One.

TEACHER: That pulls back from it. How about, "THAT'S MY RIVER!" What could be more personal? This has to be personal: "You touch my body when you pollute this river; you step on my head when you foul this earth." Anything else?

STUDENT: Thank you for your answer.

TEACHER: May your life go well.

The precept "Don't be angry" needs to be understood from multiple perspectives. From the literal point of view it means don't be angry under any circumstances because anger is based on delusion and separation. But "Don't be angry" must also be understood in terms of compassion and reverence for life. When necessary, be angry, but only out of compassion and reverence for life, not from a self-centered point of view of the separate self. The precepts are based on no-self and anger based on the precepts is the manifestation of wisdom. It is the same kind of anger as the reaction a mother has for a child when it runs out into the street. It's not self-centered; it's for the good of the child.

STUDENT: I don't know why, but I feel that every word I say separates me from the truth that I experience. There are a lot of things that come out of my mouth and I can't understand how I could say something without it being a lie.

TEACHER: What we're calling the truth is the absolute basis of reality. But you have to understand that it is only half of the picture.

STUDENT: I understand that.

TEACHER: The other half is the differences. You and I are the same thing. That's the absolute basis. But the truth is also, "I'm not you and you're not me."

STUDENT: I know.

TEACHER: Then how can you lie? In a sense you lie when you say, "All things are lying." It's not true. And you lie when you say, "All things are separate and distinct." Neither reaches the truth.

STUDENT: So, how do you deal with a world that's totally—

TEACHER: You always deal according to the circumstances. You always act according to the imperative. That's the key to the precepts. They change according to time, place, position and degree. They never function the same way in different places at different times. Your relationships change, the place changes, circumstances change. Since everything is in a constant state of change, the precepts need to be as flexible as reality and at the same time contain the fundamental and unchanging truth of the Buddha. And the truth of the Buddha includes that impermanence.

STUDENT: Should you always have one foot in the absolute when you're speaking?

TEACHER: First of all, you need to understand that the absolute always contains the relative and that the relative always contains the absolute. You need to understand that the relative emerges from the absolute, and that the absolute emerges from the relative. Then you need to understand the mutual integration of both. All five of these positions, the Five Ranks of Master Dongshan, exist and function simultaneously.

STUDENT: Sometimes it all feels as real as a dream.

TEACHER: That's what it is. Here we're speaking about a dream within a dream, which compounds the subtleties and difficulties. We create our reality by the way we use our minds.

STUDENT: For me, the truth seems to be getting further and further away.

TEACHER: Away from what? No matter how hard you try, from the absolute point of view, there is no way you can foul the nest. But from the relative point of view, every time you move you foul the nest.

STUDENT: I understand. Thank you for your teaching.

TEACHER: May your life go well.

STUDENT: In working with the precepts, do I have a choice as to the karma I want to create or do I just let things come as they come?

TEACHER: Once you really understand that what you do and what happens to you are the same thing, once you confirm for yourself that there's no separation between you and the ten thousand things, the way you act will accord with the ten thousand things. You may slip, but each time you acknowledge that slip and return to reality, you return to that particular karma. The precepts are about that level of responsibility. The Three Pure Precepts define the order of reality and harmony: cease from evil, do good, and do good for others. Everybody wants to do that. But how? The Ten Grave Precepts address that. Those ten precepts need to be understood not just from the literal point of view, the Hinayana perspective, but from the point of view of compassion and reverence for life, the Mahayana perspective, and also from the point of view of Buddhayana, which is, "Who could possibly kill what?" Who are you stealing from? The self steals from the self. The right hand steals from the left hand. It is almost hilarious.

STUDENT: At that point you don't need any precepts.

TEACHER: But all three points of view function simultaneously. They mutually integrate and are functioning in the world according to the circumstances. The action needs to be in accord with the imperative.

STUDENT: But how do you live your life in accord with all those perspectives? I mean, you can make so many mistakes! You can trick yourself. The mind is so incredibly—

TEACHER: Absolutely. It's very easy to kid yourself. You could justify lying; you could justify killing. But you have guidelines within which to work with the precepts: time, place, position, and degree. And keep in mind that actions always produce effects. All actions. Zazen produces an effect. Enlightenment produces an effect. Killing produces an effect. If you kill to protect someone, it's very different than if you kill to protect yourself. If you kill to protect yourself, you violate the precept.

STUDENT: Yes, but you could believe that you killed to protect someone and be kidding yourself, having done it for self-centered reasons. How do you recognize that?

TEACHER: As your practice continues and you follow the path studying the self, the path on which the self encounters the self—where water sees water—it is increasingly more and more difficult to hide from yourself. You can't sit with yourself every morning, every afternoon, every evening and continue to deceive yourself for very long. You can do it for a year, a couple of years—and some people do—but sooner or later, there will be no place to hide. It comes up and you see it. And either you correct it or you run away from it, one or the other. Either atonement or separation.

STUDENT: Thank you for your answer.

TEACHER: May your life go well.

STUDENT: I'm responsible for myself; I'm responsible for the ten thousand things; I'm not responsible for myself; I'm not responsible for anyone else. How? When? It changes with every situation. My morals are different from your morals.

TEACHER: That's true. But we're talking about Zen morals. My morals and my teachers' morals are based on the same principles, the Buddha's precepts. Those precepts were transmitted from generation to generation down to this time and this place. And it's those precepts that I give and that a student receives. They contain no loopholes. In general, rather than make a moral

decision where there are no clear precedents, we tend to consider such situations as free space and do whatever we want. We abuse the space between the
laws, between the guidelines. That is unfortunate. In Zen, it's well covered.
It's pretty clear. You really have to deceive yourself to claim that it is ambiguous
whether an action is appropriate or not.

STUDENT: Thank you for your answer.

TEACHER: May your life go well.

STUDENT: There was no electricity up in the cabin so Philip and I were tracing
the electrical line, trying to find the problem. We were following the wire up
the hill and there was a patch of poison ivy that the electrical line ran right
through. I'm allergic to poison ivy. I could have decided to be selfless and
continue working, but I backed off. Then I felt confused.

TEACHER: People think that going with the flow means that if they fall in the
river, they should just give up and drown. It's wise to swim and get to shore.
There are many ways through problems. You could have taken some plywood,
laid it down and walked through the patch of poison ivy. If it's unnecessary,
why suffer? Above all, don't be stupid. Jesus taught that. Buddha taught that.
The precepts teach us to take responsibility but not to be stupid.

STUDENT: Thank you for your answer.

TEACHER: May your life go well.

STUDENT: Avoid picking and choosing; avoid good and evil. I feel like I'm standing in the river up to my chin. I make a lot of mistakes. I don't understand
how it's possible not to. How do I determine what's right and what's wrong? I
understand the words, but when it comes down to making a moral decision,
I'm not sure I know what to do.

TEACHER: The precepts are the compass. They exist in the relative world of right
and wrong. They are based on the absolute but are designed to function in
the world of the relative. They are a description of how a buddha lives and
navigates their life among the myriad things. But it's not as simple as A B C:
follow these rules and everything will be cool. Life is not that simple.
Everything constantly changes. We are always in the midst of a multiplicity
of interactions. The precepts and the various perspectives that they can be
appreciated from provide the matrix for us, a matrix for a sound moral life,
and this matrix is given and received on the basis of faith, just like in any
other religion. It is an ethical code that students accept, trusting the teacher.

The students who receive the precepts here at the monastery haven't at that point confirmed the precepts for themselves, yet they take my word that they are the definition of the life of a buddha. There is mutual trust in the giving and receiving of the precepts. But before their training is over, those precepts should be a manifestation of each student's life arising from their realization of the nature of reality. And in that realization there's no picking and choosing; there's no judging, no decision making, just spontaneous action wholly in accord with the circumstances.

STUDENT: What determines what's "wholly in accord?" Suppose that I do something—

TEACHER: First of all, in "wholly in accord" there is no "I."

STUDENT: Suppose something is done without a certain intention while others read an intention into it. You consider something to fall within the confines of the precepts but someone else says it doesn't. What determines your relationship to the morality of the situation then, your view or the other person's view of it?

TEACHER: You have to understand that there is no good or bad from where you stand at that point in time, but there is good and bad in terms of society. For example, there was an old man in New Jersey whose eighty-six-year-old wife was slowly dying of cancer, suffering terribly. She cried to him every day to pull the plug. He loved her deeply. He was in constant turmoil. One day he went into the hospital and couldn't stand her agony and begging anymore. Out of deep compassion and reverence for life, he pulled the plug. He upheld the precept, "Do not kill" by doing that. But he was arrested and put in jail, and he went on trial for murder. That was the karma of his act. When you commit an act, not out of deliberation on whether it is right or wrong, but out of your own personal reality, your intuition and compassion, the consequences make no difference. You're prepared for them. It's neither good nor bad. You pull the plug; you go to jail. You get the electric chair because you committed a crime and because there's retribution in this society for that crime. And yet, you don't evaluate your act in terms of its impact on you. The act is complete when it arises out of compassion.

STUDENT: Okay, I understand now. [Laughs.]

TEACHER: Explain it to me, would you? May your life go well.

STUDENT: Yesterday, in Kingston, as I was driving by a certain house, I saw two girls about four or five years old, on a balcony, exposing their private parts to the passing cars on the street. For a minute I felt like stopping the car, running up to the house, grabbing them by the collar, knocking on the door, and telling the parents about what they were doing. Did I do right by just keeping on going?

TEACHER: You're interpreting the situation from your perspective. From the perspective of a four-year-old, there are no private or public parts. This has more to do with the parents than it does with the children. A way to handle the situation that might be a little bit more discreet is to notice the number of the house and contact the parents later, rather than grab the kids by the neck and storm through the door. If you just knock on the door and quietly say, "You know your children were attracting a lot of attention outside by exposing themselves, you'd still might get yelled at or even punched in the nose for your good deed, but if you're doing it with a pure intent, it doesn't matter what the consequences are. You really can't go wrong if your intentions are good. But, as we've been saying, it's very easy to deceive yourself.

STUDENT: In the old days, if I was doing something wrong and one of the neighbors saw me, he would just take out his belt, give me a few whacks, and take me home so I could get a few more.

TEACHER: It was a different time and a different kind of neighborhood. The neighborhood I grew up in was Italian. Everyone was Italian and it was like a huge family. Everybody outside of that area were strangers and everybody protected everyone else. If someone was going through someone's window, the whole neighborhood would immediately respond. Now, the neighborhoods are very alienated. You don't even know who lives next door.

STUDENT: Thank you for your answer.

TEACHER: May your life go well.

STUDENT: There were sunbathers out on the field. I asked them to leave and they said, "How dare you consider yourself part of a religious group and not let us enjoy this beautiful field?!" And I said, "Yes, I'm really sorry. Now, GET THE HELL OUT!"

TEACHER: Maybe you didn't have to yell. Sometimes people don't understand that it doesn't help us when they go half-undressed in the middle of the field while everyone tries to work around them. They don't appreciate what we are doing, so it may just require an explanation. Sometimes that doesn't work either. So, when you feel that you need to take a firmer stand, remember that tact is still important. Anything else?

STUDENT: Thank you for your answer.

TEACHER: May your life go well.

STUDENT: You've been at this Zen business quite some time. Your teacher has given you transmission; you've been practicing the precepts for years. Is everything you do and say in accord with the precepts?

TEACHER: Of course not. That's what it means to practice the precepts. That's why intent becomes important. If the intent is to knowingly violate the precepts in order to serve yourself, that's not practice. But if you violate the precepts, acknowledge it, let it go, and come back to uphold the precept, that's what it means to practice that precept. And practice is enlightenment. Each time you let go of delusion and bring your mind back, you manifest the life of a buddha.

STUDENT: How can you deviate from the precepts and be still instantly aware of it?

TEACHER: It depends on how much activity is going on, the intensity of the activity, and how sensitive you are to the precepts. A lot of it is very subtle. If you're really practicing and are honest with yourself, it usually all comes home on the cushion. When you're really practicing, it's hard not to reflect on your actions and take responsibility for them. When you do, it's incredibly empowering. It doesn't make you bad or wrong; it empowers and strengthens you. You let it go and come back to the precepts. And the next time you are more sensitized to it.

STUDENT: Thank you for your answer.

TEACHER: May your life go well.

STUDENT: Most of the time I feel like water splashing water, instead of water seeing anything. How do you really see the violation of the precept and let go of it? I really find it very difficult not to be hard on myself and still learn.

TEACHER: The precepts are based on no-self. Most of our problems stem from an egocentric point of view. A strong ego can head in two directions. It can say, "Look how wonderful I am. I'm so much better than everyone else." Or it can say, "Look what an asshole I am. I'm so much worse than everybody else." It takes just as big an ego to put yourself down as it does to elevate yourself.

STUDENT: What's the self seeing the self? What's different there? What's happening when the self sees the self that doesn't happen when there's a put down?

TEACHER: When you study the self, you realize what the self really is. You realize that it is much more than the aggregates—my thoughts, my feelings, my body, my history. It includes the ten thousand things, past, present, and future. It is the self that is the basis of life, the Unborn, and death, the Unextinguished. The self that compares excludes everything because of the comparisons. It takes an ego, a separate entity to do that. The self seeing the self permeates the ten directions.

STUDENT: There's nothing to compare it to?

TEACHER: There's no gain and there's no loss.

STUDENT: Thank you for your answer.

TEACHER: May your life go well.

STUDENT: I feel everyone has already asked every question.

TEACHER: Since you are last, yours has to be a wise question.

STUDENT: At this point in time, my reality is one of separation and duality. I have to make decisions, and they can be based on the precepts. I can rely on my intuition, and I feel I have to support it. Yet, in some ways my ego always gets involved and then there are all these complications. How can I handle that?

TEACHER: If you're working with your intuition, you need to learn to trust yourself. For most people that's a very hard thing to do—to trust the self. We think that trust means the fulfillment of our expectations, but trust has nothing to do with that. Following the precepts doesn't mean that everything will be wonderful. But because everything doesn't turn out to be wonderful, we stop trusting ourselves or our intuition. Trust means that no matter how things turn out, it's okay, and we still continue to trust ourselves. "That was a stupid move"; so, it was stupid. "That was a wonderful move"; so, it was wonderful! And so it is. You just keep trusting yourself. Hesitancy, uncertainty, arrogance, don't need to come into it. It all can be very gentle because of that trust.

Because we don't trust ourselves, we don't trust anybody else. So trust yourself.

STUDENT: Thank you for your answer.

TEACHER: May your life go well.

20

ZEN WARNINGS

The Gateless Gate is a collection of ancient koans collected by Master Wumen, a Chinese Zen teacher. The book contains forty-eight cases compiled by Wumen, with his appended commentaries and poems. At the very end of the collection, after having "spilled his guts," clarifying everything he possibly could clarify; after saturating us with his grandmotherly kindness by practically mouthfeeding us with dharma food, and even chewing the food for us, Wumen leaves us with a postscript he calls the "Zen Warnings":

> To observe the regulations and keep to the rules is tying oneself without a rope. To act freely and unrestrainedly just as one wishes is to do what heretics and demons would do. To recognize mind and purify it is the false Zen of silent sitting. To give rein to oneself and ignore interrelating conditions is to fall into the abyss. To be alert and never ambiguous is to wear chains and an iron yoke. To think of good and evil belongs to heaven and hell. To have a Buddha view and a Dharma view is to be confined in two iron mountains. He who realizes it as soon as a thought arises is one who exhausts his energy. To sit blankly in quietism is the practice of the dead. If one proceeds, he will go astray from the principle. If one retreats, he will be against the truth. If one neither progresses nor retreats, he is a dead man breathing. Now tell me, what will you do? Work hard and be sure to attain "it" in this life, lest you have eternal regret.

In general, we tend to see the world, problems, solutions, our lives, and relationships dualistically. Wumen directs his warnings to this tendency to move towards or dwell in the extremes. Wumen says that to keep regulations, even regulations guiding you in your spiritual practice, you're "tying yourself without a rope." Yet if you act "freely and unrestrainedly," doing whatever you want, that's "what demons and heretics do." To recognize the mind and purify it through practice is "the false Zen of silent sitting." Still, he goes on to say that "to give rein to oneself and ignore interrelating conditions is to fall into the abyss." And if you separate things, making compartments to keep things clear, by having "a Buddha view and a Dharma view," he says you'll find yourself "confined in two iron mountains." Separations restrict, hold you back, bind you. To sit quietly, peacefully retreating into zazen is the practice of the dead. How do you live and practice without falling into extremes? On the one side is the absolute; on the other side is the relative. Wumen says that if you move forward to manifest in the phenomenal world, you move away from the principle, the absolute basis of reality. Yet, if you move away from the phenomenal world back into the absolute, you miss the truth which is this very life itself. If you neither move forward nor move backwards, if you choose not to choose, you're dead, ready to be buried. How will you avoid moving neither forward nor backward? How will you attain the Way in this life? What will you do?

STUDENT: Here I am. I've come forward to challenge you in dharma encounter. That's how I'm avoiding falling into the abyss.
TEACHER: How will you attain it?
STUDENT: I have a question. Do you think I have fallen into the abyss by coming forward, or avoided falling into the abyss?
TEACHER: Is that how you will attain it?
STUDENT: How did you attain it?
TEACHER: I've never attained it.
STUDENT: Thank you for your answer.
TEACHER: May your life go well.

STUDENT: [Has a camera and takes a photograph of the teacher.] At that moment, where was I?
TEACHER: You're the only one who can answer that. Where were you?
STUDENT: [Tilts camera and takes another photograph.]
TEACHER: You've taken two pictures, both of them probably a sixtieth of a second

exposures. One was horizontal, one was vertical. They were moments apart. Are they the same, or are they different?

STUDENT: [Takes another photograph.]

TEACHER: May your life go well.

STUDENT: Thank you for your answer.

STUDENT: Zen teachers say that one should work hard and attain it. [Makes sounds like he is throwing up, spitting out something horrible.]

TEACHER: I agree.

STUDENT: What's to be done? After two years, I still get nervous coming up to face you in public.

TEACHER: What will you do about that?

STUDENT: [Sighs.] Thank you for your answer.

TEACHER: That's not good enough. You're evading the issue. What will you do about getting nervous when coming up for dharma encounter?

STUDENT: Do we really have to do dharma encounter today?

TEACHER: Better than that. [Makes frightened noises and shakes in terror.]

STUDENT: That's embarrassing.

TEACHER: It doesn't separate you. When you're intimate with your embarrassment, there is no embarrassment; no worry, no problem.

STUDENT: Thank you for your embarrassment.

TEACHER: May your life go well.

STUDENT: It's almost lunch time and my stomach is churning. [Makes growling noises.]

TEACHER: What is that addressing?

STUDENT: Not moving forward; not moving backward.

TEACHER: Is that what it's addressing?

STUDENT: It's addressing [Makes growling noise].

TEACHER: May your life go well.

STUDENT: Thank you for your answer.

STUDENT: Show me being neither a good student nor a bad student.

TEACHER: Isn't that what you are?

STUDENT: [Shouts.]

TEACHER: That's being a bad student!

STUDENT: How should I proceed?

TEACHER: What are your alternatives?

STUDENT: There aren't any.

TEACHER: Sooooo...

STUDENT: You can chase me away.

TEACHER: Impossible. Where will you go?

STUDENT: I can't go anywhere.

TEACHER: Who will go?

STUDENT: I don't know.

TEACHER: Does that answer your question?

STUDENT: I'm still here.

TEACHER: That's where you always are—here. And your coming and going always takes place right here, right now.

STUDENT: Where does the need to feel more at home come from?

TEACHER: Where does needing come from? When there's a need or a desire, it is there because you place something outside of you.

STUDENT: Then the only thing to do is to just let that be; to just be like everything else? That's everything there is?

TEACHER: What's everything there is?

STUDENT: [Shouts loudly.]

TEACHER: That's different than needing. Need and desire are based on the illusion that everything that you need is outside of you. It's not out there. What you need to do is realize that there's no inside and outside. When you realize that, there's no needing. You already have it all. It cannot be attained. Do you understand?

STUDENT: So, the way is to be the needing. Or is it to let go of the needing?

TEACHER: Needing is an idea. It's based on separation. When there's no separation, there's no needing. You're like a fish that needs water, sitting in the middle of the ocean. Surrounded by it, permeated by it, swimming through it; you want and look for water. When you realize that you are water, needing water becomes an absurdity. Desire becomes an absurdity; it no longer exists. So, forget the self and be enlightened by the ten thousand things that you think you need. Do you understand?

STUDENT: I'm here.

TEACHER: So am I.

STUDENT: Do you need anything?

TEACHER: Not right now. Do you?

STUDENT: Not right now.

TEACHER: Keep in mind there's only right now. May your life go well.
STUDENT: Thank you for your answer.

∞

STUDENT: It has taken me five months to discover that this practice takes a great deal of work, and that it's not exciting work, but slow, tedious, and sometimes boring. It reminds me of why I've never learned to play the guitar. I don't want to learn the basics. I want to jump right in and play the songs. What can I do about this?
TEACHER: You want a little excitement, yes?
STUDENT: [Laughs.] Yeah!
TEACHER: Who is the one who wants that?
STUDENT: The person who's lazy.
TEACHER: What is that person?
STUDENT: The person who's tired of struggling, sometimes tired of not struggling, and who wants the answers now.
TEACHER: But when you say "person," I don't know what you're talking about. What is that?
STUDENT: I don't know.
TEACHER: Well, find out! That should make it very exciting for you. May your life go well.
STUDENT: Thank you for your answer.

∞

STUDENT: I was pretty sick this past week and felt really confused about what to do about it. The confusion itself made me feel awful. I didn't know whether I had a right to be sick. I wondered if I was sick enough to stay in bed and just be quiet. But then I'd be in bed and think, "Maybe I'm avoiding something and should try to just be with this sickness and keep going through the day, doing my work." I really want to know how you know when you're fooling yourself, and how do you really take care of yourself? How do you know when you need to rest? How do you work through that confusion?
TEACHER: Do you know what it means to do what you're doing while you're doing it?
STUDENT: Yes, I do. I don't do it very often, but I do know.
TEACHER: When you're walking, just walk! When you're crying, just cry! There's no room to analyze it, to judge it, to evaluate it, to compare it, to understand it, to not understand it. When you're sick, be sick! [Makes sick noises.] With the whole body and mind, be sick. And when you're well, be well! Do what

you're doing while you're doing it. If you start analyzing and judging every-thing you do: "Should I blow my nose? Well, it's not running enough. Maybe I'll wait," you're going to end up like the centipede. Somebody asked the cen-tipede, "How do you manage to walk with all those legs? How do you know which one to move and how to keep them going in order, without stumbling over each other?" The centipede looked at the person, looked at his legs, looked back at the person, and from that day on never took another step. Don't be a centipede. Just do what you're doing while you're doing it. Different people, different advice. I say this to you because I know that you are very critical of yourself. If someone who is not self-critical but perhaps should be comes forward and asks the same question, I would answer very differently. In your case, just step away from it and let it be. Let it happen. Let your life happen. When you're sick, be sick. When you sit, just sit. When you walk, just walk. Anything else?

STUDENT: What about conditioning? I know that to understand it means to ana-lyze it, but so much of my life comes out of conditioning. Isn't there a way to break out of it unless I just practice?

TEACHER: What do you do when you do zazen? A thought comes up; you acknowledge it; let it go; come back to your breath. You come back to your life. Another thought comes up, and you acknowledge it, let it go, and come back to your life. You're not going to solve any of these entanglements by figuring them out. The first thing you need to do is to return to the center of your being. From that still point, you will see things very differently. When you're sick and all that evaluative chatter comes up, acknowledge it, let it go, and be sick. And if it comes up again, you acknowledge it, let it go, and be sick again. Just do what you're doing while you're doing it. May your life go well.

STUDENT: Thank you for your answer.

STUDENT: "Hello, Mr. Fenni, this is Jane Hayes from the Monastery. Could you tell me what our balance is today?"

TEACHER: What's that?

STUDENT: All is one; all is not one.

TEACHER: You were doing that before you came here.

STUDENT: Yes.

TEACHER: What have you learned from Wumen? What have you learned from your zazen?

STUDENT: "Oh, these bills! God, they're just piling up and I can't seem to pay them!"

TEACHER: That's one side. What's the other side?

STUDENT: "They make me miserable!"

TEACHER: That's the same thing. You didn't have to come here to learn how to be miserable. How do you deal with it? How do you realize it? How do you transcend the reality of bills and no bills?

STUDENT: [Screams at the top of her lungs.]

TEACHER: That's one side. How do you avoid falling into either side?

STUDENT: [Falls over to the left.]

TEACHER: That's a cop out.

STUDENT: [Falls over to the right side.]

TEACHER: That's two cop outs.

STUDENT: [Spits out something distasteful.]

TEACHER: Three strikes; you're out.

STUDENT: Yup.

TEACHER: Find out how to avoid those two extremes. May your life go well.

STUDENT: Thank you for your answer.

STUDENT: Are you having fun?

TEACHER: I just had some fun.

STUDENT: Do you enjoy the time when you're working hard?

TEACHER: Usually. Otherwise I wouldn't be doing it. I don't have any self-discipline, none at all. If I don't enjoy it, I don't do it. Do you understand?

STUDENT: [Silence.]

TEACHER: I love chopping onions and carrots; I like making soups.

STUDENT: No matter what you're doing, there will always be people who like some things and don't like other things. When you're saving sentient beings, are you trying to make them happy?

TEACHER: How do you save sentient beings? You can't make somebody happy. Can you order them, "Be happy, dammit!"? You can't do that. They have to do that. That's the way relationships work. You don't just give the other person what they want so that they will take care of you and approve of you. It doesn't work that way. You can't give anybody what they want. Only they can do that.

STUDENT: So all you can give them is the chance to give themselves what they want.

TEACHER: Absolutely. You can only help somebody help themselves. And don't look for accolades. Don't look for anyone to think that you're a wonderful person for doing this. As you are helping them with all your life, keep in mind that "life is tough, and then you die."

STUDENT: But you have fun, don't you?

TEACHER: Right. When you finally recognize that "life is tough, and then you die," then you can get on with it.

STUDENT: Don't you think there's a better way to do that? I feel so much tension, stress, and anger in trying to get everything done. Push, push, push, push. Don't you think that there's a good way and a bad way to go about it?

TEACHER: What's the tension and stress? Who did that to you?

STUDENT: My mother and father. No. [Laughs.] I did it.

TEACHER: Okay. What will you do about it now that you can't blame Mom and Dad anymore?

STUDENT: Well, I could blame you. [Laughs.]

TEACHER: There's a better way to do it. Take responsibility for that stress. That's what makes all the difference in the world.

STUDENT: So, you never have stress?

TEACHER: Right now I'm stressed out of my mind with you! [Laughs.] There are all kinds of stresses. Sometimes stress can be useful. Without it we would be very dull people. There was a Zen teacher who raised pigs. One day he was chasing a pig around the sty, hitting it with a switch, and the pig was squealing. A student asked him, "Why are you doing that?" The Roshi replied, "It gives her spirit!" It's when stress begins to be relentless, and you feel helpless and hopeless, that it becomes a problem. But whether it's healthy or malignant stress, we always create it.

STUDENT: Thank you for your answer.

TEACHER: May your life go well.

STUDENT: You say, "Thank you for feeding the dog." I say, "I don't do it for you." You say, "Oh...Woof, woof, woof, woof, woof." I don't know whether or not to thank you for being "alert and never ambiguous."

TEACHER: Did I really do that?

STUDENT: Woof, woof, woof, woof, woof!

TEACHER: Somebody feed the dog.

STUDENT: I'm on my way...

TEACHER: May your life go well.

STUDENT: Thank you for your answer.

STUDENT: Listening to Wumen's warnings, I was struck by the pointlessness of trying to understand and capture in words whatever it is that he is teaching. I also hear a caution against dismissing the questions. He talks about how sitting and purifying the mind is the false Zen, the quietude of the dead. Are there questions that don't have answers? And how do you go about asking these questions?

TEACHER: There's nothing wrong with the questions. In fact, Wumen brought up the questions. He asks a whole series of questions. Every line in that short paragraph is a koan. A genuine question is very important. It's the cutting edge of Zen training, the functioning of the great doubt. Great faith is the sense that you have the ability to break through the question. Great determination is the will not to be defeated by the doubt, the determination to see the truth clearly for yourself. But you're not going to see it intellectually. Wumen purposefully destroys all of the logical possibilities. He creates what seems like a paradox. But remember that paradox exists only in the words and ideas that are used to describe reality. Reality itself has no paradoxes. Wumen creates dilemmas and double binds, but they only have to do with words. When you go beyond the words, you find that the questions and the answers come from the same place.

STUDENT: But you don't do it simply by letting go of all the words?

TEACHER: No, you don't do it by letting go of the question. The question is going to come up. You can sit in quietude. That still doesn't answer the question. You may find yourself very peaceful, but the questions remain: Who am I? What is life? What is truth? What is reality? What is God? Those are real questions, and we should be able to understand them and live our lives out of that appreciation.

STUDENT: Thank you for your answer.

TEACHER: May your life go well.

STUDENT: I'd like to address the final line you read, "Attain it now or have eternal regret." For the past twenty years, I've brainwashed myself with the single-minded thought of attaining it, even though they say there is nothing to attain. Suddenly I hear another alternative. I could have "eternal regret." How bad is "eternal regret?"

TEACHER: Beats me.

STUDENT: Would it be something to consider as an alternative?

TEACHER: Beats me.

STUDENT: Is it something to think about?

TEACHER: Beats me.

STUDENT: Is there?

TEACHER: What do you think?

STUDENT: There's nothing to think about.

TEACHER: How will you attain it?

STUDENT: By not thinking?

TEACHER: Do you really think that you're going to attain it? Kasho Buddha sat for thirty kalpas. He never attained it. Buddha himself never attained it; Bodhidharma never attained it; Linji never attained it; Dogen never attained it. How do you expect to attain it?

STUDENT: Well, if I can't attain it, then there's no eternal regret, either.

TEACHER: Now you're getting somewhere. May you life go well.

STUDENT: Thank you for your answer.

STUDENT: I'm a new student, but I feel like I'm an old student. I've been up on the mountain top, but now I'm in the marketplace and I lost my way back. I want to explore the phenomenal world, and to achieve realization. How can I do both?

TEACHER: Do you think they're separate?

STUDENT: I've been told that they are not.

TEACHER: You have to *realize* that they are not. When we realize that, then "being in the mountain is a flower opening in the marketplace." Those who think that the mundane is a hindrance to their practice—to the sacred—only understand that in the mundane nothing is sacred. They need to realize that in sacredness nothing is mundane. When you really practice, there is no mundane. But in the mundane, there is no practice.

STUDENT: Does the search in the phenomenal realm then become meaningless?

TEACHER: "Form is emptiness, emptiness is form. Form is exactly emptiness, emptiness is exactly form." Why do you keep trying to separate them?

STUDENT: I feel so distant from realizing that.

TEACHER: Just don't separate them. Really be the phenomena with the whole body and mind. Shakyamuni Buddha held up the flower; isn't that flower phenomenal? Mahakashyapa smiled; isn't that smile phenomenal? He could have laughed instead, "Ha, ha ha! Look at Shakyamuni holding up the flower!" That was the mind-to-mind transmission. Kayashapa called, "Ananda?" Ananda responded, "Yes, Master!" Kayashapa said, "Take down the flagpole." Again, the Dharma was transmitted at that moment, in the phenomenal world. In the absolute there is no way of talking or communicating. There is no eye, ear, nose, tongue, body, or mind. How can you talk to somebody like that? What good is a person like that? That's a corpse. Your life has to be realized and manifested in the phenomenal world. May your life go well.

STUDENT: Thank you for your answer.

STUDENT: Please forgive me for being in front of you.
TEACHER: No. Forgive yourself.
STUDENT: Forgive myself? Never.
TEACHER: Then I can't either.
STUDENT: Thank you for your answer. Unless you're not finished with me.
TEACHER: How can you excuse yourself for being in front of me?
STUDENT: I said, "Thank you for your answer."
TEACHER: Ah. I would say [smacks stick on floor] "May your life go well." Do you understand?
STUDENT: [Laughs.] Thank you.
TEACHER: Thank you?
STUDENT: Whoops. Okay? I'll try again.
TEACHER: Thank you for your answer.
STUDENT: May your life go well.
TEACHER: There will be no descendants on this mountain. May your life go well.
STUDENT: Thank you for your answer.

In his "Zen Warnings" and in all of the forty-eight koans in his collection, Wumen is pointing us to see beyond the dichotomies: sacred and secular, ordinary and holy, parent and child, teacher and student, good and evil, enlightenment and delusion. The Buddha Way is the middle way; it falls into neither of these extremes. This is difficult to understand because it doesn't "compute" within our logical, conditioned matrix. The statement "form is emptiness; emptiness is form," the heart of the Mahayana teachings of Buddhism, seems contradictory. Our minds are used to function dualistically. We tend to see and appreciate everything that way. "Form is emptiness; emptiness is form" boggles the mind. "Good and evil are the same thing" boggles the mind. We have to see how these polarities co-arise and inter-penetrate. We have to realize that they are two parts of the same reality; not only realize it, but actualize it in the way we live our life.

Zen training always comes down to this actualization of wisdom. Getting up to the summit of the mountain—realizing enlightenment—is not so difficult. It's not the big deal we imagine. The real challenge is coming down off the mountain to manifest in the world—in every detail of our lives—that which has been realized. It's one thing to say "I love you." It's quite another thing to love. There is a huge gap between talking and doing, between analysis and intimacy.

"Ascending the mountain" training may take two to three years. "Descending the mountain" training lasts ten to fifteen years. In a sense, it lasts a lifetime. But unless we manifest the wisdom in the world, what good is it? Zen practice is not about secluding ourselves in some tranquil hermitage contemplating our navels. That's not what life is. That's not what the Buddha or any of the Zen ancestors did. They didn't isolate themselves, but instead functioned with abandon in the world of samsara, the world of good and evil. Unless Zen manifests there, our practice is not complete and the Buddhadharma has not been actualized and transmitted. When we say that our practice is to "give life to the Buddha," it means to practice with all of our life, with our whole body and mind. Until that happens, Zen is just a philosophy. Our lives are not an abstraction. They're flesh and blood. That is where practice needs to manifest. That is what anuttara-samyaksambodhi, complete enlightenment means: with the whole body and mind.

Acknowledgments

The project of creating this book spanned more than ten years. During that time, the difficult task of transcribing these dialogues with their many varied voices was shouldered by a number of people. Vanessa Zuisei Goddard prepared all of the transcriptions for editing, cross-checked the text for redundancies, and developed the Glossary. Ann Hoshin Ritter and Kay Senyu Larsen read through the manuscript and offered many helpful suggestions. Konrad Ryushin Marchaj and Bonnie Myotai Treace provided skillful assistance in editing these freewheeling exchanges. I want to extend my thanks to all those involved for their selfless effort, attention to detail, and perseverance in bringing this volume to completion.

I also want to express my gratitude to all those practitioners who came forth, challenging me and themselves with their openness and willingness to explore the edges of this path. Without them, there could not be any dharma encounters.

John Daido Loori, Roshi
Abbot, Zen Mountain Monastery

Glossary of Buddhist Terms

Jpn. = Japanese

ANANDA: The Buddha's disciple and personal attendant, known for having repeated all of the Buddha's discourses from memory at the First Council.

anuttara-samyaksambodhi: Supreme perfect enlightenment of a complete Buddha.

AVALOKITESHVARA: (*Jpn.* Kannon or Kanzeon) The bodhisattva of compassion; "she who hears the outcries of the world."

BAIZHANG: (*Jpn.* Hyakujo) 720–814. Chinese Zen Master; dharma successor of Mazu and teacher of Guishan and Huangbo. He founded the monastic tradition by establishing precise rules for the daily routine of a Zen monastery.

Blue Cliff Record: A collection of one hundred koans with appreciatory verses compiled by Master Xuetou (*Jpn.* Setcho), 982–1052, and with commentaries by Master Yuanwu (*Jpn.* Engo), 1063–1135; a key text in the Rinzai Zen school, it was studied by Master Dogen, who carried a handwritten copy back to Japan from China.

BODHIDHARMA: An Indian monastic known for taking Buddhism from India to China, where he settled at Shaolin monastery and practiced zazen for nine years facing the wall; the "Barbarian from the West."

BODHI MIND: Mind in which the aspiration for enlightenment has been awakened; the impulse that moves one toward self-realization.

BODHISATTVA: One who practices the Buddha Way and compassionately postpones final enlightenment for the sake of others; the ideal of practice in Mahayana Buddhism.

BODY AND MIND FALLEN AWAY: *See samadhi.*

BUDDHADHARMA: Teachings of the Buddha based on his enlightenment experience; in Zen they are not to be conceptually understood but rather personally realized and verified by each practitioner.

BUDDHA NATURE: The true, enlightened and immutable nature of all beings, according to Mahayana Buddhism.

BUDDHA WAY: The practice of realization taught by Shakyamuni Buddha; the nature of reality.

chakra: Term used in Hinduism for the centers of subtle or refined energy in the human body.

devas: Divinities who inhabit the heavenly realm.

DHARMA: Universal truth or law; the Buddha's teachings; all of phenomena.

DHARMA ENCOUNTER: Unrehearsed dialogue in which two Zen practitioners test and sharpen their understanding of Zen truths.

DHARMA DISCOURSE: *Teisho;* a formal talk on a koan or on significant aspects of Zen teachings; not an intellectual presentation or a philosophical explanation but a teacher's direct expression of the spirit of Zen.

Dharmakaya: One of the three *kayas,* bodies of the Buddha; the body of the great order, essential reality; the unity of the Buddha and the universe.

DIAMOND NET OF INDRA: A description of the universe presented in the *Flower Garland Sutra*; it depicts the interconnections and interdependence of all the facets of reality throughout time and space.

DOGEN ZENJI: 1200–1253, founder of the Japanese Soto school of Zen; Dogen established Eihei-ji, the principal Soto training monastery in Japan; he is the author of the *Shobogenzo,* an important collection of dharma essays.

dokusan: Private interview with the teacher during which students present and clarify their understanding of the Dharma.

DONGSHAN: (*Jpn.* Tozan) 910–990. Chinese Zen master; dharma successor of Yunyen. He developed the Five Ranks of the interplay between the absolute and relative, and was the co-founder of the Soto school of Zen.

EIGHTFOLD PATH: The content of the Buddha's Fourth Noble Truth, the way out of suffering; it consists of right views, right thought, right speech, right action, right livelihood, right effort, right mindfulness, and right concentration.

EIGHT GATES OF TRAINING: Training system used at Zen Mountain Monastery for complete living and realization; it includes zazen, Zen study with the teacher, academic study, liturgy, precepts practice, art practice, body practice, and work practice; it corresponds roughly to the aspects of the Buddha's Eightfold Path.

ENLIGHTENMENT: The direct experience of one's true nature.

ENTANGLEMENTS: Complications; sometimes created by the teacher to help the student see into their true nature.

Faith Mind Sutra: A poem written by Chinese Zen master Sengcan; it expounds

Zen's basic spirit; famous for its opening sentence: "The Great Way is not difficult; it only avoids picking and choosing."

Five skandhas: Five aggregates which constitute what is referred to as "the self": form, sensation, perception, mental formations, and consciousness.

Flower Garland Sutra: Mahayana sutra that constitutes the basis of the Chinese Huayen (Kegon) school; it emphasizes mutually unobstructed interpenetration of all things and states that Buddha, mind, and universe are identical to one another.

FOUR NOBLE TRUTHS: The first teaching of the historical Buddha; it addresses the nature of all suffering and points to the way of overcoming suffering; the truths are (1) life is suffering, (2) suffering has a cause, (3) there is an end to the cause of suffering, (4) the way to put an end to suffering is the Eightfold Path.

FOUR BODHISATTVA VOWS: Vows taken by the bodhisattvas, expressing commitment to postpone their own enlightenment until all beings are liberated from delusion; they are chanted at the end of each day at Zen monasteries.

Genjokoan (THE WAY OF EVERYDAY LIFE): The first fascicle and the heart of Master Dogen's *Shobogenzo*.

HAKUIN: 1689–1769. Japanese Zen Master; father of modern Rinzai Zen, he systematized koan training and emphasized the importance of zazen.

hara: Physical and spiritual center of one's body/mind; area in the lower abdomen used in centering one's attention in any activity, especially meditation.

HINAYANA: "School of the Elders" or Theravada Buddhism, prevalent in the countries of southern Asia. It bases its teaching on the Four Noble Truths, the doctrine of dependent arising, and the concepts of karma and *anatman*.

HUINENG: (*Jpn.* Eno) The Sixth Ancestor and author of the *Platform Sutra*; he is regarded as the father of the Zen tradition in China.

HUNGRY GHOSTS: Beings that suffer from greed and hunger, with immense bellies and mouths as big as the eye of a needle.

INTIMACY: the realization of complete identification of subject and object; the falling away of body and mind, as well as the truth of the unity of the self and the universe as it may be accessed through Zen practice.

joriki: Power of concentration developed through the practice of meditation; it allows practitioners to place their focus of attention where they choose for extended periods of time.

JUJING: (*Jpn.* Nyojo) 1163–1228. Chinese Zen master; and Master Dogen's teacher.

jukai: Acknowledgment and reception of the Buddhist precepts; the ceremony of becoming a Buddhist.

kalpa: A world cycle; an endlessly long period of time.

KARMA: The universal law of cause and effect, linking an action's underlying intention to that action's consequences; it equates the actions of body, speech, and thought as potential sources of karmic consequences.

KOAN: An apparently paradoxical statement or question used in Zen training to induce in students an intense level of doubt, allowing them to cut through conventional and conditioned descriptions of reality and see directly into their true nature.

LINJI: (*Jpn.* Rinzai) ?–866. Chinese Zen master; dharma successor of Huangbo and founder of the Rinzai school of Zen, one of the two schools of Buddhism still active in Japan.

LITURGIST: Person in charge of leading the ceremonies at a Buddhist monastery.

MAEZUMI ROSHI: Japanese Zen master who came to America to spread the Dharma; successor of Yasutani Roshi, Koryu Roshi, and Baian Hakuyun, receiving transmission in both the Soto and Rinzai lineages of Zen; he was the teacher of John Daido Loori, Roshi, and the first abbot of Zen Mountain Monastery.

MAHAKASHYAPA: Regarded as the Buddha's first successor in the Zen tradition; he was renowned for his ascetic self-discipline and moral strictness.

mahasattva: A perfect bodhisattva, ranking second only to a buddha.

MAHAYANA: "Great Vehicle"; the northern school of Buddhism that expresses and aims at the intrinsic connection between an individual's realization and the simultaneous enlightenment of all beings.

MANJUSHRI: The bodhisattva of wisdom.

mondo: An informal, freewheeling dialogue between the teacher and the students that centers on some relevant aspect of the teachings.

MOUNT GRIDHRAKUTA: Vulture Peak, the site of many of Shakyamuni Buddha's recorded discourses and important in Zen as the site of the first transmission from the Buddha to Mahakashyapa.

Mountain Record: Zen practice journal published quarterly by Dharma Communications, the outreach arm of Zen Mountain Monastery.

Mountains and Rivers Sutra: A fascicle in the *Shobogenzo* depicting the interrelatedness of the absolute and the relative.

Mu: One of the first koans used in koan training; the first case in Master Wumen's *Gateless Gate* collection of koans.

Nirmanakaya: One of the three bodies of the Buddha; the earthly body and manifestation that a buddha assumes to guide all sentient beings toward liberation.

NIRVANA: Union with the absolute; in Zen it is essential to realize that samsara is nirvana, form is emptiness, that all beings are innately perfect from the outset.

NO-SELF: the *anatman* doctrine is one of the essential teachings of Buddhism, stating that there is no permanent, enduring substance within any entity; "self" is an idea.

ONE BRIGHT PEARL: Symbol for the unity of the whole phenomenal universe. It was a favorite expression of Master Xuansha's, one of Xuefeng's successors.

oryoki: Jpn. "Just the right amount"; the set of bowls used in a ceremonial meal eaten in silence in Buddhist monasteries, as well as the meal itself.

Prajna: Wisdom; not that which is possessed but that which is directly and thoroughly experienced.

PRECEPTS: Moral and ethical guidelines which, are a description of the life of a Buddha, one who realizes the nature of existence and acts out of that realization.

rakusu: A small, more practical, version of the *kesa*, "Buddha's robe"; a garment worn by Zen Buddhist practitioners across their chest.

RINZAI SCHOOL: School of Zen that originated with the great Chinese Zen Master Linji in the ninth century and was reformed by Master Hakuin in Japan; it stresses koan practice and the attainment of breakthrough into the nature of reality.

roshi: "Old venerable master"; title of Zen teachers.

samadhi: State in which the mind is absorbed in intense concentration devoid of subject-object dualism, free from distractions and goals; the essential nature of the self can be experienced directly within samadhi.

Sambhogakaya: One of the three bodies of the Buddha; "body of bliss," or reward body.

samsara: Existence prior to liberation, conditioned by the three attitudes of greed, anger, and ignorance and marked by continuous rebirths.

SANGHA: Community of practitioners; all sentient and insentient beings.

sesshin: "Gathering of the mind"; an extended period of intensive meditation practice lasting between five and ten days, centered on zazen.

SHARIPUTRA: Principal student of the Buddha, and one of his ten great disciples.

SHAKYAMUNI BUDDHA: Siddhartha Gautama, the historical Buddha and the founder of Buddhism; he was a prince of the Shakya clan, living in northern India in the sixth century B.C.E.

shikantaza: "Just sitting"; form of zazen in which one practices pure awareness.

shingi: Rules or regulations for a monastic community.

Shobogenzo: "Treasury of the True Dharma Eye," a collection of writings and discourses by Master Dogen.

shunyata: Void; central principle of Buddhism that recognizes the emptiness of all composite entities, without reifying nothingness; resolution of all dualities.

shila: Precepts; guidelines of enlightened conduct.

SIXTH ANCESTOR: Huineng (*Jpn.* Eno) 638–713. Chinese Zen master to whom all modern Zen lineages can be traced; he was enlightened at the age of eighteen by listening to a line being recited from the *Diamond Sutra*.

SOTO SCHOOL: One of the schools of Zen Buddhism, founded by the Chinese Masters Dongshan and Caoshan in the ninth century; it was revitalized and brought to Japan by Eihei Dogen.

SUCHNESS: *tathata*; the absolute, true state of phenomena. It is immutable, immovable, and beyond all concepts and distinctions.

SUTRA: Narrative text consisting chiefly of the discourses and teachings of the Buddha.

SUZUKI ROSHI: 1905–71. Japanese Zen master of the Soto School. He came to America in 1958 and soon became the abbot of the San Francisco Zen Center and Zen Mountain Center, the first Zen training monastery outside Asia.

TATHAGATA: One of the titles of the Buddha, "thus-come one," referring to one who has attained perfect enlightenment.

TEN GRAVE PRECEPTS: Guidelines for activity which actualizes the life of a buddha; the functioning of the Three Pure Precepts; at Zen Mountain Monastery they are expressed as: 1 affirm life, do not kill, 2 be giving, do not steal; 3 honor the body, do not misuse sexuality; 4 manifest truth, do not lie; 5 proceed clearly, do not cloud the mind; 6 see the perfection, do not speak of others' errors and faults; 7 realize self and other as one, do not elevate the self and blame others; 8 give generously, do not be withholding; 9 actualize harmony, do not be angry; 10 experience the intimacy of things, do not defile the Three Treasures.

TEN STAGES: A schematic system delineating progressive phases of Zen training at Zen Mountain Monastery, based on the Ten Ox–Herding Pictures of Master Kuoan.

THIRD ANCESTOR SENGCAN: (Jpn. Sosan) ?–606. Dharma successor of Huike (Jpn. Eka) and author of the Faith Mind Sutra.

THREE PURE PRECEPTS: Moral and ethical guidelines which define the natural order of reality: 1) do not create evil, 2) practice good, 3) actualize good for others.

THREE TREASURES: Buddha, Dharma, and Sangha; respectively, one who is awakened, the true teachings, and the group of people living in accord with the teachings. The Three Treasures are also known as the places of refuge for Buddhist practitioners.

upaya: Skillful means; forms that the teachings take, reflecting their appropriateness to the circumstances in which they appear.

vinaya: School of Buddhism that centers its practice on strict and precise observance of monastic rules and ethical precepts; collection of Buddhist precepts.

YASUTANI ROSHI: One of the first Zen masters to be active in the West; trained in both the Soto and Rinzai schools of Zen.

zafu: Round pillow used in sitting meditation.

zazen: Sitting meditation, taught in Zen as the most direct way to enlightenment; the practice of the realization of one's own true nature.

zendo: Meditation hall.

ZHAOZHOU: (Jpn. Joshu) 778–897. One of the most important Zen masters of China during the Tang dynasty; dharma successor of Nanquan and greatly admired by Master Dogen; known for originating the koan "Mu."